Piaget
and the
Foundations of Knowledge

The Jean Piaget Symposium Series
Available from LEA

SIGEL, I. E. BRODZINSKY, D. M. & GOLINKOFF, R. M. (Eds.) • New Directions in Piagetian Theory and Practice

OVERTON, W. F. (Ed.) • Relationships Between Social and Cognitive Development

LIBEN, L. S. (Ed.) • Piaget and the Foundations of Knowledge

SCHOLNICK, E. K. (Ed.) • New Trends in Conceptual Representation: Challenges to Piaget's Theory?

Piaget
and the
Foundations of Knowledge

Edited by
Lynn S. Liben
The Pennsylvania State University

IEA LAWRENCE ERLBAUM ASSOCIATES, PUBLISHERS
1983   Hillsdale, New Jersey   London

Lawrence Erlbaum Associates, Inc., Publishers
365 Broadway
Hillsdale, New Jersey 07642

Library of Congress Catalog Card Number: 83-81920
ISBN: 0-89859-248-8

Printed in the United States of America
10   9   8   7   6   5   4   3   2   1

Contents

Preface

This volume is drawn from the Tenth Annual Symposium of the Jean Piaget Society. The theme of that Symposium, selected by the Board of Directors of the Society, was "Piaget and the Foundations of Knowledge." The goal of the Symposium was to provide a critical discussion of Piaget's views on the origins of knowledge, and to identify alternatives to those views.

To ensure a critical evaluation and the presentation of true alternatives, the individuals invited to present Plenary Addresses at the Symposium were not limited to scholars identified with Piagetian theory. Indeed, several of the Plenary speakers seemed puzzled to have been invited. One kept asking if we were certain we had the right person, insisting, "I'm not a Piagetian, you know." As a result, the contributions to this volume based on Plenary Addresses by Eleanor Gibson, Michael Lewis, Jean Mandler, Walter Mischel, David Palermo, and Marx Wartofsky, represent a diverse set of perspectives on the origins and development of knowledge.

The risk in inviting "non-Piagetians" to contribute to a Symposium and book sponsored by the Piaget Society is, of course, that there will be little direct contact with Piagetian theory. Mischel, for example, ends his contribution in this book as follows: "And we look forward to seeing how our present and future research will articulate with Piaget's work, confident that it will do so, but leaving that task to other scholars" (pp. 227–228, this volume). As a mechanism to ensure that there would be discussion of Piagetian theory, the Board invited another group of scholars to serve as discussants of the Plenary Addresses. These discussants were asked to give particular attention to the relationship between the issues raised in the presentation and Piagetian theory. The chapters in this volume by Roberta Golinkoff, Frank Murray, Ellin Scholnick, Irving Sigel, and Elizabeth Spelke are expanded versions of Symposium discussions.

Despite the great diversity evident in the resulting collection, a number of common themes emerge. One of the most central is that *context* is of critical importance to our study of the foundations of knowledge. The contributors to this volume point to the radical ways in which context must be considered, challenging, thereby, the implicit expectation that we can ever formulate a psychology or epistemology that is context independent. Contextual effects may be understood as operating at three levels—the environment, the self, and the observer of the self/environment nexus.

Environmental context is, of course, universally recognized as relevant for knowledge. Mandler (Chapter 6), for example, writes that "All schemata are formed on the basis of experiencing regularities in the environment, such as objects that regularly appear together or events that regularly follow one another" (p. 101). Lewis (Chapter 8), Golinkoff (Chapter 9), and Murray (Chapter 11) document ways in which social encounters provide the grist for the development of knowledge. Other contributors point to specific cross-cultural and contextual effects as, for example, in Mandler's (Chapter 6) discussion of the variation in subjects' performance on logical reasoning tasks which occur with variations in task materials, or in Palermo's (Chapter 4) discussion of contextual effects on the interpretation of metaphor. But this volume also contains radical challenges about those "regularities in the environment," particularly as they are assumed in Piagetian theory. Wartofsky (Chapter 1) focuses much of his chapter on this point, arguing that "Piaget fails to take fully enough into account the sociohistorical dimension of the development of child-thought and of human cognitive growth in general" (p. 1). Wartofsky challenges Piaget's implicit assumption that the objects or artifacts available for the child's manipulation are fundamentally indistinguishable over history and across cultures.

The second level at which context operates is at the level of the epistemic subject. That is, the outcomes of an individual encountering an environment (whatever it might be) are determined by the context of the self. Several components of the "contextual self" are identified in this volume. One concerns the biological constraints and predispositions of the species in general and of the individual in particular. For example, Gibson, Spelke, and Palermo (Chapters 2, 3, and 4, respectively) address ways in which "preadapted coordinations" (p. 38), "unlearned sensitivity to relationships" (p. 45), and "natural biological characteristics of the organism" (p. 57) play a powerful role in shaping the categorization and interpretation of what is encountered in the environment.

Another aspect of the contextual self is what the individual has constructed and stored from the past. These affect the individual in constructing and storing new events and objects. It is in this sense of context that the core concept of Piagetian theory—constructivism—is represented. Here, for example, are the effects of scripts and domain specific knowledge on problem solving and memory (Mandler, Chapter 6); the influence of theories of the world on the assignment of meaning (Palermo, Chapter 4); the role of logical structures on categorization

(Scholnick, Chapter 5); the effect of operational schemes on memory (Sigel, Chapter 7); and the effects of self-awareness or consciousness on the construction of knowledge (Lewis, Chapter 8).

The first two levels of context, then, refer to the environment and to the knower. But there is a third level of context, often ignored, that deservedly receives much attention in the present volume. This is the context in which the *observer* is embedded. As Lewis (Chapter 8) states, "Meaning must be constructed by those who study it, and therefore meaning is always relative" (p. 142). The context in which that scientist finds him or herself must be taken into account. The importance of the scientist's perspective in the determination, or more accurately, in the *assignment* of meaning is also noted by Palermo (Chapter 4). In discussing the foundations on which successful communication rests, Palermo notes that just as people from different cultures may have difficulty in communicating, "two scientists with different paradigmatic views of their discipline experience this kind of communication problem" (p. 67). Likewise, Murray (Chapter 11) examines the ways in which different metatheoretical assumptions influence the kinds of questions asked and the kinds of explanations sought. He illustrates this point by considering how a Piagetian might (or might not) study phenomena related to the delay of gratification research described by Mischel (Chapter 10). Another stark demonstration of the extent to which scientists' contexts influence interpretation of "truth" is provided in the exchange between Mandler and Sigel (Chapters 6 and 7, respectively). Mandler concludes her chapter by arguing that: "In the kinds of knowledge and ways of processing that I have described in this chapter, it is difficult to discern qualitative developmental changes, let alone anything that might qualify as a stage" (p. 118). Sigel says, quite simply, "I disagree" (p. 127), and presents arguments and empirical evidence to support the opposite position.

In short, just as the knowledge one acquires or constructs is influenced by variations in the environment encountered, and just as knowledge is influenced by the characteristics of the individual who is encountering that environment, so too is our scientific understanding of that knowledge influenced by our own metatheoretical assumptions and the sociohistorical context in which we make and interpret our observations.

The power of context is not the only recurring theme found in the present volume. However, an exhaustive cataloging of unifying themes is neither possible in a brief preface, nor appropriate given that individual readers' "self-contexts" will lead them to identify their own common themes. What all will find, however, is a rich, exciting range of theoretical and empirical contributions concerning the foundations of knowledge.

Lynn S. Liben

1 From Genetic Epistemology to Historical Epistemology: Kant, Marx, and Piaget

Marx W. Wartofsky
Boston University

Piaget's genetic epistemology is a radical reformation, in dynamic, evolutionary terms, of Kant's transcendental epistemology. Piaget goes beyond the fixed, essentialist notions of Kant's a priori forms of perception and of the understanding and proposes instead a notion of the development of cognitive structures. Similarly, Piaget goes beyond a biologized Kantianism, which takes the necessary and universal a priori forms of human cognition to be fixed in the genetic structures of the organism. Instead, the emphasis in Piaget's account is on the genesis of structures that emerge out of the interaction of the human cognitive organism with its environment. In this interaction, he takes the activity of the organism to be central, so that cognitive development is seen as the product of an active encounter in which the objects of cognition are not passively received or imprinted but are literally constructed. Thus, genetic epistemology is neither transcendental, nor biological in the innatist sense, nor evolutionary in the sense of species evolution, though it is conformable with such an evolutionary epistemology. Rather, Piaget wants to begin where the genetically fixed forms of perception and cognition end, where instinct is replaced by intelligence, and where phenotypic modes of adaptation and maturation develop beyond the genotype.

Yet, Piaget's approach falls short of being a fundamentally sociohistorical one in its account of child development. That is to say, Piaget seeks to discover the universal and historically and culturally invariant laws of cognitive development, and in this sense he seeks a biological explanation of human cognition as a characteristic of the species. My argument in this paper is that Piaget fails to take fully enough into account the sociohistorical dimension of the development of child-thought and of human cognitive growth in general. I take this failure to be

1

based on an inadequate view of the historicity of that very praxis, those very modes of action that genetic epistemology takes to be the source of cognitive development. I argue that what is needed is yet an additional reformation, which takes the theory of cognitive growth beyond both the transcendental structuralism of Kant and the genetic structuralism of Piaget to a historical epistemology, in which changes in modes of perception and cognition are related to changes in the modes of historical praxis and to changes in the history of science. This alternative emphasis, as a framework for developmental psychology and for epistemology, is suggested by Marx's theory of social development, namely, historical materialism. Thus, I take a historical epistemology to be the epistemological correlate of such a historical materialism; in this sense, I take it to go beyond the biologically oriented species essentialism that remains at the basis of Piaget's program.

In this paper, I begin with a brief sketch of how Piaget's genetic epistemology reconstructs and reforms Kant's transcendental epistemology. Then I review some of the historical and philosophical precedents of Piaget's developmental view. The analytical argument begins with a consideration of the question of norms, specifically, with the notion of orthogenesis, which underlies Piaget's developmental theory. Here, I argue that the sociohistorical construction of norms and the changes in norms provide a somewhat different framework of cognitive development and of maturation than Piaget proposes. In this argument, it can be seen that what is crucial is the making and use of artifacts and the activity of representation on which the capacity for internal representation, or interiorization, depends. Finally, I suggest what such a historical epistemology means as a framework for studying the growth of knowledge in the child.

FROM KANT TO PIAGET

Piaget's relation to Kant and to Kantianism is instructive, for it gives us a precise understanding of what Piaget thinks about the genesis and nature of *cognitive structures* (by which I mean both perception and thought). Though Piaget holds, with Kant, that we do not come into the world as *tabulae rasae* upon which sensations impress ideas but rather that we bring structures to bear upon our experience, he differs from Kant in holding that such structures are not innate or preformed. Yet, at the same time, he agrees with Kant that some of these structures are necessary, that is, they have a necessity that goes beyond the simple contingencies of inductive generalization or adaptation. Thus, there are a priori structures, some of which are necessary, but these are a priori in a special way: They come into being and change and therefore are only relatively a priori. In short, they develop and are neither fixed, once and for all, nor innate. On the other hand, the development of such structures, according to Piaget, is not a matter of genetic selection in the mode of evolutionary adaptation; they are not biologically a priori as aspects of heredity, for example, as instincts are. If they were—and here Piaget develops his argument against Lorenz—they would not have the plasticity that the acquisition of structure in development shows as a result of learning, nor would they have the necessity required for the proper characterization of logico-mathematical structures and the deductive necessity that marks logico-mathematical operations (Piaget, 1971a, pp. 313–317). Piaget argues, instead, that for logico-mathematical structures of cognition such necessity is achieved. He (1971a) writes:

> Their necessity is brought about by a gradual construction. In fact a study of the development of logico-mathematical structures in a child reveals that the necessity for them is imposed on the subject, not from the beginning, but . . . very gradually, often until such a time as it crystallizes very suddenly. . . . The necessary character of logico-mathematical structures, then, does not in the least prove them to be hereditary but emerges from their progressive equilibration by dint of auto-regulation [pp. 316–317].

Now this is a very interesting and revealing argument. Piaget wants to retain, with Kant, two crucial notions: (1) the role of a priori structures in the shaping or construction of experience and in the acquisition of knowledge—indeed, as preconditions for such knowledge; (2) the character of necessity which such structures have, at least in the case of logico-mathematical structures. And because, for Piaget, it is such logico-mathematical structures that characterize mature knowledge, approximating to the adult scientific world view, this necessity becomes a hallmark, for Piaget as for Kant, of scientific knowledge. As is shown later, because science is the norm of mature knowledge for Piaget, this characteristic of necessity and the achievement of this schema in thought provide a norm of cognitive development. But Piaget argues against the Kantian form of a priorism both in its transcendental mode in Kant, where it is used to assure the normative validity of scientific truth against the mere accidentality or contingency of experience as such and also in its biologized modes (e.g., in Lorenz 1943, 1957, and in a different way, e.g., in Rensch 1959, 1967), where this a priorism is seen as the selective adaptation by biological means of hereditary and therefore species-fixed modes of cognition. Piaget therefore wants to have his a priorism and eat it too. And he can, because he proposes a theory of the acquisition and change of such structures and also the complex mechanisms by means of which such construction and development take place. In short, Piaget replaces the nondevelopmental, essentialist theory of Kant with a developmental theory while retaining the very ground that for Kant required a transcendental deduction of the categories of perception and thought. The importance of this latter point bears on Piaget's antiempiricism, his rejection of inductivist, sensationist, or associationist theories of learning. But for our purposes, it bears even more importantly on the normative basis of Piaget's whole program and on the role of norms in defining knowledge. Indeed, this is what makes Piaget's program a genetic epistemology rather than a descriptive genetic psychology, for what is at issue in cognitive growth is neither simply the pragmatic norm of successful action or adaptive success nor the mere sequence of cognitive stages, but rather *truth*.

If Kant took truth to be the regulative norm satisfied by the deductive necessity of conclusions derived from necessary a priori statements, whether analytic or synthetic, then truth is grounded in the very necessity, universality, and unity of Reason itself. But Reason, with a capital R here, is taken to be transcendental and not the result or product of any development, nor the terminus of any inductive procedure. Reason yields truth, for Kant, precisely because the very possibility of knowledge—that is, of the sort of scientific knowledge yielded by Newtonian science, which is Kant's paradigm of scientific knowledge—depends on the accessibility of the object of knowledge to reason. To put it very briefly indeed, reality has to be rationable, open to rational representation, if it is to be known at all. Because for Kant, "reality" in itself, the "ding-an-sich," is a limit notion, beyond the possibility of being known, then natural knowledge must consist of knowledge of phenomena, that is, those things-for-us whose coming to be known is conditioned by the very forms under which rational knowledge is itself possible. Necessity, for Kant as for Piaget, lies not in the nature of things or of nature, but in the structures of reason itself as the conditions of the possibility of any scientific knowledge whatever. Therefore, for Kant, pure mathematics as well as mathematically rational physics (i.e., the only physics that is physics proper and not merely empirical) carry with them the necessity of synthetic a priori judgments (i.e., those that are necessarily true of all possible experience, though they are not derived from experience.) For Piaget, such a transcendental rationality as Kant posited, and which he rationally reconstructed by transcendental deduction, has to be rather the product of a cognitive development that arrives at this necessity itself by a process. Thus, though the *terminus ad quem* is one that Piaget shares with Kant, the *terminus a quo* is different and, more significantly, so is the road by which the end is achieved.

The historical precedents of Piaget's view lie both in philosophy and in biology. In philosophy, they may be generally identified with the dialectical tradition of evolutionism and developmentalism in post-Kantian thought, especially as it is elaborated in Schelling and Hegel, as well as with the tradition of Romanticist nature philosophy, in Goethe, and in a different sense, in Schopenhauer. The French roots of this tradition lie most clearly in the renaissance of Lucretian evolutionism in 18th century France, especially in the pre-Lamarckian transformism of Diderot, as well as in the preformationist views of Robinet and Maupertuis. Of course, the whole development of evolutionary biology in the late 18th and in the 19th century are the most obvious sources of Piaget's evolutionism, but with respect to theories of cognitive evolution or the evolution of thought and particularly with respect to the notion of stages of this development, the most important figure is Auguste Comte.

Now this sort of name-dropping is barely informative. What may be useful is to trace certain themes that are picked up and developed in a distinctive way by Piaget. I focus on three such themes, all of which radically revise the Kantian perspective. First, there is the notion of dialectic as the development or unfolding of the subject—in this case, consciousness itself—in the course of its activity, where this activity is seen as an interaction with another, taken as its object. This dialectic of subject and object goes beyond the Kantian synthetic activity of the understanding in that it unfolds in time and passes from "lower" to "higher" stages, in which each so-called lower stage forms the basis for the dialectical elaboration of the higher stage and in which each lower stage is incorporated and transcended or annulled (or becomes *aufgehoben*) in the higher stage. This dialectic is perhaps best known in the version that Hegel developed, particularly in his *Phenomenology of Mind,* (1807) where the active subject is consciousness itself as it attains to full self-consciousness in the course of its recognizing, and being recognized by, another self-consciousness. There is a deep affinity of Piagetan schemes of development with this Hegelian model, but Piaget makes only the briefest mention of it in his work.[1] For Hegel, as for Piaget, there are no preformed or fixed a priori structures of the mind; rather, these emerge in the course of the interactive relations between subject and object. But they emerge with a dialectical necessity determined by the end point of the development that for Hegel is the fully self-conscious self-consciousness, which incorporates all knowledge in itself and which is the identical subject–object or the totality which is identified with truth. Now the heady idealism, which is the Hegelian philosophy, is far removed from the biological emergentism of Piaget. But there is much to be studied in the formal relations between the two systems, to which I can only point here.

A second theme is that of evolutionary adaptation and transformation. In Goethe, and again in Schopenhauer, there is developed the notion that biological form is an internalization or a transformation into structure of modes of life activity. Diderot had anticipated such a view of morphological change in several of his works, but especially vividly in *Le Rêve de D'Alembert* (1875–77). Lamarck, (1809) not long afterwards, developed this as his distinctive theory of the inheritance of acquired characteristics in which forms of life activity influence heredity. In Schopenhauer (1818), this Lamarckism takes on a distinctive form (e.g., as when Schopenhauer says that teeth, throat, and bowels are objectified hunger). The emphasis here is on action and on modes of action that give rise to structures and, indeed, interiorize such structures in the changing adaptive biological forms of organisms themselves. The peculiar German-romantic form

---

[1]See, for example, Piaget, 1971a, p. 327, fn. 36, part 4. There is a brief discussion on dialectic in Piaget, 1970b, section 20, pp. 120–128, but it is mainly on Piaget's views on what Lévi-Strauss, Sartre, Bachelard, Godelier, Althusser, and others have said on the relation of structuralism and dialectic. See also the brief remarks on Hegel in Piaget, 1971b, pp. 58–59.

of this model is picked up and developed by the organicist schools of German biology and, specifically in embryology, by Driesch (1909) and von Uexküll (1909). I do not need to point to the direct connections with Piaget's thought here. Piaget's specific adoption of Waddington's (1962, 1975) model of biological adaptation and his full discussion of all these matters in *Biology and Knowledge* and elsewhere fill out the picture in detail.

The third theme, clearly related to the previous two, is the notion of stages. The historical background of this view is ancient, and it is tied in with the idea of progress, whether in theology (where the drama of salvation is marked by stages), in history, in natural history, or in the stages of consciousness. In modern thought, Buffon's *Époques de la Nature* or Robinet's *Gradation Naturelle des formes de l'Être* mark the pre-Lamarckian and pre-Darwinian notions of stages of natural history. Hegel develops perhaps the most elaborated theory of stages in all domains, whether in his philosophy of history, his philosophy of art (where Symbolic, Classical, and Romantic mark off the necessary developmental epochs of art history), his philosophy of nature, his phenomenology, or his science of logic. One may say that Hegel is stage-happy, for there is a profusion and proliferation of stages everywhere! But of particular moment is the so-called law of three stages that Comte (1830) introduces as the systematic sequence of modes of thought, namely, the theological, the metaphysical, and the positive or scientific. For Comte, these are not stages of ontogenesis, nor even of phylogenesis, but simply lower and higher stages of thought with the progress of intellectual enlightenment. The sequence is of course normative, and thus "positivism" or "positive science" is the highest stage in that it is by science alone that truth finally comes to be revealed. At almost the same time, and independently, Feuerbach (1957) proposes an entirely similar law of three stages in his philosophical critique of religion and philosophy and thus opens the way for an ideology of scientific enlightenment that has profound effects both in German science on the school of so-called "scientific materialists" in German biology and chemistry (Moleschott, Büchner, Vogt, Czolbe) and for the "scientific socialism" and "historical materialism" of Marx and Engels. Toward the latter part of the 19th century, Spencer develops his enormous synthesis of evolution and interprets it also for education and for psychology; and James outrages the Harvard establishment by introducing Spencer's text in psychology into the classroom.

Piaget's theory of stages is, of course, far removed from these earlier ideas. And his own emphasis is on the critique of philosophical theories of knowledge and of development as essentially speculative and unscientific because they are not grounded in experimental practice. But here again, the ideational structures of these historical precedents serve to sharpen our understanding of Piaget's own model both in terms of similarities and differences between them. The more immediate influences on Piaget among the historicist school of French philosophers of science (Brunschvicq, Lalande, Meyerson) lie closer to the surface, in relation to Piaget, for their emphasis is on the development of thought and upon the norms of this development, particularly in the history of science.

What emerges from this brief sketch of antecedents in philosophical and biological thought is the replacement of the ahistorical, nondevelopmental, and fixed categories of Kantian epistemology by the historicized, temporalized, developmental categories of post-Kantian philosophy, and by the organicist and evolutionary models of biological thought. Piaget is heir to both these reformations. But these models of change and development do not capture the essential feature of Piaget's program, or they do so only incidentally. Piaget's fundamental category is action or praxis. It is the features of this action that provide the motor of cognitive development and the genesis of structures. It is in the forms, the coordinations, and the schematizations of these actions that the progress of cognitive development has its grounds and the notion of stages receives its concrete interpretation. But it is also in his concept of action that I think Piaget falls short of an adequate account. The three themes of *dialectic, adaptation,* and *stages* provide at most a formal framework of the Piagetian program. Its concretization as an experimental study of the growth of child-thought depends on Piaget's characterization of the very object of experimental observation and inquiry, namely, the actions and judgments of the child. If, as Piaget claims, genetic epistemology is an attempt at a scientific theory of cognitive growth, then the fundamental entities of this science have to be specified clearly, and the fundamental criteria for making scientific judgments about these entities and their relations likewise have to be made clear. Less abstractly, we first have to examine what, for Piaget, counts as an action and then what counts as a case of development or growth of knowledge. As I hope to show, both of these concepts—action and cognitive growth—presuppose a normative framework in terms of which they are understood. Actions, for Piaget, are not merely bodily motions in space and time, as they might be for some idealized behaviorist, and cognitive growth is not merely a change in the patterns of such bodily motions. It comes as no news that Piaget is not a reductive behaviorist—indeed, who is these days? But if not, what is normative about his conception of action and his conception of cognitive growth?

ABOUT NORMS

Piaget proposes a fundamental hypothesis about the nature of cognition in general. He (1971a) writes: ". . . cognitive functions are an extension of organic regulations and constitute a differentiated organ for regulating exchanges with the external world [p. 369]." The function of cognition is, on this biological analogue, to maintain the equilibrium of the organism in the face of changes or disturbances in the environment. The presupposition here is not that an organism is a passive entity bombarded by actions upon it from the external world to which it reacts by some defensive autoregulatory compensation. Rather, for Piaget, to be an organism, a living thing, is to be a mode of activity, to encounter or to engage actively what lies beyond it. Life, then, is activity; furthermore, it is an activity that transforms its environment, indeed recreates its environment, by ingesting it, assimilating it, by making it over into a part of the organism itself. We do this in such metabolic modes as digestion, breathing, and so on. Is cognition then to be taken as a kind of metabolism, a mode of exchange between organism and environment? Well, in a manner of speaking, yes—a "highly differentiated mode." The biological norms of such organic activity are equilibrium and normal growth. Despite the biologism of the "organic regulations" metaphor and despite Piaget's seriousness in insisting on the continuity of cognition with biology, Piaget wants to avoid any biological reductionism. What differentiates the cognitive functions from other organic functions is that they are open to a development that goes beyond hereditary structures in a radical way. Piaget (1971a) puts it strikingly: "What does disappear with the bursting of instinct is hereditary programming, and this in favor of two new kinds of autoregulations, mutable and constructive. . . . What vanishes with the bursting of instinct is . . . programmed regulation, whereas the other two realities persist: the sources of organization and the resultants of individual or phenotypic adjustment [p. 366]." At this point, says Piaget (1971a), a "new cognitive evolution begins, and it begins all over again from zero, since the inner apparatus of instinct has gone [p. 367]." The dynamics of this new mode of cognition involve "two different but complementary courses: interiorization . . . and exteriorization [p. 366]."

What are we to make of these closing passages of *Biology and Knowledge?* What relevance does this have to Piaget's psychological work? Or is this simply the old man theorizing after hours? I think not. It is Piaget's attempt to provide the broadest and most systematic framework for his whole project, to place child-thought in the context of the development of human cognition in general, and to place cognition most generally into the context of its own genesis in the life-activity of organisms. But the grand schema affects the particulars very basically. For if the function of cognition is such "constructive autoregulation," as Piaget calls it in contrast to the programmed regulation of hereditary structures of action, then the very nature of human action as cognitive has to be understood in this light.

What, then, is an action? An action becomes a teleologically complex event within this scheme: It is a change in the environment brought about by an agent for the sake of maintaining or reestablishing that agent's equilibrium. But because the equilibrium in question is no longer under the regulatory system of instinctive or programmed homeostatic or homeorhetic mechanisms of equilibration, the agent has to form such mechanisms of regulation, such autoregulatory structures. And because an action is precisely undertaken to effect a change in the environment for the sake of such autoregulation, there can be no action that is not already in the service of some prior scheme of actions whose function is anticipatively autoregulative. That is to say, action presupposes a norm with respect to which the action is defined; yet this norm itself is to be the product of previous actions, and so on.

Piaget wants to avoid this infinite regress, or vicious circularity in the characterization of actions, and therefore requires the continuity with the biological modes of instinct as the original sources of actions. But the "bursting of instinct" introduces the creation or construction of norms, which now, by virtue of this construction, give rise to the range of individual and phenotypic actions no longer to be constrained by the genotype. Now this is no mere biological distinction, nor is it needless fussing over details. For what rests on this distinction between biologically inherited norms and those that come to be constructed in this postinstinctual way is the very object of cognitive activity itself, namely, knowledge. Knowledge, properly speaking, is the object of that action governed by constructed norms rather than by instinct; therefore, learning or the acquisition of knowledge is the product of such action. Piaget (1970a) writes:

> One knows an object, in effect, only in acting upon it and transforming it (just as the organism reacts to its environment only by assimilating it, in the widest sense of the term. And there are two ways of thus transforming the object to be known. The first consists in modifying its positions, or its motions or its properties in order to explore their nature: this is the sort of action which we will call "physical." The other consists in enriching the object with properties, or with new relations which conserve these properties, or with old relations among these properties, but now more fully realized by systems of classification, of ordination, of correspondence, of denumeration or measure, etc.: these are the sorts of actions which we will call "logico-mathematical" [p. 85, my trans.].

Piaget (1970a) adds: "Our knowledge proceeds not from sensation, not from perception alone, but from the entirety of our actions of which perception constitutes only the function of signalization. The proper mode of intelligence is not, in effect, contemplation, but transformation, and its mechanism is essentially operatory [p. 84]." In another place, Piaget insists on the primacy of these operative structures as the preconditions for knowledge and, indeed, on the "indisputable primacy of logico-mathematical explanations."

What this comes to, in effect, is that knowledge is systematically defined by Piaget as a normative concept in terms of the very definition of cognition as constructive autoregulation by means of successive equilibrations that are independent of biological preformation. The coordinations are fundamentally coordinations of actions that are originally sensorimotor activities of the child, which by interiorization arise to the level of logico-mathematical operations.

Thus, for Piaget, the move from genotypically fixed instinct to the "new cognitive evolution" introduces a whole range of structures that define the growth of knowledge with respect to its proper "end" or its mature form and, moreover, follow each other in what is effectively a logically necessary sequence because the higher structures (e.g., the operations) depend on the lower ones (e.g., the preoperational ones). Thus, the norm of cognitive growth is built into the norm of knowledge (as what this cognitive growth attains to), and this norm of knowledge in turn is given the validity of the deductive necessity of the sequence by which it is attained. This operates recursively, then, to establish a norm that has the force, in Piaget's sense, of deductive necessity, as the norm of cognitive growth itself. The process of cognitive development, as Piaget describes it, thus becomes orthogenic in as transcendental a sense as Kant might have desired because it has all the elements of universality and necessity that Kant demanded. We have finally achieved a theory of cognitive development that is universal and necessary. Moreover, the end state, or the validating stage of knowledge toward which this development tends—the "truth" that approximates "reality" not as a copy but as a reconstruction, as Piaget says—this truth turns out to be the present stage of the development of natural science and mathematics.

Piaget is not so naive as to think that deductive necessity attaches to the purported truths of contemporary science. In fact, he is eager to point out that science is historical and that a historico-critical approach has to be taken to its present claims. In addition, like knowledge in general, science is not a "fact" or a "given" but a process of infinite approximation to reality. Yet, in a troublesome way, the norms that define action, operation, and structure for Piaget take on a timelessness, a logico-mathematical necessity that stands in stark contrast with the historicity of contemporary science. It is as if Piaget has discovered the invariances that persist through transformations in the course of cognitive development: Cognition changes, both ontogenetically and phylogenetically—of that much Piaget assures us because child-thought is simply an accessible way to study the inaccessible cognitive development of the species in past ages. But the laws of such changes and the invariant succession or order of such changes are themselves not subject to change or development.

The very necessity that, as Piaget says, is achieved gradually in the course of successive equilibrations now seems to attach to the *sequence* of this course of development itself. It unfolds with all the inner determinateness of the Hegelian dialectic, in Piaget's reconstruction of it. One may surmise that it is achieved by the reflective abstraction that takes place in the development of genetic psychology itself, as a theory. In short, the system becomes self-certifying! Necessity attaches to the proposed laws of development and to the sequence that such laws describe, as successive equilibrations of the scientific theory take place, in the course of the "action" of scientific inquiry. We may extrapolate Piaget's account of the gradual achievement of necessity in the development of child-thought as a model of the development of scientific thought and, specifically, of the development of the science of child development.

Yet is that not precisely what we want from a science—that it will yield the laws of development not as local and time-variant laws, but as timeless, universal, and necessary truths? Or, with respect to human cognition, at least as transhistorical, transcultural, and species-wide truths?

Earlier, I suggested that I took Piaget to be a species essentialist, that is, he was proposing that there were essential features, which in effect are historically and culturally invariant in human cognition and in human cognitive development. In this respect, and in a strange way, we have come full circle back to Kant except that instead of Kant's particular form of transcendental epistemology, with fixed, nondevelopmental, a priori categories taken to be universal and necessary, we have a new set of categories that also emerges with the same universality and necessity, not as categories of our knowledge, but as categories concerning the growth of knowledge or cognitive development. What is so strange about this is that it is unsuspected: We moved away from Kantian nondevelopmental essentialism to what now appears to be a Piagetian developmental essentialism. There is surely a gain in all this, enormous in terms of what this approach yields in the way of experimental hypothesis and a rational account of development. But what is the loss? The loss it seems to me, is the relative subordination, if not the total elimination, of those features of cognitive development that cannot be encompassed under the rubric of equilibration or of the coordination of actions, in Piaget's sense. Which are these? Well, in a sense, Piaget does mention them in a relatively systematic way and even makes certain moves in the appropriate directions. And this is all the more frustrating because he stops so short of a real recognition of what he is missing. Here, as earlier in the paper, I refer to what I would call sociohistorical contexts and what Piaget calls, on the one hand, *social-structural* and, on the other, *historico-cultural*. The first is principally synchronic, and the second is diachronic. In Piaget's schema (1970a) for the four factors of development to be taken into account, he lists factors in the following order: (1) the biological factors that are "linked to the epigenetic system—interactions of the genome with the environment in the course of growth [p. 61]''; (2) the factors of the equilibration of actions (i.e., the focal group of autoregulative constructions that function in the cognitive development of the individual); (3) the social factors of interindividual coordination, specifically those that would tend to be common to all societies as structural universals; (4) what Piaget calls factors of educational and cultural transmission, which vary from one age to another (diachronically, therefore) or from one culture to another [pp. 66–67].

For the sake of brevity, let me simply report my impression that Piaget seems to underplay the social factors and tends to treat them in a somewhat defensive way, as if this might threaten his other findings. For the fourth group of historical factors (viz., those of educational and cultural transmission) he offers no more than lip service, It may be that as a biologist or even as a humanist at heart, Piaget wants to establish what is universally human and has no great interest in these other matters. Durkheim intrigues him always because Durkheim proposes such hard-core social wholes as operative constructs in his sociology that the individuals who are members of such wholes, or who are affected by them, remain alike enough as peas in a pod to satisfy any essentialist. But the role of historical change, whether in society as a whole, in modes of technological activity, or even in the history of science, seems to be ignored by Piaget as a serious factor in the course of cognitive development. Piaget (1970a) mentions the cross-cultural studies of Mohseni, Goodnow, Hyde, Boischair, and Price-Williams on the constancy of the ordering of the stages. But unless I am missing something, Piaget offers no sustained consideration of either cultural or historical factors in cognitive development.

Yet several factors urge such consideration. First, on the Piagetian grounds of the norm that adult-thought presents for child-thought, where the adult norm itself differs considerably from one culture to another or from one age to another (e.g., Aristotelian vs. Newtonian science), what effect would this have on the patterns or rates of cognitive growth? Or indeed, on the very norm of cognitive growth itself? Were ancient Greek children cognitively stunted in their growth because the adult world had not yet produced Newton and was still stuck with Aristotelian science? Or does humankind as a whole have to go through an Aristotelian stage before achieving the Newtonian or Einsteinian one? And if so, is the norm of cognitive growth itself culturally relative and diachronically changing? Moreover, where there is a major social change or revolution in the mode of life or the modes of everyday praxis, where social structures, technologies, or ideational structures change radically, what effects would such a change have on the development of child-thought or on the very norms that mark off the successive stages of cognitive development? These are the obvious questions one might expect from a Marxist consideration of Piaget's genetic epistemology, and they have been asked before (cf. the Vygotsky-Luria studies of the effects of social change in Uzbekistan in the late 1920s, only recently published, Luria, 1976; or indeed, the non-Marxist studies of the effects of culture on visual perception reported in Herskovits, Campbell, & Segall, 1969, and in later studies).[2]

These are what may be considered "external" questions. But there is what I would characterize as an internal question from the point of view of Piaget's own focus, namely, on the action-coordinations themselves and the development of cognitive structures. The first step here is a critical remark on Piaget's own apparently reasonable division of those factors, beyond the biological ones, to be considered in an account of cognitive development. These are: individual coordinations; interindividual (social) coordinations; and educative-cultural coordinations. Now, for the sake of analysis of various aspects of the growth of child-thought, the introduction of such categories may be fully appropriate. Yet, there is a methodological risk in the use of such a division, especially in the interpreta-

---

[2]See, for example, Berry and Dasen, 1974; Cole and Scribner, 1974; and Hagen and Jones, 1978.

tion of experimental results and even in the construction of experiments. This is because the world of our experience or of the child's cognitive activity and practice is not cut up in this way, and to introduce such analytic categories into the study of the child is to impose a construction that is already fragmented in a certain way upon the very object of study and thereby to risk distorting it. Results may then come to be artifacts of the experimental situation in such a way that generalizations from them about the nature of child-thought or the stages of cognitive development are false with respect to the integrity or the complexity of the phenomenon itself.

Let me make this point more specifically: Individual coordinations and the very concept of an action and of cognitive growth (which I discussed earlier) are defined by norms that are never merely the results of sensorimotor activity, *tout court*. Actions upon objects are always actions upon objects, true; but objects themselves are not abstract entities, existing in some generalized epistemological or ontological space of actions. Objects—especially those that figure in children's activity—are, in large measure, manufactured (i.e., artifacts), especially when they are the objects introduced in laboratory experiments. The world of objects is largely a world of social artifacts that bear the imprint of our intentionality, our needs and purposes, our social and technical skills and structures. What the child learns to see, to touch, to move around, to throw is a range of artifacts that already has a human significance for even the very young child. What is more, these objects of child actions are manipulated in the company of others and by the example of others, in contexts of approval and disapproval, and in the framework of questions, descriptions, and instructions, which all bring the sociality of language into the situation. The coordination of actions and the development of operative structures all take place, as Piaget agrees, in an environment where adult thought and norms play a large part in defining what is to be learned. Can such norms be regarded as so universal as not to affect the modes of cognitive acquisition and development themselves differentially? Thus, even if we start with action-coordinations at some basic level, the elements themselves are already suffused with the sociality and the intentionality embodied by the adult world of objects and language, which the child learns even in the basic sensorimotor tasks.

Further, just as sensations and perceptions only signalize the actions that give them their significance, according to Piaget, so too the actions themselves may be said to signalize the integrated world of social and historical norms and practices in which these actions take place, and which identify them as being the actions they are. What counts as a case of cognitive achievement—of equilibration or of assimilation—does so only by virtue of the fact that our cognitive norms recognize or identify it as such. But such norms, as Piaget himself agrees, are not imposed on us by the physical world of objects, either by nature or by our hereditary biological structure any longer. It is we who create these norms by our historically changing social praxis.

Thus, my argument here is that the concept of action upon which the edifice of knowledge is built by Piaget is in fact a richer concept than Piaget allows, although his emphasis on action is indubitably correct. For the action by which knowledge is achieved is also the construction of an object not only in the mind, in the internalized judgment, so to speak, but first in the external world of our practices. Objects are made or constructed things in the world. They are artifacts. They are in this sense always transformations of nature by human action or by labor. Now the child does not yet work or make things in this sense, although there is much construction in playtime activities. But the manufactured objects that constitute the child's environment, at least with respect to the "carpentered world" of artifacts, if not the world of "natural" objects, already prefigure the child's stages of cognitive development because they embody the cognitive achievements of the adult world. These stages are, so to speak, "in the objects" themselves as artifacts. For example, logico-mathematical operations are literally embodied in any object made by a machine. For the machine-made object incorporates those operations of its construction that derive from logico-mathematical norms (i.e., those norms that the machine exemplifies, and in accordance with which it was itself constructed and operates). Thus, we endow our world of artifacts with the adult world's "logic" *in concreto*. The child learns from this not simply by example but because these objects (of manipulation, of play, of child use) are already "objectifications," external representations of the structures of thought that constitute the logico-mathematical norms of the adult (scientific-technological) world. Thus, one may say that such externalized representations, "in" the artifacts, are the pictures of the adult mind, which the hcild learns to read "out there" in the objects themselves.

Piaget's concept of action may therefore be said to be weak in two ways: (1) it is not rich enough with respect to action as social, linguistic, and historically variable praxis; (2) it is not rich enough in taking into account what is already prefigured in the objects of the child's world as, so to speak, "object-lessons," which the child learns in the context of the meaning such objects have as representations of the social and technological practices characteristic of a given society. It seems to me that such a richer, more integrated conception of action is needed as a category for the analysis of child-thought and cognitive development in general. Piaget's analytical categories—biological, individual, interindividual, educative-cultural—may indeed be useful but only if the methodological risk of impoverishing the subject matter of the study is compensated for by seeing how these categories are dialectically interconnected, how each mediates or influences the others. Piaget is not unaware of this, certainly with respect to the interaction of individual and social factors; as I noted earlier, he has a subtle appreciation of the relation of biological to cognitive factors (though I believe his view is problematic here). He is less given to realizing or acknowledging the significance of the educative-cultural factors or to seeing how deeply these modify or qualify the others.

TOWARD A HISTORICAL EPISTEMOLOGY

What, then, does a historical epistemology propose as a fuller realization of genetic epistemology, and in what sense does Marx provide a richer conception of action or praxis than that used by Piaget? I can only sketch this briefly here. Basically it has to do with the recognition of the contexts of action as changing, sociohistorical contexts, whose norms cannot be abstracted from this historicity itself. The "adult world," which provides the norms of cognitive development, is itself not simply an abstract "scientific" world to which child-thought must attain as it becomes socialized and decentered. It is rather a specific concrete world, which moreover is changing, undergoing its own transformations, re-placements of norms, crises, and revolutions, whether social, technological, or scientific. This dynamic world, whatever its moments of stability or of historical "equilibration," embodies itself in the artifacts—social, technical, linguistic-cultural—which are the "objects" of child activity. Thus, what I have been calling cognitive modes are themselves subject to the very changes, and are coordinated with these changes, that take place in this world of action and objects. The sensorimotor, perceptual, and operative modes of thought are, as Piaget rightly says, action schemata and coordinations of such schemata. The logico-mathematical structures themselves are embodies not only, and not sim-ply, in the history of scientific thought, but also in the objective form of artifacts (i.e., in the products created by human beings in their social production) and within the social relations of production of a given historical period. They are also embodied in the forms of social, political, and cultural interaction that are the institutionalized forms of action of a given time and in the technological, linguistic, and value structures characteristic of an age or a given society. Thus, the adult world, which provides the normative and defining frameworks for what will count as actions, is never simply "adult" in some generic, abstract sense. It is always a given world—the specific, concrete world of Aristotelian, Newto-nian, or Einsteinian science, or of late industrial capitalist economy, of feudal-ism, of ancient Greek slave society, or of presently existing socialisms. It is also the specific, concrete world of exploitative or dominating relations, of caring, or of dutiful relations. Thus, human "action"—the operative category here—itself has a history. The specificity of this history is mapped into the aritfacts, social structures, and the very objects, institutions, and forms of communication that are the visible, palpable objectifications of a certain cognitive level of species development. Phylogenesis, in cognitive terms, is no longer biological in these contexts. It is historical, cultural, and also as Piaget says, it continues. It has not reached its final, fixed point.

But if this is true, then ontogenesis is not merely the socialization or assimila-tion of child-thought to a fixed, present-day adult world, but rather to a histor-ically changing and culturally variable one. Thus, genetic epistemology cannot, strictly speaking, set for itself the task of discovering the "universal and necessary'' features of the growth of knowledge, on the analogy proposed by Piaget of a "mental embryology" and "comparative anatomy."Such a premise takes as its norm a fixed species. But if the adult world, which provides the norms of cognitive development, is itself historically changing, then these very changes—the creation of new norms in science, in social and political practice, in technology, in art—are part of the objective world in which the actions and coordinations of children's cognitive activity take place. Such changes are then not merely reflected by thought, as accommodations to a given norm, but are created by this thought itself, as cognitive praxis. The tension in Piaget's genetic epistemology is precisely in the interplay between structure and genesis in the ontogenesis of child-thought and in the residual essentialism and ahistoricism, which persist in his search for the invariant structures of cognitive growth. The task, as I see it, is to transform the comparative anatomy of development into an evolutionary theory of the *history* of cognition (i.e., of changes in the modes of this development itself), thus from a genetic to a historical epistemology. This is not to say that all forms or stages of cognitive development will dissolve in the flux of constantly changing norms. There are, and there have to be, stabilizations of cognitive mode, which mark major historical achievements in the development of cultural, social, scientific, and technological life. And it remains an empirical question whether there are transhistorical invariants in the history of cognition, thus conceived. But this is a question that can be answered only if the "comparative anatomy of mind" is taken as a *historical* comparative anatomy of a complex species, which transforms itself by means of its own praxis in terms of the fundamental forms of its cognitive activity.

To use a metaphor from the calculus: Piaget has provided us with the first derivative, the rate of change of the vector *cognition,* with respect to the "time" of ontogenetic child development. We still need to supply the second derivative, the rate of change of the rate of change of this vector, not simply ontogenetically, nor phylogenetically, as a matter of "natural history," but rather with respect to humanly historical time (i.e., the time rate of change of human cultural evolution). For to say that cognition has a history is to say that childhood also has a history and that the modes of cognitive development of child-thought cannot be lifted out of this history.

REFERENCES

Berry, J. W., & Dasen, P. R. (Eds.). *Culture and cognition.* London: Methuen, 1974.
Cole, M., & Scribner, S. *Culture and thought.* New York: Wiley, 1974.
Comte, A. *Cours de la philosophie positive.* Paris-Rouen: 1830, Vol. I
Diderot, D. *Rêve de d'Alembert.* In *Oeuvres Complètes.* Assézat-Tourneux, Paris: 1875–77, Vol. II
Driesch, H. *Philosophie des organischen.* Leipzig: 1909.
Feuerbach, L. *The essence of christianity.* Marion Evans (tr.), New York: 1957.

Hagen, M. A., & Jones, R. K. Cultural effects on picture perception. In R. Walker & H. Pick (Eds.), *Perception and experience*. New York: Plenum Press, 1978.

Hegel, G. W. F. *Die phänomenologie des geistes,* Bamberg und Würzburg, 1807.

Herskovits, M. J., Campbell, D. T., & Segall, M. H. *A cross-cultural study of perception* (rev. ed.). Indianapolis, Ind.: Bobbs-Merrill, 1969.

Lamarck, J., de *Philosophie zoologique,* Paris: 1809.

Lorenz, K. "Die angeborenen Formen möglicher Erfahrung," *Zeitschrift für Tierpsychologie, 5,* 1943.

Lorenz, K. "Methoden der Verhaltungsforschung," in Kükenthal, Krembach, von Lengerken, Helmcke, *Handbuch der Zoologie,* vol. 8, t. 10, Berlin: De Gruyter, 1957.

Luria, A. R. *Cognitive development: Its cultural and social foundations.* Cambridge, Mass.: Harvard University Press, 1976.

Piaget, J. *Mechanisms of perception.* G. N. Seagrim (tr.), London: Routledge and Kegan Paul, 1969.

Piaget, J. *Psychologie et epistemologie.* Paris: Editions Gonthier, 1970. (a)

Piaget, J. *Structuralism.* New York: Basic Books, 1970. (b)

Piaget, J. *Genetic epistemology.* E. Duckworth (tr.), New York: Columbia Univ. Press, 1970. (c)

Piaget, J. *Biology and knowledge.* Chicago: University of Chicago Press, 1971. (a)

Piaget, J. *Insights and illusions of philosophy.* New York: World Publishing Co., 1971. (b)

Piaget, J. *Behavior and Evolution,* D. Nicholson-Smith (tr.), New York: Pantheon, 1978.

Rensch, B. *Evolution Above the Species Level,* New York: Wiley, 1959.

Rensch, B. "The evolution of brain achievements," In Th. Dobzhansky, M. K. Hecht, & W. C. Steere (eds.), *Evolutionary Biology,* I, pp. 26–68, 1967.

Uexküll, J. von *Umwelt und innenwelt der tiere,* Berlin, 1909.

Waddington, C. H. *New Patterns in Genetics and Development,* New York: Columbia University Press, 1962.

Waddington, C. H. *The Evolution of an Evolutionist,* Ithaca: Cornell University Press, 1975.

2 Development of Knowledge About Intermodal Unity: Two Views*

Eleanor J. Gibson
Cornell University

THE PROBLEM OF UNITY

Perhaps the most remarkable thing about perception is the unified quality of everything that we perceive. Courses dealing with perception frequently begin with descriptions of receptor surfaces: the retina, faceted with a dense population of rods and cones; the skin, with a fine grain of tactile receptors; the basilar membrane, a coiled surface bearing tiny hair cells; and so on. If they did not know better from the testimony of their own observations, students might expect all this to lead to a description of a totally fragmented perceptual world. But schooled or unschooled, we all know that we do not perceive fragmented, mosaic collections of components, heard, seen, or felt. What, then, do we perceive?

We perceive things and happenings in our environment—in the world around us. We perceive objects such as people, trees, furniture, and tools; we perceive places such as rooms, gardens, and tennis courts; and above all, we perceive events, changes occurring over a course of time, sometimes short and sometimes long. All of these, one might imagine, could be on a very small or very large scale—a place as small as a cavity in one's tooth or as large as Carlsbad Caverns; an event as tiny as a drop of water falling or as vast as an earthquake. There is no single-sized unit for ultimate analysis or compounding because things are nested

---

*Work on this paper was supported in part by grant (B-650) from the Spencer Foundation to Cornell University and Eleanor J. Gibson.

19

within places, small places within larger ones, and brief events within longer ones. There is structure at many levels, but levels for our perception have a size range that is ecologically appropriate for human animals, and within this range there are units, themselves structured and containing subordinate structures.

These units are structured, then, not particles; they are whole, bounded, and they have properties that are persistent enough to be described, to be specifiable, and to make them uniquely differentiable from other units. They are segregated from extended arrays surrounding them and from the temporal flow of events. We start therefore with the recognition of unity of the structures that we perceive—the objects, the places, the events. But how is this unity provided? I am going to present the problem in its most complex form, considering the multiple kinds of information available for specifying the objects, places, and events of the world. Let me begin by examining a few examples.

Objects appear to be natural units to all of us—people, animals, and artifacts such as books and tools. It is impossible to describe a person, a cat, or a pair of pliers as a compound of particles or as static snapshots. What is the shape of a cat? Because it is solid, there is no one aspect that portrays it accurately. To know its shape, it must be viewed from all sides. And because it is animate, its shape can deform as it licks a paw, stretches, sits down, and so on. The essence of catness includes tactile and aural properties as well—soft fur, scratchy claws, and, of course, a purr and a meow. But we still perceive it as a structured totality. It is specified by many stimulus properties—optical, acoustic, haptic, odorous— but all specify a cat.

Places are multimodally specified as well. My kitchen is an enclosed area bearing many distinguishing features. I can, if I try, conjure up a visual image of it—windows in the front and side walls, doors to the dining room and the hall, green linoleum on the floor, the stove, the sink under the front windows. The view I have of these things is different depending on where I stand, and as I move around something different is always occluded. There are distinctive sounds, too—the refrigerator gently humming and an annoying, dripping faucet. The floor is smooth and cool, and there is that one spot that often feels sticky. There are faint fragrances (e.g., a lingering odor of burnt toast this morning). It is one place despite all these varied ''sensations'' (as some might say), and it affords one thing—preparing meals.

Of course, events are multimodally specified, too. Consider the event of a bath for a baby. The baby can see the water, feel its warmth and wetness, and feel and hear the splashes as it kicks. But it is one event with appropriate affordances of pleasure and freedom to move one's limbs and make a noise.

All events, places, and things are specified by multimodal properties. Are these properties all modality-specific, like color, warmth, and wetness? Must a host of modality-specific properties be welded together to construct a totality? Whence comes the wholeness that is so immanent in our perceptions of the world? I shall argue that some properties of an object or an event are abstract, amodal, specifying the same invariant relation over change; that they may specify the same persisting features of a place or a face and the same affordances or meaning.

We must walk around the cat to see its shape, or it must move around. Purring, meowing, and scratching occur over time, but something persists, and the unity, boundedness, and affordances of the animal are not lost. This is the problem that I am addressing. More particularly, I want to speculate about multimodal information and how it might specify *one* object, *one* place, *one* event, segregated and unique.

TWO VIEWS

The problem I have just outlined is a very old one, as you all recognize. Although there have been a few occasions in the history of psychology when someone has made an effort to solve it (e.g., the Gestalt psychologists), we seem to be no nearer an answer. Wertheimer's laws dealt mainly with line drawings (though I have not forgotten the law of common fate, which is more useful than the rest). They are not of great help when it comes to understanding the oneness of the cat—smelly, scratchy, furry, and purry all at the same time.

One traditional view of the problem of unity is the *separatist* view, which holds that things are *not* perceived as unitary in the beginning but are integrated in the course of development. All elementaristic theories of perception have held such a view, usually conceiving of association as the welding principle. But the developmental psychologist whose impact has been greatest and whose name gives the Jean Piaget Society its title had a different conception, although I think we must still classify him as a separatist. His conception of the way objects and places become unitary is referred to as a *construction* theory. Piaget, unlike the British empiricists, has certainly never said that all relations are coincidental, arbitrary associations. But in the beginning, he conceived of perceptions as composed of "snapshots," as static and figurative. They developed (insofar as perception does develop) by way of perceptual activities. To cite one of his more recent statements (Piaget, 1971): "Indeed, perception might be characterized as a direct contact made between (1) perceptual activities carried out by the subject through an extension of assimilatory action schemata (relating and so on), and (2) objects in the environment which are reached by the intermediary of sense data in figurative form [p. 249]."

Knowledge of objects and events (e.g., causal relations) for Piaget involved cognitive processes of assimilation and organization, which are essentially constructive. How an object like a clock comes to be cognized as a ticking, metallic, hard, round, number-bearing object that has permanence and meaning had to be understood as a process of developing schemata, at first separate and eventually assimilated into one. Schemata from sight, hearing, and touch had to be coordinated. The most detailed account of this process is found in the chapters on "The Development of Object Concept" (Piaget, 1954), which is surely familiar to readers. But let me remind you, with a few pertinent quotations, of its bearing on the problem of unity.

To begin with, in Piaget's (1954) words: "A universe without objects [on the other hand] is a world in which space does not constitute a solid environment but is limited to structuring the subject's very acts; it is a world of pictures each one of which can be known and analyzed but which disappear and reappear capriciously [p. 3]." It is the activity of sensorimotor schemata that leads to construction and recognition of objects, and "every functional use (hence all primary circular reaction) of sucking, of sight, of hearing, of touch, etc., gives rise to recognitions [p. 5]." But these schemata are "heterogeneous," and until they are coordinated, there is no "continuity of pictures perceived [p. 5]." So sensorimotor schemata of looking, listening, touching, sucking, and so on are separate or "heterogeneous" in the earliest stages. Then:

> With regard to the intercoordination of schemata, that of sight and hearing may be mentioned. From the second month of life and the beginning of the third, the child tries to look at the objects he hears, thus revealing the relationship he is establishing between certain sounds and certain visual pictures. It is clear that such coordination endows sensory pictures with a greater degree of solidity than when they are perceived through a single kind of schemata: the fact of expecting to see something instills in the subject who listens to a sound a tendency to consider the visual image as existing before the perception. So also every intersensory coordination (between sucking and prehension, prehension and sight, etc.) contributes to arousing the anticipations that are assurances of the solidity and coherence of the external world [p. 7].

But in what way are anticipations "assurances" of the coherence or even the solidity of objects? Coherence (unity happens to be my preferred term) is the problem that I wish to discuss. I do not believe that anticipation of seeing something provides information of wholeness. It has to be "something" first, if it can really be anticipated. Here is one of Piaget's (1954) observations:

> Thus at 0; 2 (6) Laurent finds with his glance an electric kettle whose lid I shake. When I interrupt the noise Laurent looks at the kettle even though it is now silent; hence we may assume that he expects new sounds to come from it, in other words, he behaves with regard to the interrupted sound as he does to the visual pictures which have just disappeared [p. 10].

An astute observation, we would all agree! But the interpretation, that visual pictures have disappeared and that sounds are expected, does not explain how one can use the term *it* (i.e., the kettle).

According to Piaget (1954), the third stage, when prehension begins, brings in more schemata: "the child begins to grasp what he sees, to bring before his eyes the objects he touches, in short to coordinate his visual universe with the tactile universe [p. 13]." Piaget was giving his account here of the development of the "object concept" (i.e., of object permanence). I refer to this account because it reveals his view of how the object becomes a totality, or gains *coherence* to use his term. It is only when the schemata of touching, hearing, looking, sucking, and so forth are assimilated to one another that the object can achieve both unity and permanence. But what is the principle underlying assimilation of these schemata? On what basis are they coordinated? I accept the observations, but I find no answer to this question except "association," a principle to which Piaget seldom (if ever) appealed. As the object concept is achieved, an image of the object as a totality becomes possible (e.g., of a partially hidden toy duck). But is there no unified perception before that? Permanence, for Piaget, was achieved finally through active search in an extended space, but that does not tell us how the "polysensory complex" can become a unit. And when it does, however that may be, it is a "representation" that is unified, without reliance on prior unified perception.

Is there another way to view the phenomenon of unity? In opposition to the separatist view, there have traditionally been psychologists and philosophers who embraced a view often referred to as the *unity of the senses;* von Hornbostel (Ellis, 1938) and von Békésy (1959) have been notable among them. Von Hornbostel, for example, coined the term *super-sensuous sense perceptions.* Von Békésy emphasized the resemblances between sense impressions, especially hearing and vibration on the skin. I am uneasy with this terminology because it still appears to emphasize sense data, and I do not believe that perception starts with elementaristic, unrelated peeps, beeps, and pinpricks, even if there is some sensory correspondence between those presumed sensations. I think information is given *over* space and *over* time from the start and is relational as soon as it is picked up. I think that unity is the natural effect of multiple specification of invariant properties of things, places, and events. This is a unity theory, but not one based on sensations and resemblances between them. Multiple specification of invariant properties *is a guarantee of unity* because these properties are the same. They are not concrete in the sense of being modality-specific, but abstract.

What are these properties? In the case of objects, we think immediately of an object's size, shape, and substance as peculiarly characterizing it. These are persisting properties that do not change from moment to moment even if the object or observer moves around. Are these properties multiply specified? Indeed they are—by optic, haptic, acoustic, and often odor-bearing information. Any one of them may do for identifying an object or a place, so in that sense they are redundant. But because they specify the same thing, no integration, coordination, or even awareness of redundancy is necessary. Their redundancy of specification is itself information for unity, for oneness, with the same affordance or utility for adaptive behavior. Von Hornbostel's (in Ellis, 1938) famous quotation: "It matters little through which sense I realize that in the dark I have blundered into a pig-sty [p. 210]" can be amplified. The redundancy of information is not noted, although its identity reveals the identity of *a* place, and the affordance for the sufferer's welfare is likewise identical.

But do not objects and places have distinctive features or properties that are modality specific and are revealed even in a static array, so that dynamic relations, information revealed over time, are not in question? Yes, they do, like the numbers painted on the clock face or the features of anything painted or drawn in a picture. The relations in such cases are given in a spatial array, and insofar as they provide any information for unity, we may perhaps resort to Wertheimer's principles of proximity, continuity, similarity, and so on. I am not emphasizing these, but rather the invariant, abstract, amodal relations that are dynamic and given over time. Persisting features that characterize an object, event, or a place are seldom revealed in a static display. Many properties of an object are hidden or incompletely revealed except when the object is involved in an event. It is these properties, invariant over change, that interest me because when they are multimodally specified they provide powerful information for a bounded, segregated entity.

It is events, I believe, that we should look to first. They need to be classified in a number of ways before we can progress far in understanding them. Some are reversible and some irreversible—a very important distinction because reversibility provides information about persistence as opposed to change of form or state. Events contain different kinds of relations and transformations such as translation, passing, and causal relations. These properties characterize the event and give it distinction. Events also have dynamic properties, like rhythm, rate of change, and tempo.[1] Consider *tempo*—it can be accelerating, rising, falling, abrupt, slow, and many other kinds that you can think of. The period that is long enough to give us information for tempo is an event unit, and it cannot be any smaller. We have hundreds of words in our language to describe transformations in an event that denote tempos—explosive, luching, choppy, ambling, piercing, jerky. Jerkiness can be seen, heard, and felt. This is an amodal property that can characterize and segregate an event from sequences before and after it. It can be presented by a dancer so as to provide auditory, visual, and haptic experiences. *Choppy* is a word that derives from an action (i.e., a chopping movement), so it might be thought that it is specified only haptically. But that is not at all the case. A sea can be described metaphorically as choppy, and the property is specified by visual and vestibular information. Specification refers to the relation between actual properties of events, stimulus information for them and perceived properties with meaning and affordances (cf. Gibson, 1979), not to similarities or

---

[1]See J. J. Gibson (1979) for a discussion of invariant properties of events, and Mendelson (1979) for an outline of "amodal properties related to space and time."

resemblances between processes. Properties of energy capable of stimulating the visual system can specify choppiness, and so can energy stimulating the vestibular organs, but the energy and the receptor processes are not necessarily similar to one another any more than perception is similar to the waves of energy that make contact with a receptor surface.

DISCOVERY OF INTERMODAL PROPERTIES

Our common concern is development and theories of development. Let us consider, therefore, how discovery of abstract intermodal properties that specify the same property of an object, place, or event comes about. A metallic substance (e.g., an aluminum pot) can be detected by looking at it, striking it, and listening when it is struck. Note that all of these means describe active perceiving (i.e., searching for information). Nature has fortunately endowed the infant with endogenous motivation to explore and to seek out information. I think, myself, that the motivation extends to a search for structure and invariance. But, be that as it may, the perceptual systems are active from the start. Not only that, the perceptual systems work together from the start in an overall system of preadapted coordinations. Exploration by one perceptual system is triggered by another, with exploration by the two (or three) continuing together or by one alone if one external specifying stimulus ceases (e.g., a sound made by an object can cease and the object can still be looked at, felt, or both). These precoordinated systems can thus reveal supplementary modality-specific information about an object, or they can reveal properties that are multimodally specified, invariant over sensory systems.

So, there is a guaranteed means of extraction of the multimodal invariants and affordances that underlie and specify perceptual unity in the form of precoordinated, preadapted multimodal exploration by the perceptual systems. What are some of these preadapted coordinations? Piaget noted some of them (though he thought of them as having to *be* coordinated), but recently we have learned a great deal more.

I point out evidence from recent experiments for two or them. Systems for looking—for exploring an object in the periphery with a saccade toward a stationary target or for tracking a moving object—are present in the neonate. Both eye movements and head movements have been shown to be involved in this behavior (Bullinger, 1977). But even more interesting are eye and head movements toward sounding objects followed by visual exploration as well as continued listening if the sounds continue. Wertheimer (1961) noted that his newborn daughter turned her eyes in the direction of a clicking sound occurring to the right or left of her head. The observation roused some controversy, although there were partial replications (cf. Butterworth & Castillo, 1976). At present, with better methods of investigation and a more systematic approach to the problem, there are at least four experiments attesting to the neonate's orienting both with eyes and head toward a sound source, accompanied by visual exploration of the scene. These experiments have for the most part presented little for the infant to look at, but when they did, the baby appeared to look attentively in an extended and exploring fashion.

In an experiment by Mendelson and Haith (1976), infants 1 to 4 days old looked at a lighted field containing a vertical bar at one side or the other. Sounds (a male voice reading poetry) were presented laterally either at the same side as the bar or at the other side. The infants were sensitive to the location of the sound and scanned first toward it and then away from it. Fixations increased initially near the bars following same-side bar-sound combinations, but they eventually shifted away as if searching for a change in the stable visual environment. Mendelson and Haith (1976) report that the activity did not appear purely reflexive, but more like an "inherent information acquisition routine." The routine "enables the infant to find a visual change associated with the auditory change [p. 55]." When no such change occurred, the infants "fixated away from sound, perhaps in search of a visual change in a different place [p. 55]." Alegria and Noirot (1978) found evidence in 5-day-old infants of head turning and also eye opening toward a male speaker's voice transmitted through a loudspeaker. Occasional random head turning in a control group was not accompanied by opening the eyes.

An experiment by Haith, Bergman, and Moore (1977) strengthens the evidence that the eye movements were not purely reflex but rather exploratory. They recorded visual fixations of young infants as they scanned an adult face that was either stationary, moving, or talking. Talking produced an intensification of scanning the eye area in infants aged 7 weeks and older.

An experiment by Field, DiFranco, Dodwell, and Muir (1979) investigated whether infants of 2 months detected natural "correlations" between sight and sound from a single source or location. Auditory stimulation was a female voice reading poetry played through a speaker behind a screen, 50° to the right or left of the infant. Visual stimulation was provided by a female experimenter who raised her head above the screen at the speaker positions and smiled. There were four conditions: voice alone, face alone, face and voice in same location, and face and voice in different locations. There were also 30-second control periods when nothing was presented. Latency and occurrence of head and eye turns were recorded. The infants turned fastest to a visual presentation, whether or not it was accompanied by sound, but there was consistent head and eye orientation to the voice alone. In a second experiment, the finding of visual orientation to an auditory stimulus was replicated. Latencies were fairly long, but looking and listening behaviors were coordinated in a significant proportion of these infants.

Another experiment by Muir and Field (1979) extended these findings with infants between 2 and 7 days of age. Two rattles (plastic bottles filled with popcorn) were placed laterally at the sides of the baby's head, and one was shaken for a period up to 20 seconds. All babies turned correctly on a majority of trials. Muir and Field (1979) reported: "In general, the infants displayed lengthy and vigorous responses suggesting that they were making a deliberate attempt to investigate the locus of the shaking rattle; they hunched their shoulders, actively pulled their heads up, turned to the side of the stimulus, and then seemed to inspect the sound source visually [p. 432]." A second experiment eliminated all visual cues by recording the rattle sounds and presenting them through speakers. There was again a striking tendency to orient toward the sound. Turning latencies were slow, so continuous sounds may be optimal for eliciting the behavior. It might be noted, too, that continuous sounds provide optimal opportunity for exposure to a multimodal invariant as would normally be provided by visual and auditory information for a shaking rattle or a person talking. These results were confirmed and further amplified by Field, Muir, Pilon, Sinclair, and Dodwell (1980) with infants from birth to 3 months.

The other preadapted intermodal coordination that has received considerable attention by experimenters is looking and touching. Like the foregoing example, early experiments led to considerable controversy, perhaps because haptic exploratory systems are not as easy to observe as head turning and looking or perhaps because manual exploration is simply not ready to fucntion until later (i.e., sometime between 6 and 12 months). Even neonates appear to get haptic information about objects from mouthing them, but coordination of information about objects from visual and manual exploration may have to wait. Nevertheless, as soon as it may be available, to look and touch is of great importance for establishing unity.

Bower, Broughton, and Moore (1970b) investigated the coordination of visual and tactual activity in infants, attempting to study prehensile adjustment to size, shape, and hardness of an object presented visually. The infants were between 6 days and 6 months old. They reported that a seen object was reached for by every infant (not necessarily contacted) and that anticipatory hand-shaping occurred as early as 7 days in some infants. Haptic exploratory behavior was inexpert at this age; the information provided by the tactual system is initially much poorer than that provided visually. Bower, Broughton, and Moore (1970a) further reported that neonates exhibited different behaviors when reaching for a real, tangible object than when reaching for an intangible, virtual one. The latter situation was said to produce frustration. Further studies by Bower (1972) with neonates cited evidence of reaching toward solid objects more than photographs of them, more frequent reaching toward near objects than distant ones, and finger separation during reaching adjusted to the size of a presented object. Other experimenters (Dodwell, Muir & DiFranco, 1976; Rader & Stern, 1982; Ruff & Halton, 1978) found these observations difficult to replicate with neonates or felt that exploration was confined to the visual system. But Provine and Westerman

(1979) found that at 9 weeks all infants tested reached for and touched an object in front of their ipsilateral shoulder, although they did not as yet "cross the midline" to touch an object in front of the contralateral shoulder.

Although manual haptic exploration is surely unskilled in neonates, coordination between the two systems appears very early in that visually perceived information instigates what has been termed *pre-reaching* behavior. Bruner and Koslowski (1972) observed infants between 8 and 22 weeks of age and concluded that they were "able to make use of visual information in the regulation of early pre-reaching—information prior to that provided by feedback from early attempts at visually directed reaching [p. 13]." Infants who were not yet capable of a visually guided reach were nevertheless able to stretch their hands to the midline in the presence of a small graspable object and did so more than in the presence of a larger nongraspable object. A swiping motion, akin to palpating, was more likely to be evoked by the larger object, as I think it is toward a large surface such as a nearby wall.

Instigation of arm extension to moving objects has been studied in neonates by von Hofsten (1982). An object placed on the end of a moveable rod swung slowly past the infant. The number and distribution of arm-hand movements was examined when the object was either present or absent. There was a clear effect of fixation on the direction of forward movements. When the object was fixated, there was a higher proportion of forward arm extensions than otherwise. Analysis of the arm extensions showed that the movements performed while the neonate fixated the object were aimed closer at the objects than were other movements. In the best aimed movements, the hand slowed down as it neared the object. Von Hofsten concluded that newborns possess a rudimentary form of eye-hand coordination whose function is attentional, orienting it toward external events, rather than manipulative.

It appears then that while coordination of the systems is present at birth, skilled haptic exploration is yet to come. Knowledge of objects gained through exploratory handling seems to be minimal before 6 months or so, only appearing with appreciable force around 10 to 12 months (Gottfried & Rose, 1980; Soroka, Carter, & Abramovitch, 1969).[2] And yet, there is evidence for pickup of visual-haptic invariants that have an affordance to the child in some experiments I will describe later. One wonders whether nature has given even the human child (as occurs in greater measure in the young of many precocial species) some "wired-in" knowledge of at least a few multimodal invariant properties. I have been suggesting that the human infant is endowed originally only with the *means* of obtaining knowledge of multimodally specified invariants through precoordianted systems for exploration. A more radical assumption would be that infants

---

[2]Texture and substance might be an exception because these properties can be detected with relatively little exploration. But even the *presence* of an object in the hand, if it is unseen, draws very little attention before 10 months (Gratch, 1972).

are endowed with ability to recognize some such invariants, and their affordances, at once. Let us consider evidence that there is multimodal specification of invariants, and then ask whether young infants actually detect it.

MULTIMODAL INVARIANT PROPERTIES

A little more amplification of the term *invariant* may be needed because it is at the heart of what I wish to say and because it sometimes strikes people as a mysterious and unscientific concept. I can lay to rest any fears that it should be shunned by a scientist with some references to Einstein that I have taken from a paper by Holton (1979). On Einstein's first visit to this country in 1921, he was greeted by crowds and reporters and:

> the first question was, inevitably, how the content of relativity theory could be made clear in a few sentences. Einstein had a ready answer: ''If you don't take this response too seriously and see it only as a sort of joke, I can make it clear in the following way: It used to be thought that time and space would remain if all things in this world disappeared. According to relativity theory, however, space and time disappear with things'' [p. 13].[3]

Time and space are not disembodied but are joined in identifying the occurrence of events. The word event was frequently stressed by Einstein, and according to Holton (1979): ''Until 1913 Einstein still referred in print to the 'so-called relativity theory,' and his correspondence shows that he would have preferred the exact opposite, the much more accurate term, invariance theory, because he was concerned primarily with the constancies behind change [p. 19].''

That is exactly what perception psychologists are concerned with—the constancies behind change and, in the present case, how perception of them develops. What is perceived as constant are things with constant properties. The things themselves are units—bodies located with reference to a persisting surface (i.e., the ground) and with reference to events of which they are part—not assemblages of arbitrary properties in a disembodied universe. Perception of this unity depends on invariant information that specifies both unity and constancy over change. Invariant information for unity and constancy is abstract and relational. It must be, to be invariant over change. It may only be described in abstract terms, like those of mathematics, but that makes it no less powerful.

What I wish to do now is give examples of invariant properties of an event, an object, and a place, show that they are specified in such a way that an affordance

---

[3]It is interesting to compare this statement with Piaget's (1954) speculations about an infant's experience of a ''universe without objects'' as a ''world in which space does not constitute a solid environment [p. 5].''

may be perceived, and show that this information is multimodally specified, guaranteeing that the event or thing can be perceived as a structural unit from the start. I begin with an event, the event of impending collision, sometimes referred to as *looming*. The event involves an object moving through a place, but it is the change, the transformation occurring over time, that has interested many experimenters. The invariant information for the event itself—impending collision—can be mathematically specified (see Fig. 2.1).

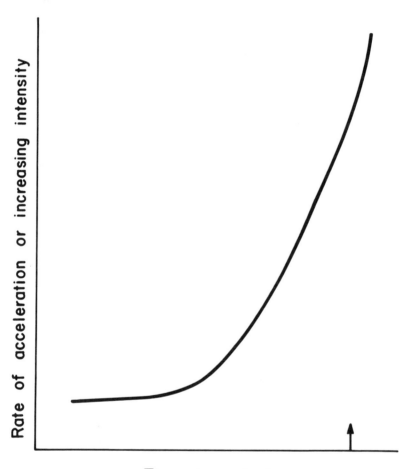

Time to contact

FIG. 2.1 Hypothetical curve of an approaching object. An optical expansion pattern, or increasing acoustical or tactile intensity can be so represented as time to contact approaches. The arrow represents contact, or the nearest point in the trajectory of approach. The process represented is abstract, without reference to any particular "modality" (redrawn from Bower, 1979a).

The first experiments on impending collision were performed by Schiff (1965) with a shadow-casting apparatus. The subjects were stationed in front of a large screen. Behind the screen at a distance of 1 meter or so was a point source of illumination; between the screen and the point source was a small object that cast a shadow on the screen. The object was mounted on or suspended from a trolley and, as it moved from the screen toward the source of illumination, the shadow magnified progressively at an increasingly accelerated rate until it flooded the entire screen in a final explosive burst. The subjects (animals in Shiff's case) winced, retreated, blinked, and so on. The pattern of expansion or accelerated magnification specifies imminent collision, and the effect is compelling even to a sophisticated adult viewer. The experiment has been repeated many times now (Ball & Tronick, 1971; Bower et al., 1970b; Yonas, Bechtold, Frankel, Gordon, McRoberts, Morcia, & Sternfels, 1977; Yonas, Petterson, Lochman, & Eisenberg, 1980) with human infants. Some have reported avoidance or defensive behavior as early as 1 or 2 weeks, and some (Yonas and his colleagues) find compelling, reliable evidence of startle (indicated by blinking) only later, around 3 to 4 months, but they find it, nevertheless, in this very unorthodox situation. Differentiation of a collision course from a "miss" course is present before the 3rd month in human infants (Ball & Tronick, 1971). Children are seldom subjected to experiences of imminent collision in the real world. But if they were, it would be specified as well by a rush of air of increasing force against the skin and sometimes sounds increasing in intensity and changing frequency as the object or surface approached and finally collided.

Evidence that this event is multimodally specifiable and is therefore an abstract, amodal invariant has been provided by White, Saunders, Scadden, Bachy-Rita, and Collins (1970) in the course of testing a prosthetic device for the blind. The device consists of a 20 × 20 matrix of vibrators placed against the user's skin. A television camera takes a picture of a scene or event, and the image is transformed electronically into a vibrotactile image. In the authors' words (White et al., 1970), it is a "sensory substitution system that converts a visual image into a tactile one [p. 23]." The system was shown to be capable of demonstrating to its wearers size constancy and impressions of external localization of objects as the camera moved over appropriate displays, but more interesting still were: "the occasions when Ss gave startled ducks of the head when the tactile image was suddenly magnified by a sudden turn of the zoom lever on the camera [p. 25]." This is a demonstration of a startle response to "tactile looming." To quote Hatwell (1978), a psychologist specializing in blindness:

The main contribution of White and Bach-y-Rita et al. is to show that when an area of the skin is treated as a retina, that is, when it receives plane projections of a three-dimensional world, the spatial information extracted from this tactile stimulation is exactly the same as that extracted from the visual one, provided that the same conditions of active transformation of the stimulus array are allowed [p. 515].

Bower (1979a;b) has written of an analogous substitution of auditory for visual information about spatial aspects of events. He had a sonic guide device developed by Kay modified to be worn by a very young blind child. The guide is an ultrasonic echolocation system that continuously irradiates the environment with ultrasound and converts reflections from objects and surfaces such as walls into audible sound. The sounds are coded to provide information about distance, size, and texture of the reflecting surfaces. Informal experiments with the device were tried with blind infants of various ages (4 months, 6 months, 13 months). As an object was made to approach the 4-month-old infant, interposition of the hands between the face and object occurred, behavior often reported in a visual looming experiment. Reaching and swiping occurred with appropriate presentation to right and left. In the 13-month-old infant, who walked with one hand held, walking was aimed away from walls and toward doorways after a short experience. An accelerating intensity pattern (acoustic in this case) was information for something approaching or being approached, and an aperture (i.e., a doorway) was distinguished from an obstacle (i.e., a solid wall). Features of a *place,* in other words, can be specified by multimodal invariants, providing information for where to walk or not. The pitch-intensity change function presents information that is invariant over modalities and is comparable to that presented optically and on the skin in the analogous examples, All three specify the same kind of change when there is a missle, a barrier, or an obstacle that affords collision.

I chose this case because it is such an elegant example of an intermodal invariant that specifies the same event, which has been studied experimentally. Something rather similar actually happens frequently in the daily life of an infant, though it always stops short of collision. An adult approaches the infant's room and then its crib, heralded by footsteps, sometimes a voice becoming louder and louder, and a figure presenting an optical expansion pattern approaching at the same time, eventually looming over the infant as it is picked up. Does an infant detect the optical-acoustic invariant in the continuing series of transformations of this event? There is good reason to think that it does, at least by the age of 4 months, as demonstrated by Spelke's experiments (1976, 1978, 1979).

Spelke's method was to present two filmed events projected side by side on a small screen in front of an infant. A sound track was made for each film, but only one of the two was played, from a source at the center of the screen. A hidden observer monitored the baby's visual fixations to see if the infant would detect the event that was appropriate for the accompanying sound and watch it. Babies did indeed select the appropriate film and watch it significantly more often than the comparison film. This selective attention confirms the infant's ability to pick up invariant information specifying the same event, thus unifying the event. Both real, natural events (e.g., a woman playing peekaboo, a hand playing some percussion instruments or a xylophone, a game of pat-a-cake[4]) and artificial, unfamiliar events (e.g., puppets marching to unfamiliar sounds and rhythms) provided evidence for the baby's ability to identify the unified event. Synchrony of rate, tempo, and other temporal invariants provided abstract, amodal information for unity.

It may be that common *affordances* also provide a basis for unity. Both voice and face can specify the affordance for friendly, comforting treatment, versus hasty or rough handling, or even neglect. Walker (1982) presented infants with films of a woman either smiling, cheerful, and talking happily or behaving in a depressed or an angry fashion. Infants definitely preferred the happy film, but nevertheless an appropriate sound track drew their attention to the event specified in the film, even when expressions ware sad and angry. These infants, 5 and 7 months old, still selected the appropriate film when the sound was played out of phase with it, so that synchrony could no longer unify the event. The common affordance, itself invariant, may well have done so. The multimodally specifiable event that I discussed earlier, impending collision, has an obvious common affordance whether it is specified optically, acoustically, or haptically. Indeed, it is the behavior telling us of the affordance that gives us an objective criterion for testing the psychological reality of a multimodal invariant. The invariant can be mathematically described, whether it is functional or not, but it becomes of theoretical interest to developmental psychologists when it is responded to.

Objects as well as events have properties that are multimodally specified. They are constant, persisting properties such as size, shape, and substance. That size and shape of an object are specified both optically and haptically is obvious, and that the invariant, amodal information is picked up by quite young children and even animals has long been known (Davenport & Rogers, 1970; Gibson, 1969). What is new is research carrying this work into infancy. Bryant, Jones, Claxton, and Perkins (1972) found some evidence of cross-modal discrimination by infants under 12 months between objects that could be both visually and haptically differentiated by curvilinear and angular contrasts. Gottfried, Rose, and Bridger (1977) investigated pickup of visual-haptic invariants in 12-month-old infants, again with pairs of objects differing in curvilinear and angular properties. They used two procedures, one in which the infants were familiarized with a small object orally and then given a pair of objects, the familiarized one and a contrasting new one, for a visual preference test. There was a preference for looking at the novel object, and it was reached for more often than the old one. The other method employed manual-haptic familiarization followed by a visual preference test. Again there was a preference for the novel object.

Ruff and Kohler (1978), in a somewhat similar experiment, worked with 6-month-old infants. They were familiarized manually with a cube or a sphere hidden under a cape. The experimenter placed the object in their hands and

---

[4]Playing the xylophone and the game of pat-a-cake were filmed and tested by Bahrick and Walker (1978).

moved it around. A visual preference test followed, in which the infants looked longer at the familiar object. These results were not as clear as those with older infants appear to be, probably because manual exploration was not sufficient and also not self-instigated. For that reason, an experiment by Meltzoff and Borton (1979) with infants only 1 month old is especially interesting. Haptic familiarization was accomplished by inserting a small hard rubber object mounted on a pacifier into the infant's mouth for 90 seconds of oral exploration. Two objects, one similar to the familiarization object and one contrasting in surface texture, were then presented for a visual preference test. (Both objects were spherical in shape, one of them covered with nubs and the other smooth.) The infants spent significantly more time in the preference test looking at the object resembling the one that had been mouthed.

The implication of this research for Meltzoff and Borton is that infants recognize an "intermodal match" without benefit of experience in simultaneous haptic-visual exploration. This may be so. I am more comfortable with the hypothesis that what is built-in is a preadapted coordination of exploratory systems, not intermodal knowledge. Intermodal knowledge is obtained through active exploration of the perceptual systems. Multimodal invariants are detected that specify properties of the object, including its unity. In the Meltzoff and Borton experiment, the infants detected the invariant directly both from mouthing and from looking at the objects, or they discovered the affordance of "roughness," or both. Either way, I do not think that they "matched" because the invariant, abstract information that is extracted specifies the same property in both cases.

A property of objects that is certainly as important as shape is the substance they are made of—hard or rigid as compared with chewy, elastic or soft. These are constant properties that are very important for adaptive action. To an adult, their affordances are obvious, no matter how the information is obtained. Hard things can be used as weapons, spongy and elastic ones can be chewed, liquid ones can be drunk, soft ones afford comfort. Properties of rigidity and elasticity are specified optically as invariant by types of motion (rigid motion or perspective transformations vs. deforming motion). For adults, perceiving certain motions as invariant information for rigidity is well-documented (Fieandt & Gibson, 1959; Gibson & Gibson, 1957) and, indeed, according to Jansson and Johansson (1973) information for rigidity enjoys a privileged status in that the perceptual systems are biologically constrained to extract it easily. Rigid motion (i.e., motion of a rigid figure) is defined by projective properties that remain invariant under perspective transformations of a figure. An example of such invariance (Johansson, von Hofsten & Jansson, 1980) is the cross-ratio between sets of elements (points) on a straight line:

> When the line is rotated relative to the eye (either by locomotion of the perceiver or by motion of the object), the metric distances of the proportions of any four points

on the picture plane (representing the retina) of course will change very much. The cross ratio between these points on any such projection will remain constant, thus carrying mathematical information about the constant distances on the moving real line [p. 31].

This information for rigidity of a surface is perceived as such by adults. Indeed, when a display is created artificially so that rigid motion (rotation) or stretching can be perceived, adult observers perceive rigidity preferentially (Jansson & Johansson, 1973). It is as if the system is attuned to pick up information for a rigid, nonstretchy world presenting surfaces that persist. It is now clear that infants, by 3 months, detect invariant optical information specifying rigidity and differentiate it from information, provided by deforming motions, for elasticity (Gibson, Owsley, & Johnston, 1978; Gibson, Owsley, Walker, & Megaw-Nyce, 1979; Walker, Owsley, Megaw-Nyce, Gibson, & Bahrick, 1980).

These properties are specified acoustically and haptically as well. Bahrick (in press) has shown that infants of 4 months differentiate rigid, hard objects from plastic, spongy ones on the basis of acoustic specification. Two events were filmed with accompanying sound tracks. One portrayed blocks being struck together, the other water-filled plastic sponges being squeezed. When a single sound track was played with both films displayed, infants looked preferentially at the appropriate film. Acoustic invariants specifying hard versus soft or elastic substances have not yet been clearly defined but are carried in part by temporal information.

Haptic differentiation of rigidity from plasticity is specified through exploration both by mouth and by manual manipulation. Its differentiation and identification with the appropriate visually given invariant has been investigated in our laboratory with 1-month-old and 1-year-old infants (Gibson & Walker, 1982). The question is whether an infant, after exploring a hard or a spongy substance haptically (by mouth at 1 month, manually at 1 year), will recognize it visually on the sole basis of differential motions specifying rigidity or elasticity of the substance. It is essential that the infant manipulate the substance actively in order to get haptic information about its properties. Manual exploration is late in maturing and is very difficult to obtain in infants under 1 year. We therefore chose subjects 1-year-old for our first experiment with manual exploration. Subjects sat on their mother's lap in a dark room. On a table before them lay an object of either an elastic (soft) or a rigid (hard) substance. Aside from the substance, the objects were alike. A dot of luminescent paint on an object made the presence of something detectable. A baby was left to itself to find an object, pick it up and manipulate it, its actions meanwhile recorded on videotape in infra-red light. When a baby had accumulated 60 seconds of time spent manipulating an object, the object was withdrawn and two movies were projected on a small screen in front of him. The films were of similar objects, the same shape as those handled and a little larger, but one was moving in a rigid pattern characteristic of a hard substance while the other moved in a deforming pattern characteristic of an elastic substance. The subjects' eye movements were monitored by an observer. The infants' first looks were directed significantly more often at the object related to the substance that had just been handled. The duration of first looks at an object of a familiarized substance was also significantly longer than that to the nonfamiliarized.

The experiment with 1-month-old infants was similar in design, but haptic familiarization was accomplished by placing a cylinder of either a hard or a spongy substance in the infant's mouth and allowing it to mouth it for 60 seconds. The visual preference test was conducted with real objects instead of film. Two otherwise identical-looking cylinders were moved simultaneously before the infant, one in a rigid pattern and one deforming. Again there was a looking preference, this time for the novel substance. The shift from a familiar preference in the first experiment to a novel preference in this one was probably attributable to the greater similarity of the preference situation to the familiarization situation in the experiment with younger infants. But in both cases, looking behavior was influenced by prior haptic familiarization, providing evidence for intermodal detection of invariants specifying substances with different affordances.

My last example of an intermodal invariant is for a *place*. A cliff is a horizontal surface ending in a drop-off. One can walk or crawl to the edge and feel manually or by putting out a foot that the surface of support affords locomotion only so far. It is a ground only to the edge, and terrestrial animals fall if they proceed over the edge. But adults, if they are looking, do not do so, and neither do precocial animals of many species, such as newborn kids (Walk & Gibson, 1961). They do not have to poke with a hand, foot, or cane to know where the surface of support stops because there is visual information for a surface of support provided by characteristic texture, reflectance, and layout. The transition at the edge is optically well-defined by differential texture gradients, motion parallax, and progressive occlusion of texture elements of the surface below as the animal's head is moved. The affordance of haptic and visual information for the drop-off is so identical that a creature at a cliff edge is quite unaware of modality-specific experiences; the experience is perfectly unified, and the cliff is avoided. The concordance of the information and its affordance does not seem to have to be learned by the young of some species. That may not be true for human infants, although length of crawling experience does not appear to be a good predictor of cliff avoidance (Rader, Bausano, & Richards, 1980). Whether or not the invariant and its affordance is learned by simultaneous exploration with haptic and visual systems, the common invariant information specifying a drop-off is unified and functional about the time that locomotion begins in most infants.

MODAL PROPERTIES

It may seem, in my emphasis on the wholeness of our experiences of events and things, that I have forgotten about modality-specific knowledge such as color, warmth and cold, musicality in an auditory event, and so on. Objects do have some modality-specific properties, which as adults we are well aware of, can dissociate from our perception of the total object or event, and speculate about. Preadapted coordinations, like the auditory system's capability of alerting the visual system, serve the function of directing the alerted system to explore for modality-specific properties, as well as providing the opportunity for simultaneous bimodal exploration. That is a kind of bonus in my opinion. Although I have very little evidence to go on, I would speculate that such specific knowledge is rarer in infancy than knowledge of intermodal invariant properties. For example, there is evidence that shape, an intermodal property, is attended to and remembered preferentially in comparison to color by young infants (Strauss & Cohen, 1980).

I do not wish to push that point, but I would push the hypothesis that modal properties, as separate dimensions of things and events, are differentiated developmentally from an originally more primitive "whole" experience unified by abstract, amodal invariants. Separating modal dimensions from one another with awareness of doing so seems to me, as has been said before (Bower, 1974), a sophisticated achievement. Certainly children cannot analyze and talk about such modal separation until rather late. In an experiment by Walker (1982) on preferential looking at two films of facial expressions with only one accompanying sound track, a 4-year-old was shown the films side by side and asked: "Which lady was talking?" He picked the right one, of course. When asked how he knew, he said, "I heard her." So he did—the sound, to an adult and undoubtedly to him, appears to move to the correct side when the tape is changed and to be localized behind the correct event. He localized it with the appropriate visually perceived event, but it seemed from his immediate report that he was simply perceiving a film of a happy person, without any analysis of sensory properties.

SUMMARY AND HYPOTHESES

I have contrasted two approaches to the problem of how it is that we perceive unitary objects, events, and places in the world given their multimodal properties. One approach emphasizes construction of representations by coordination of originally separate modally specific schemata. The other emphasizes pickup of invariant properties of things and events through multimodally specified information, by actively searching perceptual systems. Invariance of multimodal information has utility for facilitating perception of unity of an object or event by defining a segregated whole. The information that specifies the same environmental source by different perceptual systems, whether distal object, event, or place, is itself abstract and amodal. Spatial coincidence of such information is not the critical factor, although it may help. The invariant information is relational and structured over time as well as space. We need therefore to look to events and actively operating pickup systems to identify this information as it exists in the world and in experiments designed to investigate it.

The essential contrast with the construction theory is the hypothesis that distal objects and events in the world are multiply specified by proximal information that is abstract and invariant over change, itself specifying and thus defining a unique, segregated whole, and that this kind of information begins to be picked up early in the lives of individuals, allowing them to perceive events and things with unique affordances for behavior. The process is not one of *construction* but of *extraction* of structured information that is present in the light, in the air, on the skin, in short, in the world.

I suggested a few hypotheses about how the developmental course might proceed:

1. There are preadapted coordinations of the perceptual systems, ready to go at birth or relatively early in infancy. They give rise to active exploration simultaneously or in tandem.
2. The coordinated exploration by these systems provides a means for detection of amodal invariants, basic information for unity of what is experienced.
3. Modal qualities, like color, are also detected in the course of this activity, but they are not *associated* with other properties; rather they are differentiated or dissociated from the whole, which is more primitive.

Finally, I think that perception is essentially detection of what objects and events afford for adaptive behavior. We may turn this proposition around, and look for the multimodal invariants by using as our criterion behavior that reflects identical affordances however it is instigated, as has been done in a few cases like the studies of looming. The affordance of surfaces that are extended and rigid, resistant to impact so that they can be walked on, is perceived very early, as we know from experiments with the visual cliff. The affordances of properties of objects that are specified by looking at, hearing, and touching, like the property of substance, appear also to be realized quite early. Important affordances like potential for locomotion, for collision, for a safe path around obstacles, and for chewing may have a privileged status in biologically constrained perceptual systems tuned or biased to detect them. Although the answers to the questions thus posed will be a while in coming, a fruitful domain for research is clearly marked.

REFERENCES

Alegria, J., & Noirot, E. Neonate orientation behaviour towards human voice. *International Journal of Behavioral Development,* 1978, *1,* 291–312.

Bahrick, L. E. Infants' perception of substance and temporal synchrony in multimodal events. *Infant Behavior and Development,* in press.

Bahrick, L. E., & Walker, A. S. *Infants' perception of amodal information in natural evetns.* Paper presented at the meeting of the Eastern Psychological Association, Washington, D.C., April 1978.

Ball, W. A., & Tronick, E. Infant response to impending collision: Optical and real. *Science,* 1971, *171,* 818–820.

Békésky, G. von. Similarities between hearing and skin sensations. *Psychological Review,* 1959, *66,* 1–22.

Bower, T. G. R. Object perception in infants. *Perception,* 1972, *1,* 15–30.

Bower, T. G. R. The evolution of sensory systems. In R. B. MacLeod & H. L. Pick, Jr. (Eds.), *Perception: Essays in honor of James J. Gibson,* Ithaca, N.Y.: Cornell University Press, 1974.

Bower, T. G. R. The origins of meaning in perceptual development. In A. D. Pick (Ed.), *Perception and its development.* Hillsdale, N.J.: Lawrence Erlbaum Associates, 1979. (a)

Bower, T. G. R. Visual development in the blind child. In V. Smith & J. Keen (Eds.), *Visual handicap.* Spastics International Publications, 1979. (b)

Bower, T. G. R., Broughton, J. M., & Moore, M. K. The coordination of visual and tactual input in infants. *Perception & Psychophysics,* 1970, *8,* 51–53. (a)

Bower, T. G. R., Broughton, J. M., & Moore, M. K. Infant responses to approaching objects: An indicator of response to distal variables. *Perception & Psychophysics,* 1970, *9,* 193–196. (b)

Bruner, J. S., & Koslowski, B. Visually prepared constituents of manipulatory action. *Perception,* 1972, *1,* 3–14.

Bryant, P. E., Jones, P., Claxton, V. C., & Perkins, G. M. Recognition of shapes across modalities by infants. *Nature,* 1972, *240,* 303–304.

Bullinger, A. Orientation de la tête du nouveau-né en présence d'un stimulus visuel. *L'Année Psychologique,* 1977, *2,* 357–364.

Butterworth, G., & Castillo, M. Coordination of auditory and visual space in newborn human infants. *Perception,* 1976, *5,* 155–160.

Davenport, R. K., & Rogers, C. M. Inter-modal equivalence of stimuli in apes. *Science,* 1970, *168,* 279–280.

Dodwell, P. C., Muir, D., & DiFranco, D. Responses of infants to visually presented objects. *Science,* 1976, *194,* 209–211.

Ellis, W. D. *A source book of Gestalt psychology.* New York: Harcourt, Brace, 1938.

Fieandt, K. von, & Gibson, J. J. The sensitivity of the eye to two kinds of continuous transformation of a shadow pattern. *Journal of Experimental Psychology,* 1959, *57,* 344–347.

Field, J., DiFranco, D., Dodwell, P., & Muir, D. Auditory-visual coordination of 2½–month-old infants. *Infant behavior and Development,* 1979, *2,* 113–122.

Field, J., Muir, D., Pilon, R., Sinclair, M., & Dodwell, P. Infants' orientation to lateral sounds from birth to three months. *Child Development,* 1980, *51,* 295–298.

Gibson, E. J. *Principles of perceptual learning and development.* New York: Appleton-Century-Crofts, 1969.

Gibson, E. J., Owsley, C. J., & Johnston, J. Perception of invariants by five-month-old infants: Differentiation of two types of motion. *Developmental Psychology,* 1978, *14,* 407–415.

Gibson, E. J., Owsley, C. J., Walker, A. S., & Megaw-Nyce, J. Development of the perception of invariants: Substance and shape. *Perception,* 1979, *8,* 609–619.

Gibson, E. J., & Walker, A. S. Intermodal perception of substance. Paper presented at the International Conference on Infant Development, Austin, Texas, March, 1982.

Gibson, J. J. *The ecological approach to visual perception*. Boston: Houghton Mifflin, 1979.

Gibson, J. J., & Gibson, E. J. Continuous perspective transformations and the perception of rigid motion. *Journal of Experimental Psychology*, 1957, *54*, 129–138.

Gottfried, A. W., & Rose, S. A. Tactile recognition memory in infants. *Child Development*, 1980, *51*, 69–74.

Gottfried, A. W., Rose, S. A., & Bridger, W. H. Cross-modal transfer in human infants. *Child Development*, 1977, *48*, 118–123.

Gratch, G. A study of the relative dominance of vision and touch in six-month-old infants. *Child Development*, 1972, *43*, 615–623.

Haith, M. M., Bergman, T., & Moore, M. J. Eye contact and face scanning in early infancy. *Science*, 1977, *198*, 853–855.

Hatwell, Y. Form perception and related issues in blind humans. In R. Held, H. Leibowitz, & H. L. Teuber (Eds.), *Handbook of sensory physiology: Perception* (Vol. VIII). Berlin: Springer-Verlag, 1978.

Hofsten, C. von. Eye-hand coordination in the newborn. *Developmental Psychology*, 1982, *18*, 450–461.

Holton, G. *Einstein's task as universe builder: His early years*. Paper presented at the American Academy of Arts and Science, Cambridge, Mass., April 1979.

Jansson, G., & Johansson, G. Visual perception of bending motion. *Perception*, 1973, *2*, 321–326.

Johansson, G., von Hofsten, C., & Jansson, G. Event perception. *Annual Review of Psychology*, 1980, *31*, 27–63.

Meltzoff, A. N., & Borton, R. W. Intermodal matching by human neonates. *Nature*, 1979, *282*, 403–404.

Mendelson, M. J. Acoustic-optical correspondences and auditory-visual coordination in infancy. *Canadian Journal of Psychology*, 1979, *33*, 334–346.

Mendelson, M. J., & Haith, M. M. The relation between audition and vision in the human newborn. *Monographs of the Society for Research in Child Development*, 1976, *41*, No. 167.

Muir, D., & Field, J. Newborn infants orient to sound. *Child Development*, 1979, *50*, 431–436.

Piaget, J. *The construction of reality in the child*. New York: Basic Books, 1954.

Piaget, J. *Biology and knowledge*. Edinburgh: Edinburgh University Press, 1971.

Provine, R. R., & Westerman, J. A. Crossing the midline: Limits of early eye-hand behavior. *Child Development*, 1979, *50*, 437–441.

Rader, N., & Stern, J. D. Visually elicited reaching in neonates. *Child Development*, 1982, *53*, 1004–1007.

Rader, N., Bausano, M., & Richards, J. E. On the nature of the visual-cliff-avoidance response in human infants. *Child Development*, 1980, *51*, 61–68.

Ruff, H. A., & Halton, A. Is there directed reaching in the human neonate? *Developmental Psychology*, 1978, *14*, 425–426.

Ruff, H. A., & Kohler, C. J. Tactual-visual transfer in six-month-old infants. *Infant Behavior and Development*, 1978, *1*, 259–264.

Schiff, W. The perception of impending collision: A study of visually directed avoidant behavior. *Psychological Monographs*, 1965, *79*, (Whole No. 604).

Soroka, S. M., Carter, C. M., & Abramovitch, R. Infants' tactual discrimination of novel and familiar stimuli. *Child Development*, 1979, *50*, 1251–1253.

Spelke, E. Infants' intermodal perception of events. *Cognitive Psychology*, 1976, *8*, 553–560.

Spelke, E. *Intermodal exploration by four-month-old infants: Perception and knowledge of auditory-visual events*. Unpublished doctoral dissertation, Cornell University, 1978.

Spelke, E. Perceiving bimodally specified events in infancy. *Developmental Psychology*, 1979, *15*, 626–636.

Strauss, M. S., & Cohen, L. B. *Infant immediate and delayed memory for perceptual dimensions*. Paper presented at the International Conference on Infant Studies, New Haven, Conn., April 1980.

Walk, R. D., & Gibson, E. J. A comparative and analytical study of visual depth perception. *Psychological Monographs,* 1961, *75,* (Whole No. 519).

Walker, A. S. Intermodal perception of expressive behaviors by human infants. *Journal of Experimental Child Psychology,* 1982, 33, 514–535.

Walker, A. S., Owsley, C. J., Megaw-Nyce, J., Gibson, E. J., & Bahrick, L. E. Detection of elasticity as an invariant property of objects by young infants. *Perception,* 1980, *9,* 713–718.

Wertheimer, M. Psychomotor coordination of auditory and visual space at birth. *Science,* 1961, *134,* 1692.

White, B. W., Saunders, F. A., Scadden, L., Bach-y-Rita, P., & Collins, C. C. Seeing with the skin. *Perception & Psychophysics,* 1970, *7,* 23–27.

Yonas, A., Bechtold, A. G., Frankel, D., Gordon, F. R., McRoberts, G., Norcia, A., & Sternfels, S. Development of sensitivity to information for impending collision. *Perception & Psychophysics,* 1977, *21,* 97–104.

Yonas, A., Petterson, L., Lochman, J., & Eisenberg, P. *The perception of impending collision in three-month-old infants.* Paper presented at the International Conference on Infant Studies, New Haven, Conn., April 1980.

3 Constraints on the Development of Intermodal Perception

Elizabeth S. Spelke
University of Pennsylvania

To make sense of any perceptual array, we must be able to carve that array into stable, persisting units—parcels, so to speak, possessing internal coherence and external boundaries. The ability to perceive what goes with what in the world is so basic that it is hard to imagine it could ever be lacking, at any age. Yet, perhaps the most influential theories of perceptual development—associationist theories—have proposed that this ability is entirely learned. According to these theories, newborn perceivers experience independent sensations within and across modalities of stimulation. As infants grow, they gradually discover contingent relationships among those sensations. Ultimately, they will put together into units the sensations whose appearances have been most highly associated in the past.

Now, a strict associationist account leaves many questions unanswered. For example, how do perceivers discover that bundles of associated sensations pertain to things in the external world? And again, how do they discover that some associated sensations (e.g., the sight of the mother and the sound of her voice) pertain to a single object, whereas other associated sensations (e.g., the sight of the mother and the feeling of contentment she evokes) pertain to different things? And finally, how can associative learning lead to the formation of perceptual units at all, if only sensations are initially experienced? To learn about a unitary object or event, we presumably must have repeated or extended encounters with the same pattern of sensations. Yet the sensations evoked by an object are diverse and changing. It is hard to see how we could ever profit from multiple encounters with an object if we could not already perceive that something stable and persisting was there.

Partly in response to such problems, many psychologists have looked for a different explanation for the development of perceptual unity. Two explanations

43

have received the greatest attention: those of Jean Piaget and Eleanor Gibson. Piaget and Gibson explicitly reject associative learning as a principle of perceptual development. Yet neither theorist is a nativist. They stress, in different ways, that knowledge of perceptual unity develops through exploration. For Piaget, this knowledge develops as the child exercises, extends, and coordinates innate actions. For Gibson, this knowledge develops as the child seeks and abstracts invariant perceptual information.

By rooting perceptual development in exploration, Gibson and Piaget seek to endow children with as little initial structure as possible. Yet for children to gain knowledge by exploring, their exploration must be guided by mechanisms that are already attuned to certain structures in the world. Neither Piaget nor Gibson seems to me to describe these innate mechanisms sufficiently. To illustrate what I see as the gap in each of their accounts, I will focus on Piaget's and Gibson's very different ideas about the development of perception of an object that is both seen and felt (for a discussion of other relevant phenomena, see Spelke, in press).

PIAGET'S THEORY

Piaget proposes that children enter the world with a repertoire of simple actions and an overarching tendency to respond to the environment in an adaptive, organized fashion. Children's innate actions are not coordinated with each other, and each is confined to one modality. Children, moreover, have no knowledge of the world around them, because the development of such knowledge depends on the development of coordinated activity. Thus, newborn infants can look at things and grasp things reflexively, but they cannot systematically direct their eyes to that which they grasp. And if infants should happen to grasp the object at which they are looking, they will not appreciate that they are seeing and feeling the very same thing.

Infants gain these abilities as they grow. Looking and grasping become coordinated with each other and with other actions in the normal course of development, bringing knowledge of perceptual unity. According to Piaget, the functions of adaptation and organization insure that these developments will occur. The child is born with the tendency to assimilate and adjust reflex actions to objects and to each other and with the tendency to organize these actions into stable structures. These tendencies lead to the development of intermodal perception.

More specifically, Piaget proposes that intermodal perception develops largely through *reciprocal assimilation* (Piaget, 1952). He has illustrated that concept by describing what happens as a child of several months accidentally looks at his moving hand:

> On the one hand, he is led, by visual interest, to make this spectacle last—that is to say, not to take his eyes off his hand; on the other hand, he is led, by kinesthetic

and motor interest, to make this manual activity last. It is then that the coordination of the two schemata operates, not by association, but by reciprocal assimilation. The child discovers that in moving his hand a certain way (more slowly, etc) he conserves this interesting image for his sight . . . [p. 107].

This theory is intriguing, but as Gibson (this volume) has pointed out, it leaves certain questions unanswered. In particular, how does the child discover that the acts of looking at the hand and moving the hand are related? At any given time, an infant will be doing a multitude of things: breathing, blinking, pursing his lips, wiggling his toes, and digesting food, as well as moving his hand and looking in that hand's direction. Each of these actions involves a number of interrelated movements. What leads the child to the notion that one subset of all these movements is related to another subset? By proposing that knowledge of objects comes from action rather than from perception, Piaget does not avoid the problem of unity—the problem of figuring out what goes with what. He only poses that problem in a different way.

Piaget seems to provide no specific account of how the child discovers that certain actions go together. Although he rejects the associationist solution, it is not clear what he offers in its place. But Piaget always emphasized that action is structured and that this structure underlies the development of knowledge. In the spirit of his thinking, one might propose that infants are innately sensitive to certain structural relationships among their acts. Children might discover that looking at a hand is related to moving the hand because those acts share similar or complementary structures—structures that children are predisposed to detect. At any given time, looking at a hand and moving a toe will also be related under some structural description, but children may not be predisposed to detect those relationships.

This view seems close in spirit to Piaget's theory. But notice what it assumes: (1) the children's acts are structured—a familiar Piagetian assumption; (2) different acts on the same object are structurally related in some special way that distinguishes them from different acts on distinct objects; (3) children are able to detect these special structures, without needing to learn to do so; and (4) when they detect these special structural relationships, children perceive that activities of the hand are linked to activities of the eye. We have moved a long way from independent, uncoordinated reflexes in this version of Piaget's theory. Children's discovery of intermodal relationships is guided by an innate sensitivity to certain kinds of structure in their actions.

My proposal does not provide the only possible solution to the problem of putting the right actions together. It might not be the solution Piaget would have preferred. I suggest, however, that any such solution must grant children an initial sensitivity to relationships of some kind between acts that are directed to each other or to the same external object. If children had no unlearned sensitivity to relationships among their actions, they could never discover that certain actions go together.

GIBSON'S THEORY

Let us turn to Eleanor Gibson's account of the development of intermodal perception. Gibson endows children with innate capacities to seek invariance and so to perceive certain properties of objects, events, and the spatial layout. Many properties of things are multiply specified: They are visible, audible, and tangible. When children detect invariants that specify the same property in different modes, they perceive a unitary episode.

For example, there is invariant optical information specifying the rigidity or nonrigidity of a moving object. As an object moves rigidly, light from the object projects changing patterns onto the eyes' receptor surfaces, but these patterns are equivalent in projective geometry. All the properties that are preserved under projection, such as the cross-ratio of any four collinear points, are invariant. If the same object is deformed, on the other hand, it will typically project to the eyes a changing pattern of images which are not projectively equivalent. Gibson has shown that infants can perceive the rigidity of an object that undergoes a series of projective transformations (Gibson, Owsley, & Johnston, 1978). They may do this by detecting properties that are invariant over these transformations. If infants can also manipulate a rigid object and detect invariant relationships specifying its rigidity to their touch, then they should be able to perceive a unitary object by looking and touching. Recent evidence suggests that infants do this as well (Gibson & Walker, 1982).

Gibson's account is of great interest, but I feel that it is incomplete. In order to explain the development of perception of a unitary world, it seems necessary to endow the child with more than a general tendency to explore and seek invariance. One needs to endow the child with rich and quite specific mechanisms for detecting some particular set of invariant relationships and not other sets. To clarify this idea, let us look further into the concept *invariant*.

In principle, an invariant is any stimulus property or relationship that remains constant as other properties and relationships change. But by this general definition, the concept cannot explain how we discover the unity of an object or event. For most invariants seem to provide no information for unity. Consider, for example, invariants in topology. A doughnut and a picture frame are topologically equivalent objects. Each can be continuously transformed into the other mathematically; their topological properties are invariant over this transformation. Yet suppose one allowed a child first to feel the frame and then to see the doughnut. The child should not perceive these two objects as one unitary entity in the way that one perceives the sight of a cat as united with the feel of its fur. Topological invariants are mathematical relationships that should *not* lead children to perceive a unitary object.

Examples such as this can be multiplied: One can imagine indefinitely many invariants that carry no information about the unity of an object. Indeed, one can select any two sensory patterns, as different as one pleases, and there will always be some abstract description under which they are the same. In order for children to perceive a tactile pattern as specifying one visible object and not another, there must be constraints on the class of invariants that they detect for this purpose.

This point is not new to Gibsonian theorists. James Gibson has proposed a new field of study for perception psychologists—"ecological optics"—the goal of which is to discover what invariants people detect and what properties of the world we thereby perceive (see J. Gibson, 1979). In her investigations of perceptual development, Eleanor Gibson's goals are similar. For a number of years, she has been attempting to build an "ecological optics of infancy" (see E. Gibson, 1982). I only wish to emphasize one implication of this undertaking: To say the infant perceives objects and events by detecting invariant relationships is to endow the infant with considerable innate structure. Infants who perceive visible, tangible objects by detecting the appropriate intermodal relationships, for example, have much more than a general capacity for exploring and detecting invariance. They have perceptual mechanisms that are attuned to some relatively small set of invariant properties: mechanisms that select—from all the logically possible stimulus relationships—just those relationships that specify the amodal properties of an object. With development, perceptual mechanisms may become more differentiated, and new mechanisms may mature. But perception cannot begin in an unstructured state.

CONCLUSION

Jean Piaget and Eleanor Gibson have provided two alternatives to the associationist account of the development of intermodal perception. Their theories are very different. According to one theory, the development of perception of intermodal unity depends on the capacity to act, and to extend and adjust one's actions to new objects. According to the other theory, this development depends on the capacity to seek and detect invariance in stimulation and so to perceive properties of the world. These differing commitments serve as a springboard for debate at the very heart of theories of perception, cognition, and development.

Yet despite their differences, Piaget's and Gibson's theories prompt the same question: What are the innate structures that make development possible? Proponents of Piaget's action-based theory need to study the detailed structure of children's earliest actions. They also need to investigate children's ability to detect relationships among different action structures. Proponents of the Gibsons' invariant-detection theory need to describe the class of invariant relationships that specify the amodal properties of the world, and to investigate children's ability to detect those invariants. If future investigations were to focus on these tasks, they might reveal a great deal about humans' initial sensitivity to certain kinds of structure, both structure in our own acts and structure in the environment we perceive.

ACKNOWLEDGMENTS

Preparation of this chapter was supported by a grant from the National Institutes of Health (HD-13248). I thank Jeanette Brack for her helpful comments on an earlier draft.

REFERENCES

Gibson, E. J. The concept of affordances in development: The renascence of functionalism. In W. A. Collins (Ed.), *Minnesota Symposia on Child Psychology* (Vol. 15). Hillsdale, N.J.: Lawrence Erlbaum Associates, 1982.

Gibson, E. J., Owsley, C. J., & Johnston, J. Perception of invariants by five-month-old infants: Differentiation of two types of motion. *Developmental Psychology, 1978, 14,* 407–415.

Gibson, E. J., & Walker, A. S. *Intermodal perception of substance.* Paper presented at the International Conference on Infant Studies, Austin, Tex., March 1982.

Gibson, J. J. *An ecological approach to visual perception.* Boston: Houghton Mifflin, 1979.

Piaget, J. *The origins of intelligence in children.* New York: International Universities Press, 1952.

Spelke, E. S. The development of intermodal perception. In L. B. Cohen & P. Salapatek (Eds.), *Handbook of infant perception.* New York: Academic Press, in press.

4 Some Thoughts on Semantic Development*

David S. Palermo
The Pennsylvania State University

> *"All knowledge, ... of whatever nature it may be, raises the problem of the relations between subject and object, and this problem can lead to many solutions according to whether one attributes such knowledge to the subject alone, to an action by the object, or to the interactions of both. Now, since the subject is one aspect of the organism, and the object a sector, as it were, of the environment, the problem of knowledge, seen from this point of view, corresponds to the problem of the relations between the organism and its environment—undeniably the most general question in the whole of biology."*
> —Piaget, 1967. Translated by Beatrix Walsh, *Biology and Knowledge*, 1971. p. 51.

Piaget (1971) in discussing the nature of knowledge and, in particular, the act of knowing, notes that there are three subproblems associated with the understanding of knowledge: (1) the relations between the subject and object in knowledge involving some part of the innate; (2) the relations between the subject and object in learning and the knowledge drawn from experience; (3) the relations between the subject and object in the regulation and equilibration of knowledge and the establishment of operational structures. Piaget's theoretical efforts were directed toward explicating how the child acquires a meaningful interpretation of the

---

*The present chapter is a modified version of a paper which appeared under the title, "Theoretical issues in semantic development," in S. Kuczaj, II (Ed.), *Language development, Vol. 1: Syntax and semantics*. Hillsdale, N.J.: Lawrence Erlbaum Associates, 1982.

world, which makes it possible for the child to deal with and interpret that world at successively higher levels culminating in formal operational thought.

In this paper, I focus on the relation between the child's developing knowledge and the child's ability to talk about the world and the objects and events in it. A prerequisite to the discussion of language acquisition, however, is an understanding of the knowledge possessed by the child at any particular developmental period when language is being used. The necessity of understanding the former as prerequisite to the latter may account for Piaget's relative neglect of language in his theorizing. Thus, although portions of this chapter focus on the child's acquisition and use of language, the major part of the chapter relates to the problems raised in the introductory quotation from Piaget. Piaget points to the relations between organism and experience, and his theory was concerned with the structures that enter into the interpretation of experience by the organism. The problem is how we make sense of, or give meaning to, our experiences. Notice that the issue is one of giving meaning to our experiences, not deriving meaning from our experiences. The meanings are not out there in the real world waiting to be discovered, but rather, they are in the person who encounters the real world and imposes a meaning upon it. To say that a person provides the meaning is not, however, to say that the objects and events of reality have no structure that influences the organism that assigns the meaning to them. As has been pointed out by Piaget (1969) and others (e.g., Macnamara, 1982), there are important distinctions between perception and meaning. The point is that even though the real world is structured, it is ambiguous, and meaning is assigned to objects and events by people; it is not given by, or picked up from, information present in the external world.

Subsidiary to the question of how we assign meaning are questions related to how we establish similarities that allow for categories or classes and thereby make distinctions that separate classes or categories. What are the dimensions we are capable of discriminating and the dimensions we are likely to use or ignore as we formulate classes? For example, why do children classify static objects as a category distinct from moving objects rather than basing their classification system on some other set of dimensions that cut across the static–dynamic dimension? Equally important, we know little about the basis of our conceptualizing the relations among classes. It is not at all clear, for example, why we should classify some plants or animals as more closely related than others. There is no obvious reason that Chihuahua and Saint Bernard are considered to be in the same class, whereas Chihuahua and kitten are in different classes. One cannot appeal to our scientific knowledge of the biological relations among these animals because the classifications of such taxonomic categories by people unaware of the science of biology reveal similar systems of relations (Berlin, Breedlove, & Raven, 1973).

The last question, subsidiary to the previous two questions and upon which this paper focuses, has to do with how we develop the ability to convey our categories and the relations among those categories to other persons. How do we transfer the ideas in one mind to another mind in the meaningful manner, which we call communication? Viewed in light of the previous questions, it becomes clear that language is but a tool that makes it possible for people to convey concepts and relations among concepts to other people. Language acquisition, then, is the learning of the use of a tool for communicating that which is already known in the form of concepts and concept relations.

THE STRUCTURE OF CONCEPTS

It is assumed here that the child, as the adult, uses language to represent concepts and relations among those concepts. Words represent concepts and relations for which objects and events are exemplars. The concepts and relations are abstract and specified in terms of a set of differentially weighted, context-sensitive rules. The rules that specify the structure of the concepts and relations allow one to classify particular exemplars of those concepts and relations encountered in the real world. The particulars in the real world may vary in terms of their exemplariness of the abstract categories. Some will be classified as good or prototypic, others as poor or peripheral, and still others as nonmembers of the class or relation in any particular context. Therefore, the structures are assumed to be of two types: (1) those specified by the set of rules underlying what we usually refer to as nouns in the language; (2) those specified by the set of rules underlying what we usually refer to as verbs[1] in the language. Thus, there are category or class structures and relational structures, the latter serving the function of relating the former.

The nature of the rules that establishes the structure of a concept is difficult to specify because the rules form a part of the tacit knowledge system of the conceptualizer. At this point we have less understanding of these rules than of syntactic rules, which also form a part of the tacit knowledge system. We do not know, for example, what rules we use to decide that armchairs, rockers, Chippendale chairs, and beanbag chairs are all members of the category *chair,* whereas tables, stools, and rocks are members of other categories. It may be possible, however, to understand more clearly the structure of a concept, be it relational or categorical, by examining the relations among the set of exemplars encompassed by that concept. The tacit rules specify those exemplars that fall within the category and those that fall outside the category in any particular context. In addition, the rules specify the relative position of the exemplars within the conceptual space defining the category. In most cases of natural categories, some

---

[1]Obviously many adjectives and adverbs are used to convey relational meanings. It is assumed that these linguistic forms are closely related to verbs, as many linguists since Plato have noted (Lyons, 1969).

exemplars are more central to the meaning of the concept, and others are more peripheral. One way to think of the relations specified by the rules is in terms of a spherical metaphor. Thus, the rules identify the prototypicality of a particular exemplar, and they also specify the relative similarity or position of the exemplars in the spherical space. Prototypes are at the center of the sphere, whereas other exemplars are positioned in the infinite number of directions emanating from the central core. Thus, the tacit rules for any concept determine the basis for deciding whether any particular object or event in the real world is to be included in the conceptual category, establish the prototypicality of that exemplar with respect to the conceptual category, and specify the similarity relations among exemplars within the category.

Those advocating prototype theories (e.g., Anglin, 1977; Nelson, 1974; Palermo, 1978a, 1978b; Rosch, 1973, 1975) have tended to emphasize the wholistic nature of the conceptual meaning derived within specific contexts, but Rosch and Mervis (1975) have suggested that the problem of similarity among exemplars may be handled within the framework of family resemblance, which they borrowed from Wittgenstein (1953). Although there are no defining sets of features for a concept, which determine whether a particular exemplar is a representative of that concept, exemplars of a concept do have some attributes (as opposed to distinctive features) in common so that there is a family resemblance among them. Some exemplars are more prototypic of a concept in that they may be characterized as having more attributes in common with other exemplars of the concept, whereas other exemplars have fewer common attributes and are, therefore, more peripheral to the concept. It should be noted that the idea of partially accounting for the relations among exemplars of a conceptual category in terms of family resemblance allows for a similarity metric, which not only relates prototypic exemplars to peripheral exemplars but also helps to account for relations among peripheral exemplars where close similarities and vast differences may exist depending on the positions in the spherical space of the peripheral exemplars. For example, the difference between Chihuahuas and Saint Bernards is large, whereas that between malamutes and elkhounds or Salukis and greyhounds is small, although all of these pairs might be considered peripheral exemplars of the dog category. Rosch and Mervis (1975) have demonstrated in several contexts how the relations among meanings of prototypic and peripheral exemplars may be, in part, a function of attribute overlap of the exemplars.

The principle of family resemblance not only helps to account for the relations among exemplars of a class but also has the advantage of making clearer an aspect of prototype theory that has been problematic for feature theories. If a set of criterial features define a cateogry as feature theorists have suggested, then all exemplars of the category must have all of the criterial features and, therefore, should be equally representative of the category. As suggested earlier and as several investigators have demonstrated empirically (e.g., Andersen, 1975; Labov, 1973; Rosch, 1975), this is not the case for most natural categories. Rather, almost any object or event may be categorized as an exemplar of almost any conceptual category if the context is such as to focus upon an aspect of the exemplar that is relevant to the concept (Palermo, 1978a). For example, there are many exemplars of the concept *furniture* ranging from those close to the core meaning (e.g., chair or table) to those more peripheral to the core meaning (e.g., rug or lamp). Seldom would rocks or logs be considered as a part of the furniture category, but they could be considered furniture in the context of a campfire where people were sitting on logs and placing their food on rocks. Thus, the meaning of furniture may be extended to include logs and rocks in appropriate contexts, although logs and rocks would not be considered close to the core meaning (i.e., prototypic exemplars) of the furniture category. The focus on the functional aspects of rocks and logs in this context permits the extension of the concept meaning to these particular exemplars. Similar extensions based upon perceptual, affective, social, or other aspects of exemplars could be constructed as well, as is often done in the case of figurative uses of language. Consider the following mundane examples of instances of such extensions: "The basketball player is a tower among ordinary men." "The man is a dirty rat." "She is a social butterfly." Such focusing, or foregrounding, points to the need for recognizing the context-sensitive nature of conceptual rules that take into account the relative salience and/or weighting of different attributes of exemplars of a concept yielding different meanings for those exemplars in varying contexts.

In discussing a prototype semantic theory, I have suggested (Palermo, 1978a, 1978b) that there may be other contextually determined effects on the rules defining the meaning of a concept. Context may lead to transformations of the rules or to the generation of new rules that change the relations among exemplars of the concept (i.e., the relative positions of exemplars encompassed by a concept may vary in the semantic space defined by the concept). Thus, the core meaning of the concept *furniture* might be expected to shift in the context specified by "living room" furniture, or "kitchen" furniture. Although some shifting in meaning would be expected as a function of contextual variations, if it should be the case that the meaning of a concept (c.g., *furniture*) were to change completely as a function of context, then a prototype theory of meaning cannot account for the commonality of meaning across contexts. Each new context would require a new prototypic structure analogous to the theoretical need for a new set of features required of feature theories faced with the same problem. Both the stability and the variation in the meaning of words and their conceptual referents are something that needs to be taken into consideration.

A recent set of experiments conducted in our laboratory bears on this question (MacKenzie & Palermo, 1980). Our concern was related to the stability of the normative data collected by Rosch (1975) establishing the prototypic structure of sets of exemplars for several conceptual categories. Rosch established the category norms in the context of the category name alone. In addition, she demonstrated that exemplars close to the core meaning of the concept, defined in terms of the normative data, are classified faster as members of the conceptual category than are peripheral exemplars (Rosch, 1975). We focused upon the effects of contextual manipulation on the category structures. For example, it is known from Rosch's norms that "table" is a prototypic exemplar of the category *furniture* and "rug" is a peripheral exemplar. It is also known from Rosch's experiments that it takes less time to classify prototypic exemplars as members of the category than peripheral exemplars. If the normative data do reflect the conceptual structure of the categories, and if that structure is not ephemeral, then it should be the case that performance affected by that structure will reflect the same relationships among the exemplars of a concept regardless of the context in which the concept is used. In terms of the furniture exemplar, it should be the case that the prototypic exemplar "table" and the peripheral exemplar "rug" should maintain their relative positions in the *furniture* concept regardless of the context in which the concept may occur.

After demonstrating the replicability of Rosch's (1975) findings that classification time is relatively faster for prototypic exemplars of conceptual categories than peripheral exemplars in a linguistically barren context and in the context of the category name, the category names were placed in adjectival and sentential contexts designed to be appropriate for the prototypic or the peripheral exemplars of the concepts. The relative classification time for exemplars varying in normative prototypicality were compared and used as a basis for inferring the effect of context on the structure of the categories. For example, subjects were required to decide whether the normatively prototypic exemplars "apple" and "pear" and the normatively peripheral exemplars "coconut" and "date" are members of the category *fruit* in the contexts:

1. He climbed the orchard tree to pick the ripe / fruit/.
2. He climbed the palm tree to pick the tropical / fruit/.

The context of the first sentence was designed to be appropriate for the prototypic but inappropriate for the peripheral exemplars, whereas the second sentence was appropriate to the peripheral but inappropriate to the prototypic exemplars. Preliminary research established that prototypic exemplars were, in fact, called to mind in the first context and peripheral exemplars in the second.

The results indicated that in the sentential contexts appropriate to the prototypic exemplars, those exemplars were classified more rapidly than peripheral exemplars, as expected. The sentential contexts appropriate to peripheral exemplars led to slower classification of good exemplars and faster classification of poor exemplars, relative to the other contexts, but there was no reversal in classification speed of prototypic and peripheral exemplars. In both contexts, classification of prototypic exemplars was faster. There was no evidence that peripheral became prototypic nor that prototypic became peripheral exemplars when the context was deliberately constructed to be appropriate for peripheral exemplars and inappropriate for prototypic exemplars. The same results were obtained when the category labels were presented in the context of a modifying adjective (e.g., living room furniture and kitchen furniture).

These experiments provide evidence that the tacit rules used to classify common objects of the real world into categories and to specify their structural relations are sensitive to contextual manipulations, but at the same time, the classification and the structural relations remain relatively stable regardless of the context in which those semantic categories occur. The effort in these experiments was directed to providing contexts in which exemplars ordinarily considered peripheral to the meaning of a category might be considered central (i.e., prototypical) and normatively prototypical exemplars might be considered as peripheral. Insofar as the task and categories used were sensitive to structural changes in the meanings of the categories due to contextual modifications, the experiments reflected changes only in the relative positions of exemplars of a category with respect to each other and failed to show absolute changes in the relations among exemplars. The contextual manipulations expanded or contracted the structural distances among exemplars, but the results provided no evidence that the basic categorical structure was modified. Contexts designed as appropriate to prototypic exemplars of a category yielded results that suggested a topological expansion of the semantic space, whereas contexts designed as appropriate to peripheral examplars of a category yielded results that suggested a topological contraction of the semantic space as reflected in the differences in response speeds between prototypic and peripheral exemplars in the two contexts. In short, contextual changes led to changes in topological relations among exemplars, but no exemplars peripheral in one context became prototypical in another or vice versa.

Both the stability and the variability in meaning that are reflected in the results of these experiments are of importance to any theory of semantics. The problem for those concerned with these issues, regardless of their theoretical approach, is the two-horned dilemma that words or other linguistically meaningful units are used to convey different meanings in different contexts and yet maintain some, as yet poorly specified, commonality of meaning across contexts. The theoretical problem centers around the need to account for both the *commonality* and the *variability*, which are readily apparent in the modifications in meaning that occur when contexts are changed as in the experiments just described as well as others (e.g., Barclay, Bransford, Franks, McCarrell, & Nitsch, 1974). Perhaps more important, we need to account for the seemingly broader commonality– variability problem evident in the figurative use of language. It is clear, for example, that when Shelley wrote in *Prometheus Unbound* that "My soul is an enchanted boat," the meaning conveyed by the phrase both preserves the basic structure of the meanings of the words involved and, at the same time, modifies them in an as yet unspecifiable, but presumably rule-governed, way that may be understood by others who also have a tacit knowledge of those rules. To say that the meanings of the words are fixed to certain readings is to say that Shelley's phrase is anomalous or meaningless, which is absurd. On the other hand, to argue that words may convey any and all meanings would suggest that Shelley could have substituted "dog" in the phrase and conveyed the same meaning, which is equally absurd. The particular words used by Shelley were selected both because of the stable aspects of their meaning and because of the variable aspects of their meaning, which allowed them to be brought together in that phrase to generate a specific meaning appropriate to the concepts the author wished to convey in that context. Tacit knowledge of the rules underlying the concepts and the relations into which those concepts may enter make it possible both for the creation and the understanding of a metaphor such as that created by Shelley.

Another aspect of conceptual structure implied in the discussion to this point should be made explicit. Most natural categories have no well-defined boundaries, a point made most clearly by Rosch (1973). The meaning of a concept is best exemplified by some objects or events encountered in the real world, but boundaries that specify what belongs within the conceptual category and what should be excluded appear to be fuzzy because they are strongly influenced by context. Furthermore, as Rosch and Mervis (1975) have shown, peripheral exemplars are more likely to be classed in more than one category. The fuzzy boundaries of different conceptual categories may overlap, as for example Labov (1973) and Andersen (1975) demonstrated. In addition, categories may be included within other larger categories as in the case of hierarchical relations. The core meaning of a concept is specified by the rules that define the abstract concept, but depending on context, what counts as an exemplar of that concept will vary as will the relation of the exemplars to the core meaning. It would appear to be the case that the rules defining what exemplars may be included in the category are themselves generative of other rules dependent on the context so that exemplars included in one context are excluded in other contexts.[2] The nature of the rules that specify the structure of any natural concept and how those rules are modified by contextual constraints are, unfortunately, not specifiable at this point.

Some significant subset of the rules specifying the structure of concepts is surely determined naturally in the sense that the human organism classifies in particular ways as, for example, Rosch (1973) has reported for colors and geometric forms and Berlin et al. (1973) have reported for taxonomic classes. The basis for forming classes appears to include at least functional, perceptual, so-

---

[2]Weimer (personal communication) argues that boundaries of concepts are never fuzzy. Boundaries appear to be fuzzy because some exemplars are counted in the class in some contexts and out of the class in other contexts. The result is that across contexts the concept boundaries appear to be fuzzy. Weimer's point is that the rules defining a concept generate rules appropriate to contexts specifying exactly what are to be counted as exemplars in any particular context.

cial, and affective dimensions, but we have little guidance at this point as to the nature of these abstract dimensions or the rules into which they enter as variables. There are hints coming from a variety of sources, however, as researchers are beginning to look at the manner in which infants and young children categorize the world about them. Consider, for example, the recent research and theoretical account of infant visual behavior provided by Haith (1978, 1980). He has suggested that newborn infants follow a specified set of rules that guide visual search activity. According to Haith, the basic rule, or principle, governing the infant's scanning is to maximize visual cortical firing rate. He proposes an Ambient Scan Routine and an Inspection Scan Routine. The first facilitates the detection of visual stimuli, and the second generates eye movements, which maximize visual cortical firing rate. With these two principles, Haith accounts for scanning in darkness and formless light fields, fixation of edges and bars, crossing of edges, scanning of stimuli with varying edge density, acquisition of accommodation, and binocular convergence, as well as speculations about later visual activity as maturational development occurs.

Although Haith's theory deals with perception rather than cognition as such, his approach suggests the beginnings of principles underlying classificatory dimensions, which will play a part in subsequent cognitive development. It might also be noted that Haith points out that the natural movements of the eyes are on a horizontal plane. This natural biological characteristic of the organism makes it more probable that the infant's initial perceptual classes will be divided on the basis of vertical contours because the scanning patterns are more likely to encounter vertical than horizontal contours. It is not that the infant cannot scan vertically, only that it is more natural to scan horizontally, and this biological characteristic influences the infant's perceptual experience. It seems very likely that there are many other naturally determined constraints on the perceptual differentiations made by infants. Recent research has demonstrated, for example, that infants have an innate capacity for shape constancy (Schwartz & Day, 1979), and other research concerned with infant visual capacities assumes a natural ability to distinguish figure from ground. Other aspects of the innate organization of perception are currently being explored in research with infants (cf. Cohen & Salapatek, 1975).

In the auditory realm, we now have impressive evidence of the natural classificatory capabilities of the infant on dimensions relevant to speech (e.g., Eimas, Siqueland, Jusczyk, & Vigorito, 1971; Molfese, Freeman, & Palermo, 1975; Trehub, 1973). Again, at least some of these classificatory abilities appear to be based upon the biological characteristics of the organism (Molfese & Molfese, 1979). Similar research on the gustatory and olfactory senses yields indications of natural dimensions demarking classes there, too (e.g., Crook & Lipsitt, 1976; Reiser, Yonas, & Wikner, 1976).

There are also well-documented indications of natural relational concepts. Chang and Trehub (1977) have demonstrated relational processing of auditory stimuli at 5 months. Certainly, aspects of movement are naturally conceptualized relations, regardless of conclusions about object permanence (Moore, Borton, & Darby, 1978), but it would seem that static relations are less likely to prove natural. Macnamara (1972) has argued that this should be the case, and Nelson (1973, 1975) has provided evidence that children's early meanings in many instances may be closely tied to function and to changing aspects of referents as opposed to static attributes of those referents. One might also expect that process verbs would appear before state verbs in language acquisition, and Brown's (1973) data seem to support this hypothesis. There must be many as yet unknown natural dimensions forming the basis of relational concept formation that are common to most humans. Certainly, there are individual differences, but as Macnamara (1972) has pointed out, the child seldom forms bizarre concepts indicating that there must be some constraints on what is classed together. Further research specifically oriented to establishing what those constraints are, both in infancy and at later maturational developmental periods, should prove helpful in expanding our understanding of the perceptual systems and their relation to the rules and structure of the abstract conceptual system.

Acquired concepts presumably derive from or are induced from objects and events classified, in part, on the basis of natural dimensions in complex interrelations with distinctions acquired perforce through the child's interactions with his or her environment. In the latter case, a distinction may be made between those concepts based upon the tradition of rules and practices that form the culture into which the child is born and those specifically or deliberately learned distinctions (Hayek, 1978). It is clear that certain classes (e.g., colors and animals) are naturally categorized because of the human biological construction, but other categories may be formed in addition to the natural categories. The categories of furniture and sport, for example, are not likely candidates for natural categories. They are, however, likely to be formed on the basis of some abstract dimensions that are natural, some that are culturally acquired, and some that are deliberately learned. Those dimensions, in turn, are related by natural and acquired relational rules allowing us to generate which exemplars belong to the categories furniture and sport and where in our conceptual space the exemplars for each category fall. Finally, it should be noted that although some bases for forming conceptual categories may be more natural than others, it is clear that seemingly unnatural classes can be formed with deliberate effort as, for example, the classes required in relating spoken to written or printed language necessary in learning to read. The letter-sound relations are clearly unnatural as is obvious from the fact that establishing the relation between print and the conceptual system requires conscious effort. The relation between speech sounds and the conceptual system is much more natural and yet culturally acquired. Witness the fact that children learn different languages in different speech communities at about the same rate. The abstract dimensions and rules that compose the conceptual system, therefore, emerge from biological, cultural, and rational sources.

It should be noted that the sense of words (i.e., the conceptual structure that the words represent), in the case of at least some natural categories, must be known to the child and adult alike as a function of the nature of the organism. The communality in conceptual structure, and therefore in the meaning of words representing that structure, is assured by the commonality in the structure of the biological organism. As has been demonstrated (Mervis, Catlin, & Rosch, 1975) for example, the child's prototype of a natural color concept is the same as that of an adult, although the boundaries of the color concept may differ for the two age groups. In the case of words representing acquired concepts, however, the commonality of meaning is a function of the commonality of the abstracting characteristics of the organism and the particular exemplars and context experienced by the individual organism. There is, therefore, likely to be greater variability in the sense, or meaning, of words representing acquired concepts than words representing natural concepts.

Some research is beginning to appear in the literature exploring the development of what might be viewed as acquired concepts. In the case of the concept of *human face* or *dog,* for example, it might be expected that the conceptual structure may initially be a function of the particular exemplars, pictures of exemplars, and verbal input from others about exemplars of the concept in question. Cohen and his colleagues, for instance, have recently demonstrated that infants as young as 30 weeks of age form prototypically structured concepts of human faces based upon several varying exemplars (Cohen & Strauss, 1979; Strauss, 1979). Strauss interprets his research as indicating that the infant uses some sort of averaging procedure over experienced exemplars to form a prototype for the category *human face.* The hypothesis that infants register each exemplar and compute a running average, however, seems to be a rather simplistic account of what is surely a much more complicated process. At least two factors argue against Strauss' hypothesis. First, Schwartz and Day (1979) have shown, using the habituation technique, that 8-week-old infants have shape constancy (i.e., different orientations of the same object are categorized by the child as the same object). If the averaging hypothesis were correct, it would be impossible to establish shape constancy because the infants would average the various retinal images of any particular shape viewed from different perspectives and respond differentially to the averaged retinal image rather than to retinal images that differ markedly from the average. The infants, however, habituated to one version of the shape and treated all others as the same shape (i.e., they showed evidence of knowing the relations among the shapes rather than averaging all the exemplars presented). Schwartz and Day's experiments, incidentally, provide strong support for the innate abstract classificatory capacities of the infant (i.e., all exemplars with the same perceptual relations are classed as the same shape).

The second type of evidence arguing against the averaging hypothesis is provided by Nelson and Bonvillian (1978) who have shown that children may form concepts on the basis of a single exemplar. They presented children with a single exemplar of a new concept and found that such a single positive exemplar resulted in generalization of the concept to similar objects. It is not necessary to have a number of different exemplars to form a concept. Thus, although the Cohen and Strauss (1979) and Strauss (1979) experiments are of considerable interest in demonstrating the conceptual abilities of very young infants and the prototypic structure of those conceptual categories, a theoretical account of the results in terms of either feature averaging or feature frequency (Goldman & Homa, 1977) seems unsatisfactory.

In any case, at least some of the child's acquired concepts are likely to be different from those of an adult resulting in overextending or underextending the use of words associated with those concepts to exemplars that adults might exclude or include. Both overextension and underextension should be anticipated in early language acquisition because the child's concepts may be, at least in part, a function of the particulars a child encounters. Note, however, that the child's concept is not an incomplete version of the adult concept; rather, it is a complete concept that may be different from an adult's with respect to the abstract rules defining the concept, especially with respect to the boundaries and relations of the concept to other concepts. Thus, children may not, in the case of the dog concept, for example, draw the same line between wolves and dogs that an adult might. Similarly, the child may not have the concept that dogs are in a category of animals that bite when teased. Given some minimal experience with dogs, however, the child is quite capable of forming the concept *dog* much as the adult does. We have worked with 3-year-olds who had no difficulty at all identifying over 300 breeds as exemplars of the category *dog* distinct from other animals. Most concepts of child and adult, both natural and acquired, are likely to be the same. It is only the number of conceptual classes, their relations, and the recognition and use of these classes and relations that are likely to differ from child to adult.

In summary, concepts are defined in terms of a tacitly known set of rules, which identify abstract categories and the basis for relating categories to each other. The tacit rules, in turn, provide a basis for classifying exemplars encountered in the real world as members or nonmembers of the category. Concrete exemplars of the abstract category vary with respect to how well they fit the conceptual specification for the category. The structural relations among exemplars of an abstract category may be conceived metaphorically as spherical in shape. Prototypic exemplars are located at the core of the sphere, and poor exemplars are toward the surface or periphery of the spherical semantic space. What counts as an exemplar of a category is contextually related. Thus, the boundaries of concepts appear fuzzy in the sense that some exemplars are counted as members of the category in some contexts but not in others, and the topological relations among exemplars in the spherical conceptual space will vary with context. In short, the rules defining a conceptual category are generative in that they may create rules appropriate to specific contexts.

Concepts are both natural and acquired. More appropriately, concepts are relatively natural and relatively acquired in the sense that some are determined primarily by the biological structure of the organism, others are acquired rather naturally in the cultural milieu, and others are acquired by rational effort devoted to dimensions and rules that are less related to the biological nature of the organism. Different animals and different maturational levels of the same animal may conceptualize differently. Natural concepts provide a common base for conceptualization across individuals within a species. Culturally acquired concepts provide a common base for conceptualization across individuals within social groups of a species. Acquired concepts are based upon rules for combining natural dimensions for making distinctions and acquired bases for making distinctions. Acquired categories, therefore, vary across individuals, and the exemplars included within those categories vary as a function of individual differences in the rules for forming the abstract classes.

Finally, words in particular and language in general are used to communicate the conceptual system in terms of the particulars, or exemplars, encountered in the world of the language user.

MEANING AND THE AMBIGUITY
OF EXPERIENCE

Thus far, we have been discussing the specific questions of how we classify. Let us now turn to the larger question of how we make sense of, or give meaning to, our experiences. One thing that has become particularly clear in the wake of Chomsky's influence on psychology is the pervasiveness of ambiguity. Until fairly recently, most psychologists have treated ambiguity as a curiosity exemplified in visual phenomena such as the Nekker Cube, the vase-face figure, and the Ames rooms. Chomsky added sentences to the psychologist's list of ambiguous curiosities. More importantly, of course, Chomsky pointed to the necessity of making a distinction between the surface or exemplary level of a phenomenon and the abstract or deep structural level of that phenomenon in accounting for the meaning of ambiguous sentences (Chomsky, 1957). As Weimer (1973, 1974; see also Hayek, 1969) points out, Chomsky focused upon the primacy of the abstract.

It has taken some time for psychologists to accept the implications of ambiguity for a theory of the mind. Many psychologists have assumed that Chomsky treated ambiguity as a special case, too, albeit requiring drastic changes in scientific conceptualizations and research approaches to the study of mind. That interpretation led to the study of ambiguity as a particular type of phenomenon, a class of sentences that required separate analyses in contrast to apparently unambiguous sentences. Recent work by psychologists has now made it clear that ambiguity is the rule rather than the exception. The work of Bransford and his colleagues (e.g., Bransford & McCarrell, 1974), for example, has made it evident that any visual or verbal stimulus (and surely any other stimulus) may be interpreted in more than one meaningful way. In short, all surface structure phenomena are ambiguous.

Given a world of stimuli all of which are ambiguous with respect to their meaning and given that we as individuals are very seldom confused by, nor even aware of, that ambiguity, the question immediately arises as to why we fail to note the ambiguity. Some theorists (e.g., Jenkins, 1977; Ortony, Reynolds, & Arter, 1978; Ortony, Schallert, Reynolds, & Antos, 1978) have argued that the context of a sentence or other stimulus acts to disambiguate that sentence or stimulus. In its simplest form, the argument is that the ambiguity of a sentence, for example, is eliminated by the sentences that precede or follow it. The problem with this account seems obvious. The sentences that precede or follow an ambiguous sentence are themselves ambiguous. There is no way, in principle, that something which is itself ambiguous can act to disambiguate another ambiguity.[3]

Given this state of affairs—that the surface form of one sentence cannot disambiguate the surface form of another sentence, even when the independent deep structure forms of those sentences are examined—the meanings of the sentences must be related at some more abstract level. Furthermore, the sentences must be related to the ambiguous context in which they occur, those contexts must be related to the contexts in which they occur, and so on. It seems clear that the only manner in which a sentence, or any other stimulus, can become meaningful (i.e., unambiguous) derives from the meaning placed on it by the person who is interpreting the sentence or stimulus. The constraints upon meaning (i.e., that which determines the particular meaning selected from the many possible meanings) must come from within the person and not from the stimuli without. In short, people, not stimuli, create meaning for objects and events in their environment on the basis of their world view. They must have some sort of theory about the world, which allows them to interpret what goes on about them in a systematic way (Weimer, 1973).

By a theory of the world I mean a set of rules used by the person to interpret the events, objects, and relations with which he or she comes into contact internally and externally in everyday living. The theory is what one uses to make sense of one's senses. The theory of the world each of us has allows us to place single meanings upon specific empirical experiences that have an indeterminant number of possible meanings. Furthermore, the theory allows us to construct a systematic integration of those empirical experiences.

By systematic, I do not necessarily mean logically consistent. Individuals will

---

[3]In making this point in another occasion, it was pointed out to me that the sentence, $a + b = 12$ is ambiguous and that the additional sentence, $a = 4$ completely disambiguates it. Although the example is clear, the disambiguation rests upon the presupposition of a theory of arithmetic, which is precisely the point to follow.

develop schemata, or theories, over limited domains, which may not necessarily be logically consistent with schemata they have developed in other limited domains. An individual's overall theory of the world may provide rules that allow for inconsistencies of schemata in different domains, or the schemata will be changed when inconsistencies among schemata and the total theory become apparent. Such changes may occur via social interactions, as Piaget (e.g., Piaget & Inhelder, 1969) has noted, by the person's inability to interpret events meaningfully within the framework of the theory in hand, or by maturational changes in the biological organism, which may lead to spontaneous internal reorganization of the conceptual system. The lack of a totally logical system is evidenced at all levels of human development and in many related spheres of cognition. Piaget has referred to a part of what is implied here in his concept of horizontal décalage, although I believe that the lack of logical consistency is broader than implied in his presentations. For example, the social psychological phenomenon of prejudice fits nicely with the conception presented here. Prejudice within this framework is conceived as an exception in the way one interprets the meaning of the behaviors of some identifiable group. The rules for conceptualizing people in general are suspended for some specified group to whom another set of rules is applied.

The general theoretical position taken here, however, is not unlike that proposed by Piaget and others. As Piaget has formulated his position, through interactions with the world children develop abstract intellectual structures that allow them to make sense of the intellectual problems and challenges with which they are faced. Those structures change as a function of the interactions of the child with the world, and thus, the meanings placed upon the events, objects, and relations experienced by the child change. The meaning of a ball, the modification of the shape of an object, or the relation of sticks graded in size to a child in the sensorimotor stage is not the same as the meaning of those same objects, events, and relations at the concrete operations or formal operations stages. At each level the child's theory of the world has changed. As Piaget described it, the cognitive structures that define the stages are modified or developed through the child's interactions with the environment. Although Piaget discusses the evolving nature of cognitive structures and processes, he tends to focus on the organism-environment interaction in the development of the child's theory, and he deemphasizes the direct effects of the hereditarily determined biological structures on the cognitive processes (Piaget, 1971, 1977). I feel that the evidence today suggests some rather direct biological constraints on cognitive processes. Furthermore, it seems likely that some of those biological constraints may be directly related to maturational changes that occur in the developing child and account for the transitions in the child's theory of the world, which are associated with the stages proposed in Piaget's theory.

There are other theorists who have also taken positions similar to that outlined here. Beck (1976), for example, has suggested that the clinical syndrome of depression is a product of an individual's particular theory of the world. A depressed person views the world as a negative place in which to exist, and most events that occur in the life of the depressed person are interpreted (i.e., given meaning) as negatively related to the person. The depressed person's theory includes a view of the self as incompetent to deal with the misfortunes of life. Finally, the depressed person's theory of the future includes little hope for change in the present state of affairs. The same events interpreted by one person as hopeful, encouraging, or inconsequential are interpreted within the depressed person's theoretical framework as discouraging, and the outlook is futile. Beck's behavioristically oriented therapeutic techniques are cognitively directed to changing the depressed patient's theory so that different meanings are imposed upon the same events in reality.

Still another theorist with a similar approach was Lewin (1946). He argued that the goals, motivations or forces, valences, and conceptualizations of the relations of the self with the environment are given meaning in terms of the individual's theory, represented at any particular moment by the person's phenomenological life space. Two persons with the same external goals will view them differently, according to Lewin, as a function of the structure of each individual's life space. Lewin provided a comprehensive account of the developmental changes in the life space. At the time Lewin proposed his theory, he received a hostile reception from his behavioristic colleagues because he could not operationalize what he meant by the life space. Today, operationalism is no longer as strong a requirement, but theory is. We need a way of conceptualizing the phenomenological world of the person to allow something more than after-the-fact accounts of the cognitive processes.

In all these theories, and in some others as well, the theoretical concern is with the abstract mental structures (and, to a lesser extent, with processes) used by developing children to give meaning to the concrete individual objects, events, and relations that make up their experiences. Those objects, events, and relations are indefinitely ambiguous in and of themselves with respect to their possible meanings. Each theorist, explicitly or implicitly, has proposed that individuals construct the meaning of experience in terms of a theory they hold. In order to disambiguate our experiences we must have a theory of how the world is constructed and how it operates. The theory we hold permits us to interpret or disambiguate the empirical experience in a meaningful way. In fact, the theory gives us such a clear view of the world that we seldom notice ambiguity. For the most part, ambiguity only becomes apparent when two people see the world differently because they hold different theories about aspects of the world. Note also that our theories of the world, yours and mine, are theories of how the world ought to be, and not how it actually is (Proffitt, 1976). That is, we make certain assumptions about the world and predicate other aspects of our theory on the basis of those assumptions. We make decisions, judgments, and act according to our theories of how we expect the world to be. On those occasions when we err, we are faced with the fact that our theory, as all other theories, is fallible.

It must be the case that we have some sort of theory of the world from the time of birth. Otherwise the world of the infant would be the blooming, buzzing confusion suggested by James (1890). Furthermore, without a theory, the behavior of the infant with respect to the world would be in a similar random state. That neither of these states appears to be the case makes it clear that some organizational principles are available allowing the infant to interpret and respond to the world in a meaningful way insofar as the infant is concerned. Children's conceptions, or theories, of the world certainly change with age, but they always have a theory that provides for the organization or meaningful integration of the environment and their behavior with respect to that environment. The child, as the adult, has a set of rules establishing abstract concepts and organizing those concepts in abstract relations, which provide for the interpretation of concrete events and responses to those events. The theory is a grammar of the world and the person's relations to that world.

Accepting the idea that a theory of the world allows us to interpret our particular empirical experiences (i.e., gives them meaning), we are faced immediately with at least two general types of questions. The first concerns the source of the theories we possess. How is a theory developed? This is the ontogenetic question of how a particular person develops a particular theory. More broadly, however, the question is an evolutionary one pertaining to the way in which the human has evolved and the commonalities in the species, which are reflected in the commonalities in the theories of individual members of the species.

The second question relates to how two persons can communicate, given that they may not necessarily have the same theory of the world. Although there are species commonalities, there are also individual differences in both biological composition and in empirical experience. The biological and empirical similarities will make for common theories, whereas the individual variations will lead to different theories. How do we overcome the latter for the purposes of communication? As already implied, the ontogenetic or evolutionary question and the communication question are inevitably related. We can begin by looking at the second question and then turn to the first.

The basic assumption of our theories of the world is that the world is meaningful. We assume without question that the world can be rendered coherent, regular, and predictable. The world is dependable, and it can be understood. Obviously there are some matters that we admittedly cannot understand, but we make the assumption that there is some principle, some structure, some sort of organization even if we cannot comprehend it at the moment. Despite our conscious lack of knowledge, we are forced to deal with our environment, and we do so within the framework of our conceptualization of it (see Martin, 1982, for a somewhat different position).

Given the assumption of a meaningful world, it follows that when we talk with other people, we assume that some meaning can be given to that empirical experience. When we try to interact or communicate with other people, animals, plants, or even objects, we believe that it will be possible to impose some meaning on that experience. In the case of language, at least, we assume a contractual relation between ourself and the person with whom we are communicating. That agreement involves the commitment to be meaningful, to make sense, to be relevant, and to tell the truth. Grice (1975) has discussed this relationship between speakers in terms of conversational implicatures. Proffitt and his colleagues (Cutting & Proffitt, 1979; Proffitt, 1976) have spoken of contractualism in the broader perspective of perceptual modes and other experiential relations. The point is that all empirical experiences including those involving language assume meaning, and therefore, it is up to the receiver of the message to assign a meaning to it. Thus, for example, when we encounter Shelley's phrase, "My soul is an enchanted boat," we do not throw up our hands in disgust. Instead, assuming Shelley was abiding by the contract to make sense, we create a meaning for the phrase and proceed. In fact, given the contractual assumptions made in communication situations, we give meaning where none may have been intended. Boswell (1977), for example, has shown that people can readily interpret metaphors created from a random selection of nouns randomly assigned to the syntactic frame, "A ———is a———." Furthermore, graduate students in English could not differentiate metaphors created in this way from metaphors created and used by noted poets. Metaphors from both sources were judged as equally difficult. These findings point up both the importance of the contractual assumptions between communicators and the theoretical position that the meaning of an utterance or written statement is imposed or created by the person interpreting it and does not reside in the statement per se.

There are times, however, when the rules or contractual assumptions in communications appear to have been disregarded. When we encounter such situations we usually ask questions about words used, interpretations of sentences, presuppositions, and implications. In such conversational situations, one speaker stops the flow of the conversation to ask, "How are you using the word X?" "Are you assuming Y?" "What is implied by Z?" and so on. Upon clarification, that is, once meaning has been agreed upon or at least stated more clearly, the conversation proceeds. When we cannot clarify the meaning by questioning, as in the case of a book or a lecture, oftentimes we will leave the field. It is too much work to provide a meaning, and we put the book away or turn off the lecturer. Children often do this to parents, teachers, and other adults. In fact, when adults are communicating with children, one might expect ambiguity to prevail. Such ambiguity, however, would be most likely to occur when the adult or child does not take into account the different theory of the other person. As is now well-documented, this seldom occurs because the adult takes the child's theory into account as do older children when talking to younger children (Slobin, 1975).

Sometimes, however, the receiver's theory is so different from the communicator's theory that communication is very difficult. At such times, the conceptual referents of words differ, assumptions about the world differ, and communication breaks down because the two persons have conceptualized the world in seemingly irreconcilable ways. People from different cultures often have such problems. In the scientific community, as Kuhn (1970) and more recently Weimer (1979) have argued, two scientists with different paradigmatic views of their discipline experience this kind of communication problem.

At still other times, communication is so bizarre as to cause us to define the other person as psychotic. But, in general, we have no reason to question the contractual arrangement in communication situations. We assign meaning to our empirical experiences within the framework of our own theory. The fact that we assign meanings does not, however, guarantee that the meaning the speaker assigns and the meaning the listener assigns are the same. It seems unlikely that the two are ever exactly the same. We are not, after all, robots. There is, however, considerable overlap between meanings of speaker and listener in most cases. Consideration of the commonality of meaning for two persons leads to the ontogenetic and/or evolutionary developmental question raised earlier.

The fulfillment of the contractual arrangements assumed in our ambiguous environment is made possible by the commonalities in the theories of the world that different people hold. Those commonalities within a species are assumed to be based at one level upon the commonalities that must exist in the biological structures of the organisms involved. In the same sense that dogs can communicate with dogs, birds with birds, and chimps with chimps, humans communicate with humans because each species has a biological commonality that forms a part of the basis for the theory of the world held by that species. The genetic characteristics of humans passed from one generation to the next and set in motion for the individual at the time of conception establish part of the sensory equipment—central nervous system, glandular, muscular, and other biological characteristics, which underly the common structure we, as humans, will impose upon our world. That common biological structure establishes, in part, the manner in which we will be predisposed to classify and to relate, given any empirical experience. The biological structure constrains the theory we will develop.

There are some empirical experiences that cannot be classified because the biological organism cannot sense them. Ultraviolet light and high frequency sounds are examples of sensory stimuli of which we are not aware, but something about which we know because of machines and inferences made on the basis of the responses of other animals. There are some stimuli that humans prefer to classify in one way rather than another, although when forced to they can classify the same stimuli in many ways. The recent child literature on classification has provided a number of examples here (e.g., Nelson, 1977; Smiley & Brown, 1979). The point is that there are natural ways of classifying, conceptualizing, or theorizing about the world. As human beings, we have an increasingly ordered set of natural conceptualizing rule systems in common from the point of conception. The natural conceptual base has evolved over time as human evolution has taken place.

At a second, and not entirely independent, level, the commonalities in our theories of the world are made possible by the commonalities in the culture in which societal members are immersed. The cultural commonalities, too, have evolved over time as the evolution of society has taken place. The cultural characteristics of a society are passed from one generation to the next and extablish, among other things, particular languages and the rules and practices of conduct and custom that govern the conceptualization of interactions among humans in groups (Campbell, 1975; Hayek, 1978).

Thus, the child has a theory of the world from the very beginning. The child has an abstract classification system, presumably prototypic in structure, and a system of relating the abstract classes. In short, there is a conceptual framework with which the child can understand the particulars of the world. That conceptual framework, or theory, is a system of rules for making judgments about what is and ought to be.

Once the children become capable of language, they contract with others to talk about how to talk about the world, which they already know or understand in terms of the theory of the world they possess. Children know the meaning because they have a theory. What they must learn is not the meanings of words but, rather, what words are used to convey the meanings that they already know. Language acquisition, on this view, is a matter of determining the contractually agreed upon language mechanisms people in a particular language community ordinarily use in talking about the concepts and relations among concepts that are natural to humans.

As suggested earlier, the child already has a concept of, for example, dog, which allows the classification of Chihuahua and Saint Bernard. What the child needs to learn is that in English (if that is the language of the community) the word *dog* is used when one wishes to communicate that concept. The concept of dog is not as rich in relations for the child as for the adult in the sense that the child does not know that teasing dogs leads to biting or that dogs have a particular phylogenetic status among animals. The child does know, however, how to classify in terms of fur, bark, weight, ears, animateness, and so on. The child has a concept of dog that is a synthesis used to identify particular exemplars of dogs, to separate dogs from other conceptual categories, and in turn, that concept allows for an analysis of the concept in terms of some of the attributes of dog.

In summary, the human organism organizes its empirical experiences in terms of a cognitive system that encompasses and provides a structure for the concepts and relations used to give meaning to individual events encountered in those empirical experiences. The cognitive system has been referred to here as a theory of the world. The theory of each individual makes it possible for the individual to create a meaning for the empirical experience and thus avoid the inherent ambiguity of that experience. The very fact of communication among individuals makes it clear that individuals share a commonality in their theories of the world. The commonality of theory is assumed to derive from the sameness of the genetic and cultural endowment passed from one generation to the next and manifest in the biological systems of individual organisms and the societal systems of groups within a species. The variations in theory are assumed to derive from individual differences in biological and cultural endowment and from the particular empirical experiences of individuals.

Children's cognitive development reflects the maturational changes in the biological system and the modification of the theoretical system of the child brought about by failure to confirm the theory with respect to the way things ought to be in the empirical experience. Thus, the biologically established abstract dimensions and relations are organized and reorganized in terms of the biological changes that have their effects upon the theory at any moment of development and the failure of that naturally determined theory to account for the actual experiences viewed from the perspective of that theory.

METAPHOR AND MEANING

In this section, I would like to consider briefly the potential in the study of metaphor for the elucidation of some of the theoretical issues considered in the previous sections. The enigmatic nature of metaphor created by relating exemplars of two diverse conceptual categories to generate a new relation or meaning may be a key to the understanding of the abstract, tacit conceptual system. Although it may seem improbable that we might use metaphor as a key to unlocking the mysteries of the mind in light of its continued intractable status after such a long intellectual history, there are reasons for being optimistic.

Metaphor, as every introduction to the topic relates, has received the attention of scholars from the time of Aristotle. Since that time, we find that many philosophers have struggled to account for the nature of the metaphoric form of figurative language. In addition, metaphor has drawn the attention of poets, linguists, anthropologists, and psychologists, among others. Actually, Aristotle was concerned with metaphor less as a philosophical problem than as a pedogogical tool. He considered metaphor rather narrowly as a rhetorical and poetic device used to infuse liveliness, vividness, pleasantness, clearness, charm, and a distinctive style into one's communication. Aristotle assumed this linguistic ability to be natural and otherwise acquired only by long practice. Others since Aristotle have viewed metaphor primarily as a linguistic device (e.g., Beardsley, 1962), some have suggested that metaphor is more a reflection of thought in language (e.g., Richards, 1936; Wheelwright, 1962), and others have argued that metaphor is basic to all of human cognitive processes (e.g., Cassirer, 1946). As Cassirer has suggested, perception of reality is a human construction, and metaphor is a construction on that construction. It is the latter point of view that suggests the importance of metaphor in understanding the cognitive processes of humans.

Regardless of the breadth of scope assumed to be encompassed by metaphor, there is general agreement that a metaphor is composed of a tenor or subject, a vehicle or object, and a ground or relation, which allows the tenor and vehicle to come together in a meaningful way (Richards, 1936). It is, of course, the unstated ground relating tenor and vehicle that is the riddle of metaphor. The issue concerns the manner in which one person can create a relationship between two distinct concepts and, without stating the relationship explicitly, communicate it to another person. There is no surface structure hint in a metaphor as to the underlying meaning conveyed by bringing together the disparate conceptual domains of the tenor and vehicle, which form the metaphor. Three major accounts of the nature of the relationship have been offered. The first, offered initially by Aristotle, is that there is a resemblance between tenor and vehicle. Understanding a metaphor, by this account, involves determining the similarity dimension relating the two parts. The second account is that metaphor creates thoughts of two different things together, and the meaning derives from their interaction. It is not the similarity of one part to the other but the interaction of the two parts that yields the meaning (Black, 1962, 1979; Richards, 1936). By interaction is meant the selection of properties of the vehicle meaning, construction of implications for the tenor from those meaning properties, and a reciprocal change in the vehicle as a result of the construction for the tenor (Black, 1979). Finally, the third account suggests that the meaning emerges from the whole metaphor as a unit rather than some kind of composition of the separate parts (Beardsley, 1962; Cassirer, 1946; Perrine, 1971; Wheelwright, 1962). From this perspective, metaphor is composed of two elements, tenor and vehicle, each of which has its own conceptual sphere, but the very bringing together of those elements into a metaphor creates a new conceptual sphere, which cannot be broken down into its elements without losing the concept that is the metaphor.

As several investigators have noted, in order to understand metaphor, we need a comprehensive theory of semantics or meaning because metaphor is only part of a larger problem. As Black (1962) has indicated, such a theory will have to encompass pragmatics and context as well as language itself. Cassirer (1946) and Verbrugge (1979) add that the theory will have to account for artistic metaphor as well as linguistic metaphor. Furthermore, others have noted that other forms of figurative language such as simile, proverb, hyperbole, oxymoron, and even riddles are not basically different from metaphor and, therefore, must be encompassed by the theory.

Careful consideration of metaphor reveals the inherent complexities for any theory. To begin, linguistic metaphors are created in at least two forms: *A is B* and *A:B as C:D*. The latter form, called the proportional metaphor, is often considered superior to the simple metaphor as a rhetorical or poetic device. In addition to the analogy inherent in the proportional metaphor, the latter metaphors are further complicated by the fact that often some parts of the proportion do not appear in the surface form (e.g., "Billboards are warts on the landscape''). Such omissions require creation of the full proportion as well as the ground in the process of comprehension. Simple metaphors are considered by some writers as simpler than proportional metaphors, but others have argued that simple metaphors are really proportional metaphors with two elements of the proportion omitted. For example, ''The man is a fox'' should be understood as something like ''The man is clever as the fox is sly.''

On another level, several students of metaphor have noted the necessity of taking into account the nature of the tenor and the vehicle in the metaphoric relationship and the frame of reference in which the metaphor itself is created. Barfield (1928), for example, has argued that the poet's metaphors create relations between objects and other objects, between objects and feelings, and between objects and ideas. Upton (1961), also moving away from a consideration of the words per se in the metaphor, argues for a consideration of the frame of reference of the speaker and listener in the understanding of metaphor. He suggests that the logical, sensory, and affective point of view of the creator of the metaphor must be captured by the comprehender to obtain the meaning.

Others have taken the position that in order to understand metaphor fully one must know the etymological history of the words involved (e.g., Barfield, 1928). The meaning of a metaphor from this perspective involves not only the current meanings of the words but also aspects of the historical meanings each word brings to the metaphor. Many historical linguists, approaching the problem of metaphor from yet another perspective, have argued that shifts in the meanings of words have been initiated through the creation of metaphors (e.g., Sturtevant, 1917; Ullman, 1957). As particular metaphors capture the imagination of the language community, they are passed from one generation to the next as a part of the culture. In the process, the metaphors change from interesting creations to dead metaphors, to words with new meanings. Tracing the history of particular words in the metaphor through this history, there is an initial meaning for the word, followed by a polysemous stage when both new and old meanings are available, to a final stage when only the new meaning is used (e.g., *sharp tongue*). Because metaphoric creations are unpredictable, the expanding and shifting semantic space encompassed by words is difficult to anticipate. Several linguists, however, have suggested that at least some of the changes attributable to metaphor are based upon universal semantic relations (Fernandez, 1972; Upton, 1961; Williams, 1976). There is some evidence that the same metaphors have appeared in widely different cultural linguistic groups providing support for this hypothesis (Dezso, 1979).

From an anthropological perspective, it has been argued that metaphors have social-behavioral influences in different cultures. Conceptions of people, for example, may be created in either an adorning or disparaging manner by metaphor. Particular grounds used to relate tenor and vehicle, however, are related to the culture in which the persons exist (Fernandez, 1972). At the same time, Dickey (1968), among others, has noted that because metaphor involves the mind of the individual, it is necessary to take into account the history brought by that particular mind to each word in a metaphor and, hence, to the metaphor itself. Dickey is, therefore, recognizing idiosyncratic as well as general meanings for metaphors. The universal nature of some metaphoric creations, the cultural influences on others, and the individual creativity involved in still others reveal the complexity of the problem with which any theory of meaning must deal.

Although there are a number of hypotheses advanced to account for metaphor, it is viewed by most psychologists as a special case, which when encountered in a linguistic environment creates a tension in the comprehender because literal processing routines cannot be applied to achieve meaning. The distinction between literal and nonliteral statements, it is assumed, requires a separate conceptualization of the nonliteral metaphor. Most psychologists have taken positions that are variations on the theme that metaphor can best be understood in terms of similarity and analogy (e.g., Miller, 1979; Ortony, 1979; Sternberg, Tourangeau, & Nigro, 1979). Metaphor is conceived as a disguised simile, which at base is an analogy of the form A is similar to B as C is similar to D. The basic problem is to establish similarity metrics for the $A–B$ and $C–D$ relations (e.g., Tversky, 1977) and the processes or rules for forming the analogy involved. The difficulty with this approach is in many ways the same as the difficulties in analyzing the meaning of a word in terms of the compontential features of which it is composed. The meaning of the metaphor is assumed to be the sum of the parts, albeit complicated by similarity and analogy relations as well as the often unspecified need to create some of the assumed parts of the analogy, which are frequently omitted from the surface form of the metaphor.

Two points may be noted here. First, there does seem to be some, at least qualitative, difference between sentences that are clear cases of what are called literal sentences and clear cases of metaphor. For example, the sentence "Billboards are signs on the landscape" is literal in the sense that it provides a piece of information that may be evaluated in terms of its truth of falsity. On the other hand, "Billboards are warts on the landscape" is a metaphor that engenders generation of its meaning rather than its truth. It is conceivable that the difference between the strategies engendered by the two types of statements may be important to our understanding of sentences in general and metaphor in particular, although to my knowledge no one has scrutinized the question.

Second, although it is obvious that the meaning of a metaphor, as any sentence, is constrained by the components of which it is composed, it does not follow that the meaning of any sentence, metaphoric or otherwise, can be derived from an analysis of those components. As is the case with a word, a metaphor is a unit and must be analyzed as such. A componential analysis presupposes a knowledge of the object being analyzed, and the sum of the components does not, in itself, yield the object. It is, of course, possible, and maybe fruitful for some purposes, to analyze the metaphoric unit into components just as it is possible to analyze words into features. Such analyses, however, are at different levels dealing with different units and, as a result, cannot be used to explain questions about processing, for example, at other levels of analysis.

In this context, it is worthwhile to recognize that a metaphor is composed of at least two words set in a kind of equivalence relation (i.e., X is Y). The two words, in turn, are exemplars of conceptual categories. It is, therefore, the case that the creation of a metaphor brings together two diverse or unrelated classes and subsumes them under a higher level concept in which the two no longer are exemplars but, rather, are merged as a new conceptualization. This being the case, it may be useful to examine the dimensional structure and the rules used to generate the exemplars of those conceptual categories. The rules of any category will not only generate the exemplars of the category but also the transformations of the category structure, given a particular context. In the case of metaphor, we have a tenor in the context of a vehicle undergoing transformation in conceptual structure. We might anticipate that the position of the tenor and vehicle in their respective conceptual structures would influence the meaning of the metaphor (Sternberg et al., 1979). Prototypic exemplars of a concept might, for example, affect metaphoric meaning differently than peripheral exemplars. More important, perhaps, is the system of interrelationships between tenor and vehicle brought about by the metaphor (Verbrugge, 1979; Verbrugge & McCarrell, 1977). The vehicle influences the conceptualization of the tenor via some transformational rules analogous, in some ways, to the syntactic embedding of one sentence into another. In both cases, the matrix and embedded portions of the whole undergo changes themselves and at the same time impose constraints upon the nature of the final product, which emerges as a result of those transformational rules.

The importance of metaphor lies in the potential that the study of metaphor processing holds for revealing the characteristics of the abstract dimensions and rules used in creating a meaning for them. If we think of metaphor as the creation of a new meaning from the merging of two unrelated meanings, we can begin to ask questions about the nature of the emergent meaning in terms of the constraints imposed by the unrelated meanings, the context in which the metaphor is created, the developmental characteristics of the person creating or comprehending the meaning, and most important, the characteristics of the abstract dimensions and generative rules used to achieve the meaning.

Given the metaphor, "My uncle is a pretty summer" or "Love is a dressed-up doll"—the first a randomly selected set of words placed in a metaphoric syntactic frame (Boswell, 1977) and the second from Keat's *Modern Love*—we can begin to look for the answers to how they are interpreted. We can ask about what meanings emerge from these metaphors. How are the concepts of "uncle" and "love" expanded or transformed by their merging with "pretty summer" and "dressed-up doll"? Do those meanings vary as a function of larger contexts in which they are embedded? What cultural variations affect the meanings? What

changes in meaning occur as a child grows conceptually? Are there commonalities across persons regardless of age, culture, and context? Are there
commonalities within cultures and individuals that differ across cultures and
individuals? We can study individuals as they reveal meaning of the same metaphors in different settings and of commonalities of meanings across individuals
in the same contexts. We can identify persons with apparently different theories
of the world and establish their meanings for particular metaphors. We can
establish the structure of the concepts for the words used in the metaphors and
their influences on the emergent meaning of the metaphor. Research in this area
has only begun to scratch the surface of the potential insights available here (cf.
Gardner, Winner, Bechhofer, & Wolf, 1978; Hoffman, in press; Pollio, Barlow,
Fine, & Pollio, 1977; Verbrugge, 1979).

SUMMARY

I have attempted here to elaborate a theory of the structure of concepts, to
advance a theory of how a child develops a framework within which to impose
meaning on experience, and to illustrate how the investigation of metaphor may
be an empirical entree to an examination of the theory advanced. It has been
suggested that the biological organism is structured in a way that constrains the
manner in which the world is explored and predisposes the organisms to a
conceptual system with prototypically organized concepts. These concepts, in
turn, are molded by cultural contexts and individual learning, and they relate to
each other within the framework of a continually changing theoretical system,
which allows the child to understand the environmental experiences that he or
she encounters. Such an approach places the emphasis upon the abstract system
of rules, mostly tacit in nature, which within any particular context define the
meaning of any experience for the person. By implication, any empirical approach to the study of language acquisition and, more broadly, the cognitive
development of the child must focus upon the abstract if we are to gain an
understanding of the problems Piaget raised concerning the relation of subject
and object and the nature of our knowledge.

ACKNOWLEDGMENTS

I would like to thank James E. Martin and Walter B. Weimer for their critical readings of
portions of this paper. They stimulated further thinking, modification of some ideas, and
correction of others. They cannot, however, be held responsible for problems that may
remain.

REFERENCES

Andersen, E. S. Cups and glasses: Learning that boundaries are vague. *Journal of Child Language*, 1975, *2*, 79–104.

Anglin, J. M. *Word, object, and conceptual development*. New York: Norton, 1977.

Barclay, R. J., Bransford, J. D., Franks, J. J., McCarrell, N. S., & Nitsch, K. Comprehension and semantic flexibility. *Journal of Verbal Learning and Verbal Behavior*, 1974, *13*, 471–481.

Barfield, O. *Poetic diction*. London: Faber & Faber, 1928.

Beardsley, M. The metaphorical twist. *Philosophy and Phenomenological Research*, 1962, *22*, 293–307.

Beck, A. T. *Cognitive therapy and the emotional disorders*. New York: International Universities Press, 1976.

Berlin, B., Breedlove, D. E., & Raven, P. H. General principles of classification and nomenclature in folk biology. *American Anthropologist*, 1973, *75*, 214–242.

Black, M. *Models and metaphors: Studies in language and philosophy*. Ithaca, N.Y.: Cornell University Press, 1962.

Black, M, More about metaphor. In A. Ortony (Ed.), *Metaphor and thought*. Cambridge, England: Cambridge University Press, 1979.

Boswell, D. A. *Metaphoric processing in maturity*. Unpublished doctoral dissertation, The Pennsylvania State University, 1977.

Bransford, J. D., & McCarrell, N. S. A sketch of a cognitive approach to comprehension: Some thoughts about understanding what it means to comprehend. In W. B. Weimer & D. S. Palermo (Eds.), *Cognition and the sybolic processes*. Hillsdale, N.J.: Lawrence Erlbaum Associates, 1974.

Brown, R. W. *A first language: The early stages*. Cambridge, Mass.: Harvard University Press, 1973.

Campbell, D. T. On the conflicts between biological and social evolution and between psychology and moral tradition. *American Psychologist*, 1975, *30*, 1103–1126.

Cassirer, E. *Language and myth*. New York: Harper & Brothers, 1946.

Chang, H. W., & Trehub, S. E. Auditory processing of relational information by young infants. *Journal of Experimental Child Psychology*, 1977, *24*, 324–331.

Chomsky, N. *Syntactic structures*. The Hague: Mouton, 1957.

Cohen, L. B., & Salapatek, P. *Infant perception: From sensation to cognition* (Vols. 1 & 2). New York: Academic Press, 1975.

Cohen, L. B., & Strauss, M. S. Concept acquisition in the human infant. *Child Development*, 1979, *50*, 419–424.

Crook, C. K., & Lipsitt, L. P. Neonatal nutritive sucking: Effects of taste stimulation upon sucking rhythm and heart rate. *Child Development*, 1976, *47*, 518–522.

Cutting, J. E., & Proffitt, D. R. *Modes and mechanisms in the perception of speech and other events*. Unpublished manuscripts, Weslayan University, 1979.

Dezso, B. *Prospectus on metaphor comprehension and comparison*. Unpublished manuscript, 1979. The Pennsylvania State University.

Dickey, J. *Metaphor as pure adventure*. Lecture delivered at the Library of Congress, 1967. Washington: Library of Congress, 1968.

Eimas, P. D., Siqueland, E. R., Jusczyk, P., & Vigorito, J. M. Speech perception in infants. *Science*, 1971, *171*, 303–306.

Fernandez, J. Persuasions and performances: Of the beast in everybody and the metaphors in every man. *Daedalus*, 1972, *101*, 39–60.

Gardner, H., Winner, E., Bechhofer, R., & Wolf, D. The development of figurative language. In K. Nelson (Ed.), *Children's language* (Vol. 1). New York: Gardner Press, 1978.

Goldman, D., & Homa, D. Integrative and metric properties of abstracted information as a function of category discriminability, instance variability, and experience. *Journal of Experimental Psychology: Human Learning and Memory,* 1977, *3,* 375–385.

Grice, H. P. Logic and conversation In P. Cole & J. L. Morgan (Eds.), *Syntax and semantics Vol. 3: Speech acts.* New York: Academic Press, 1975.

Haith, M. M. Visual competence in early infancy. In R. Held, H. Leibowitz, & H. L. Teuber (Eds.), *Handbook of sensory physiology* (VIII). Berlin: Springer-Verlag, 1978.

Haith, M. M. *Rules that infants look by.* Hillsdale, N.J.: Lawrence Erlbaum Associates, 1980.

Hayek, F. A. The primacy of the abstract. In A. Koestler & J. R. Symthies (Eds.), *Beyond reductionism.* New York: Macmillan, 1969.

Hayek, F. A. *The three sources of human values* (L. T. Hobhouse Memorial Trust Lecture). London: The London School of Economics and Political Science, 1978.

Hoffman, R. R. Metaphor in science. In R. P. Honeck & R. R. Hoffman (Eds.), *Cognitive psychology and figurative language.* Hillsdale, N.J.: Lawrence Erlbaum Associates, in press.

James. W. *The prinicples of psychology* (2 Vols.). New York: Holt, 1890.

Jenkins, J. J. Remember that old theory of memory? Well, forget it. In R. Shaw & J. D. Bransford (Eds.), *Perceiving, acting, and knowing.* Hillsdale, N.J.: Lawrence Erlbaum Associates, 1977.

Kuhn, T. S. *The structure of scientific revolutions.* Chicago: University of Chicago Press, 1970.

Labov, W. The boundaries of words and their meanings. In C. J. N. Bailey & R. W. Shuy (Eds.), *New ways of analyzing variation in English.* Washington, D.C.: Georgetown University Press, 1973.

Lewin, K. Behavior and development as a function of the total situation. In L. Carmichael (Ed.), *Manual of child psychology.* New York: Wiley, 1946.

Lyons, J. *Introduction to theoretical linguistics.* Cambridge, England: Cambridge University Press, 1969.

MacKenzie, D. L., & Palermo, D. S. *The effect of context on semantic categorization.* Unpublished manuscript, 1980.

Macnamara, J. Cognitive basis of language learning in infants. *Psychological Review,* 1972, *79,* 1–13.

Macnamara, J. *Meaning.* In W. B. Weimer & D. S. Palermo (Eds.), *Cognition and the symbolic processes* (Vol. 2). Hillsdale, N.J.: Lawrence Erlbaum Associates, 1982.

Martin, J. E. Presentationalism: An essay toward self-reflexive psychological theory. In W. B. Weimer & D. S. Palermo (Eds.), *Cognition and the symbolic processes.* Hillsdale, N.J.: Lawrence Erlbaum Associates (Vol. 2), 1982.

Mervis, C. B., Catlin, J., & Rosch, E. Development of the structure of color categories. *Developmental Psychology,* 1975, *11,* 54–60.

Miller, G. A. Images and models, similes, and metaphors. In A. Ortony (Ed.), *Metaphor and thought.* New York: Cambridge University Press, 1979.

Molfese, D. L., Freeman, R. B., Jr., & Palermo, D. S. The ontogeny of brain lateralization for speech and nonspeech stimuli. *Brain and Language,* 1975, *2,* 356–368.

Molfese, D. L., & Molfese, V. Infant speech perceptions: Learned or innate. In H. A. Whitaker & H. Whitaker (Eds.), *Advances in neurolinguistics* (Vol. 4). New York: Academic Press, 1979.

Moore, M. K., Borton, R., & Darby, B. L. Visual tracking in young infants: Evidence for object identity or object permanence. *Journal of Experimental Child Psychology,* 1978, *25,* 183–198.

Nelson, K. Structure and strategy in learning to talk. *Monographs of the Society for Research in Child Development,* 1973, *38,* Nos. 1–2, 1–135.

Nelson, K. Concept, word, and sentence: Interrelations in acquisition and development. *Psychological Review,* 1974, *81,* 267–285.

Nelson, K. The nominal shift in semantic-syntactic development. *Cognitive Psychology,* 1975, *7,* 461–479.

Nelson, K. The conceptual basis for naming. In J. Macnamara (Ed.), *Language, learning, and thought*. New York: Academic Press, 1977.

Nelson, K. E., & Bonvillian, J. D. Early language development: Conceptual growth and related processes between 2 and 4½ years of age. In K. E. Nelson (Ed.), *Children's language*. New York: Gardner Press, 1978.

Ortony, A. The role of similarity in similes and metaphors. In A. Ortony (Ed.), *Metaphor and thought*. Cambridge, England: Cambridge University Press, 1979.

Ortony, A., Reynolds, R. E., & Arter, J. Metaphor: Theoretical and empirical research. *Psychological Bulletin*, 1978, *18*, 919–943.

Ortony, A., Schallert, D. L., Reynolds, R. E., & Antos, S. J. Interpreting metaphors and idioms: Some effects of context on comprehension. *Journal of Verbal Learning and Verbal Behavior*, 1978, *17*, 465–477.

Palermo, D. S. *Psychology of language*. Glencove, Ill.: Scott, Foresman, 1978. (a)

Palermo, D. S. Semantics and language acquisition: Some theoretical considerations. In R. N. Campbell & P. T. Smith (Eds.), *Recent advances in the psychology of language: Formal and experimental approaches*. NATO Conference Series, Vol. 4B, 1978, 45–54. (b)

Perrine, L. Psychological forms of metaphor. *College English*, 1971, *33*, 125–138.

Piaget, J. *The mechanisms of perception*. New York: Basic Books, 1969.

Piaget, J. *Biology and knowledge*. Chicago: University of Chicago Press, 1971.

Piaget, J. Chance and dialectic in biological epistemology: A critical analysis of Jacques Monod's theses. In W. F. Overton & J. M. Gallagher (Eds.), *Knowledge and development* (Vol. 1). New York: Plenum, 1977.

Piaget, J., & Inhelder, B. *The psychology of the child*. New York: Basic Books, 1969.

Pollio, H. R., Barlow, J., Fine, H. J., & Pollio, M. *The poetics of growth: Figurative language in psychotherapy and education*. Hillsdale, N.J.: Lawrence Erlbaum Associates, 1977.

Proffitt, D. R. *Demonstrations to investigate the meaning of everyday experience*. Unpublished doctoral dissertation, The Pennsylvania State University, 1976.

Richards, I. A. *The philosophy of rhetoric*, Oxford: Oxford University Press, 1936.

Rieser, J., Yonas, A., & Wikner, K. Radical localization of odors by human newborns. *Child Development*, 1976, *47*, 856–859.

Rosch, E. On the internal structure of perceptual and semantic categories. In T. E. Moore (Ed.), *Cognitive development and the acquisition of language*. New York: Academic Press, 1973.

Rosch, E. Cognitive representation of semantic categories. *Journal of Experimental Psychology*, 1975, *104*, 192–233.

Rosch, E., & Mervis, C. B. Family resemblances: Studies in the internal structure of categories. *Cognitive Psychology*, 1975, *7*, 573–605.

Schwartz, M., & Day, R. H. Visual shape perception in early infancy. *Monographs of the Society for Research in Child Development*, 1979, *44*,(7, Serial No. 182).

Slobin, D. I. On the nature of talk to children. In E. H. Lenneberg & E. Lenneberg (Eds.), *Foundations of language development* (Vol. 1). New York: Academic Press, 1975.

Smiley, S. S., & Brown, A. L. Conceptual preference for thematic or taxonomic relations: A nonmonotonic age trend from preschool to old age. *Journal of Experimental Child Psychology*, 1979, *28*, 249–257.

Sternberg, R. J., Tourangeau, R., & Nigro, G. Metaphor, induction, and social policy: The convergence of macroscopic and microscopic views. In A. Ortony (Ed.), *Metaphor and thought*. Cambridge, England: Cambridge University Press, 1979.

Strauss, M. S. Abstraction of prototypical information by adults and 10-month-old infants. *Journal of Experimental Psychology: Human Learning and Memory*, 1979, *5*, 618–632.

Sturtevant, E. H. Linguistic change. Chicago: University of Chicago Press, 1917.

Trehub, S. E. Infants' sensitivity to vowel and tonal contrasts. *Developmental Psychology*, 1973, *9*, 91–96.

Tversky, A. Features of similarity. *Psychological Review*, 1977, *84*, 327–352.

Ullmann, S. *The principles of semantics*, (2nd edition). Glasgow: Jackson and Oxford, Blackwell, 1957.

Upton, A. W. *Design for thinking: A first book in semantics*. Stanford, CA: Stanford University Press, 1961.

Verbrugge, R. R. The primacy of metaphor in development. New Directions for Child Development, 1979, *6*, 77–84.

Verbrugge, R. R., & McCarrell, N. S. Metaphoric comprehension: Studies in reminding and resembling. *Cognitive Psychology*, 1979, *9*, 494–533.

Weimer, W. B. Psycholinguistics and Plato's paradoxes of the Meno. *American Psychologist*, 1973, *28*, 15–33.

Weimer, W. B. Overview of a cognitive conspiracy: Reflections on the volume. In W. B. Weimer, & D. S. Palermo (Eds.), *Cognitions and the symbolic processes* (Vol. 1). Hillsdale, N.J.: Lawrence Erlbaum Associates, 1974.

Weimer, W. B. A conceptual framework for cognitive psychology: Motor theories of the mind. In R. Shaw, & J. D. Bransford (Eds.), *Perceiving, acting, and knowing*. Hillsdale, N.J.: Lawrence Erlbaum Associates, 1977.

Weimer, W. B. *Notes on the methodology of scientific research*. Hillsdale, N.J.: Lawrence Erlbaum Associates, 1979.

Wheelwright, P. E. *Metaphor and reality*. Bloomington, Ind.: Indiana University Press, 1962.

Williams, J. M. Synaesthetic adjectives: A possible law of semantic change. *Language*, 1976, *52*, 461–478.

Wittgenstein, L. *Philosophical investigations*. New York: Macmillan, 1953.

5 The Implications of a Semantic Theory for the Development of Class Logic

Ellin Kofsky Scholnick
University of Maryland, College Park

Inevitably, debates about Piaget's theory produce a common set of questions. These questions arose when Wartofsky discussed the nature of development and when Gibson and Spelke speculated on the origin of intermodal perception. We return to these questions in my discussion of Palermo's paper (Chapter 4), which is not a bad way of beginning a discussion on the nature of classes! There are two frequent criticisms of Piaget's theory and research. Piaget uses formal logic as a basis for describing what the child must acquire, but formal logic does not describe natural thought processes. Either because Piaget used the wrong conceptual analysis or because Piagetians do not present children with tasks that seem natural to youngsters, Piaget seriously underestimated the cognitive capacities of young children (e.g., Carey, 1980; Donaldson, 1978; Gelman, 1978) and presumed unwarranted discontinuities in development.

This paper briefly sketches the kind of evidence that prompts attacks on the use of logic as a model of human reasoning and on the use of the Piagetian timetable as evidence for a stage theory of development. The review, although sketchy, should place Palermo's points in a more general context. The paper continues with a more specific discussion of the evidence for a different kind of categorical logic than what Piaget studied and for different ages of mastery than Piaget proposed. Finally, some proposals, including Palermo's, to deal with the evidence are discussed and evaluated.

THE CHALLENGE TO PIAGETIAN THEORY

Is Logic a Model for Human Reasoning?

Piaget's theory of conceptual development ties the acquisition of concepts to the acquisition of logic. Therefore, any controversy about the nature of logic and the timing of its acquisition is of central relevance to the validity of the Piagetian position. But the mapping of conceptual development onto formal logic has run into difficulty. It is well-known that descriptions of performance on tasks requiring the use of propositional reasoning pose problems for cognitive psychologists. There is a discrepancy between ordinary language and logic. The logician's "or" refers to inclusive disjunction. "Bobby will invite Mary or Jane to his party" implies in logic that the boy could invite one guest, the other, *or both*. In natural language, choices are often exclusive or incompatible alternatives—Bobby will or will not invite Mary to his party. Thus, on logical tasks the subject interprets "or" in the exclusive sense referring to one alternative or the other but *not* both, whereas the logician defines "or" inclusively to refer to either possibility or both (e.g., Neimark, 1970).

The logician's "if-then" refers to conditional relations. "If it rains, then I will take my umbrella" implies to the logician that wet weather leads to carrying a parasol, but in dry weather, the fate of the umbrella is uncertain. The individual may or may not carry it. But in natural logic, most adults interpret if-then statements differently. Some adopt biconditional logic. The presence of rain is associated with carrying umbrellas and the absence of rain with leaving an umbrella at home. Others infer that once we know that it is raining, we can predict what is carried, but no inferences are permissible under other circumstances (e.g., Braine, 1978; Taplin, Staudenmayer, & Taddonio, 1974). We cannot say any outcome is likely or anything at all. Similar problems arise in interpretations of "unless." Although it is the logical equivalent of "if-not," many adults think it means "if." Thus, they interpret "Unless it snows, I'll stay home" to mean that snowy weather is perfect for indoor activity, but the sentence suggests that dry weather leads to staying inside (e.g., Scholnick & Wing, in press).

Does Mastery of Formal Operations Coincide with Mastery of Propositional Logic?

The differences in interpretation of logical connectives lead to different claims about the time of comprehension of them and facility in reasoning with them. If understanding of propositional logic requires interpreting "or" as inclusive disjunction, "if-then" as a conditional, and "unless" as denial, then even adults, who are presumably formal operational, fail to use propositional logic (e.g., Lunzer, Harrison, & Davey, 1972; Wason, 1969). If instead we examine only those circumstances where logic and natural usage coincide, then mastery of propositional reasoning is evident in children who are presumed to be too young to be at the stage of formal operations (e.g., Hill, 1961). The problem is more fundamental than simply defining a criterion of mastery. There are circumstances where young children appear to derive inferences in a precocious way. The domain must be very familiar and very salient so that children can rely on environmental support to reduce the complexity of the task, and the children's own interest should motivate optimal deployment of their resources (e.g., Donaldson, 1978). Trabasso (1975) even argues that children's failures on logical tasks are due to problems in ancillary constraints on task performance rather than to failures in logic itself. He studied transitive inference. An example of a transitive inference problem is: "If Mary is taller than Sally, and Sally is taller than Joan, who is the tallest?" Numerical reasoning incorporates transitive reasoning, and hence transitive reasoning is vital to concrete operations. However, Trabasso demonstrated that children much younger than the age ordinarily associated with attainment of concrete operations could solve problems requiring transitive inference if they were trained to remember the initial premises or givens in a problem. Trabasso's critique of Piaget is actually more radical than the claim that task solution depends on memorial capacity. Although good memory is a prerequisite for task solution, success with combining premises is not based on logic at all. The child simply constructs a perceptual continuum by lining up the terms (e.g., girls), and then the child reads the terms off the line to solve the problem. Hence, the issue of timing of task solution raises not merely questions of experimental design. It raises fundamental questions about what develops—logic or the loosening of constraints upon logic (e.g., Gelman & Gallistel, 1978)—and about the psychological processes that underlie task solution (e.g., perceptual or logical strategies).

CLASSIFICATION RESEARCH

Misinterpretations and Reinterpretations of Class Logic

The controversy over the nature of logic and the timing of acquisition of reasoning skills extends to class logic. There is a discrepancy between ordinary language usage of "all" and "some" and their use by logicians (e.g., Revlis, 1975). Often adults misinterpret "all" to refer to an equivalence relationship when it refers to class inclusion. If told that "All oilmen are rich," they conclude that "All of the oilmen are all of the wealthy population." The two terms, oilmen and rich refer to the same population. Although "all" *can* denote equivalence (e.g., "All panthers are black leopards"), "All A are B" *often* refers to an inclusion relation where all of the A are some of the B. Such is the case with the oilmen, who presently constitute only a portion of the wealthy.

In logic "some" and "all" have overlapping meanings. "Some" refers to anything from one instance to the entire class, whereas "all" refers only to the entire class. In everyday speech, "some" and "all" are mutually exclusive: "We say some but not all wealthy people have oil stocks." Hence, adults who are well aware of the logic of class inclusion often fail to reason accurately on categorical syllogisms that contain the term "some" (e.g., Neimark & Chapman, 1975; Neimark & Slotnick, 1970).

Objections to using class logic as a model for conceptual reasoning are deeper than simply differences about language comprehension. The arguments focus on whether class logic is understood through the processes Piaget postulated and whether classes are defined appropriately. Markman (e.g., Markman, Cox, & Machida, 1981; Markman, Horton, & McLanahan, 1980; Markman & Seibert, 1976) has asserted there are two kinds of hierarchical relations, classes and collections, with the latter being more natural. Oak–tree is a class-inclusion relation, whereas oak–forest is a collective part–whole relation. In a class relation, membership is defined by the presence of a criterial set of attributes. Every member of the class possesses those criterial attributes, which we call the intension of a class. All trees are plants with woody trunks and high branches. In addition, classes have extensions. An extension is the scope of the class, the instances to which the class label applies. Once you define a tree, every oak belongs in the class. Everything with the defining attribute or attributes is a member of the class. In a class-inclusion relationship, there is a superordinate class, which is defined by a small number of attributes, and a set of subordinate classes, which is defined by additional attributes. Oaks are woody plants with high branches; they are also deciduous. Thus, all of the oaks are only some of the trees because trees may also include evergreens like pines. Oaks are part of the superordinate class of trees.

Oak–forest also exemplifies a part–whole relation, but the part–whole relationship is different from oak–tree. The oak–forest relation is not one of shared intension. A forest is not a homogeneous entity because it contains many kinds of plant and animal life. The extension of a collection like forest is not defined by its intension. Any of its members could exist outside of a forest, but an oak is necessarily a tree. The collection relation is based on spatial proximity, not shared attributes, and spatial proximity is very salient to children. The relation between an object and the collection to which it belongs can be perceived directly, whereas the relation of an object and a class requires analysis of the properties that an object and a class share. Thus, although part–whole relations in a collection are readily accessible in the perceptual array, class-inclusion relations must be constructed through perceptual analysis. Markman therefore suggests that collections are the earlier and more natural form of hierarchical relations. Children may misunderstand class inclusion because they lack the analytic skills needed to isolate and compare intensional relations. They learn class inclusion as they generalize from perceptually linked part–whole relations to conceptually organized abstract inclusion relations. Children readily grasp collective relations but not the less natural class relations.

Palermo deals with the same issue from a different perspective. He, too, argues that there is another kind of relation that may be more accessible and psychologically relevant than the relation of instance equivalence. He draws attention to the data on semantic development and sorting tasks to show both that children apprehend these natural relations and that the apprehension is much earlier than predicted by the Piagetian timetable for the acquisition of categorical logic. Word meanings reflect the individual's conceptual structure, which does not correspond to the equivalence classes defined by formal logic. In formal logic, every instance of a class possesses the same criterial attributes. All of the possessors of the attributes are in the class. But Palermo draws on the work of Rosch (e.g., 1973, 1975; Rosch & Mervis, 1975) to claim that natural categories have a different structure defined by disjunction or family resemblance. A member of a category may possess one criterial attribute, or a second, or both. There is a pool of attributes that differ in their salience, the degree to which they apply to all class members, and the degree to which they distinguish class members from instances that do not belong in the class. Exemplars vary in the number and type of defining attributes they contain. Some class members, the prototypes, contain a large number of defining and distinctive attributes, whereas others contain so few that they are borderline rather than core exemplars of the category. If birds are typically small, feathered songmakers, a sparrow is a bird prototype, but the large, flightless ostrich is not. In semantic categories, class membership is based on family resemblance, and categories have fuzzy boundaries. Dolphins and bats are both mammals, but they are unusual ones. In contrast, logical classes are sharply demarcated, and every instance of the class is as good an instance as other members.

There is also a discrepancy between Piaget's descriptions of the development of category logic in the early school years and Palermo's contentions that the contents of natural categories, their defining attributes, and the rules by which those categories are constructed are innate. Palermo argues that there is evidence for the construction of logical categories even before the child can speak. Cohen and Strauss (1979) have reported that 7-month-olds exposed to several versions of the same face in different orientations habituate to the faces and do not recover from habituation when a new face is presented. Similarly, Cohen and his colleagues (Cohen & Younger, 1983) have shown that 7-month-olds habituate to a series of diverse stuffed animals and fail to recover when a new stuffed animal is presented, and Caron, Caron, and Myers (1981) demonstrated that 7-month-olds habituated to various exemplars of smiling faces and showed dishabituation when the same faces expressed surprise. In each of these studies, younger infants did not show the same pattern of selective recovery to instances of a different class although data on slant perception (Caron, Caron, & Carlson, 1979) show the early formation of shape invariance across shifts of perspective. Ten-month-olds exposed to extreme exemplars of the distribution of facial features recognize a prototype or average composite of a face and attend less to that novel prototype than to a familiar extreme exemplar that they have already seen (Strauss, 1979). Older children appear to grasp more abstract concepts. One- to two-year-olds habituate to stimuli from diverse conceptual categories such as food (Ross,

1980). When 2-year-olds use terms like "more" or "another," they appear to be referring to an additional instance of class (Bloom, 1970). When 2½-year-olds are given a couple of examples of a novel concept, they name and select new instances of the concept (Nelson & Bonvillian, 1978).

Therefore, if we examine the recognition of categories and the production and generation of labels, it appears as if categories are formed early in development. Like Carey (1980), Palermo argues that much of conceptual development simply consists of adding domain-specific knowledge. The child fills in more examples such as adding emus and egrets to the category of birds. The child also decides the appropriate distance metric on which to arrange examples of categories or category relations. We add peripheral examples of categories, and we make finer subdivisions or more inclusive groups (see also Mervis & Mervis, 1982; Rosch, Mervis, Gray, Johnson, & Boyes-Braem, 1976). Because the network of category relations is context sensitive, we also learn the contexts that alter the salience or centrality of certain category exemplars. For example, wastebasket is less central an item of furniture in a living room than in a study. Just as performance on tasks of propositional logic challenges Piaget's theory of the structure and nature of formal operational logic (e.g., Ennis, 1976), studies of semantic development challenge the Piagetian explanation of the structure and acquisition of concrete operations.

It can also be argued that even if we examine tasks of classification and class-inclusion relations within the Piagetian framework of equivalence classes, many tasks thought to tap classification logic are developmentally insensitive (e.g., Gelman, 1979; Markman et al., in press; Siegel, McCabe, Brand, & Matthew, 1978). Children are more likely to group together only those things that are alike, as opposed to constructing designs, if they put objects in bags rather than in boxes. They are more likely to form equivalence classes if the class is relatively homogeneous (e.g., breeds of dogs) rather than very broad (e.g., species of animals). The age of success on class-inclusion tasks depends on variables like the perceptual arrangement or variety of contrast classes in the inclusion hierarchy and the child's understanding of the language of the question (see Winer, 1980). These data seriously weaken Piaget's attribution of the mastery of equivalence class logic exclusively to comprehension of concrete operations.

IMPLICATIONS OF THE DATA

Is the Only Kind of Classification Innate "Natural" Categorization?

It is indeed tempting to argue that Piaget (Inhelder & Piaget, 1964) has used the wrong model of classification to investigate the origin of category logic. But before we discard equivalence classes for prototypically organized semantic concepts, we must realize that conventional equivalence classes do exist in more than the minds of logicians. Scientific thought is based on equivalence categories. Suppose, like Mandler and Johnson (1977), we wished to examine the recall of stories. We must categorize the parts of stories such as setting events or outcomes to see if stories have a similar structure. We must also ascertain the relationship between story nodes such as temporal, enablement, and causal connections. There may indeed be marginal examples of each story node and relation, but if there were not a high degree of reliability in coding relations and nodes, we could not reduce the multiplicity of stories into some predictable structure, nor could we determine the factors associated with recall or comprehension. In many areas of scientific reasoning, we try to predict discrete categories of events, not the best exemplars. Conventional logical categories based on equivalence rules help sharpen boundaries, produce abstractions, and develop predictions (e.g., Rosch et al., 1976). To ignore equivalence categories is to ignore an important component of conceptual functioning. There must be at least two kinds of categorization used by children.

Is either kind innate? What is innate? Palermo suggests that attention to some dimensions may be innate, but he does not specify what those dimensions might be in any detail. In many instances, categories claimed to be innate undergo radical transformation in development, and dimensions that were initially salient may decrease in importance during development. Carey (Carey, Diamond, & Woods, 1980; Diamond & Carey, 1977) found that perception of faces, the very example Palermo cites, shifts in preadolescence, and organization of biological concepts shifts in the early school years (Carey, 1980). Early semantic and syntactic categories seem to be much narrower in preschoolers than in adults. A prime difficulty in using models of case or transformational grammar to describe early speech is that the child's linguistic categories lack many of the properties included by adults (e.g., Bowerman, 1973; Braine, 1976). Children do not just add exemplars to categories; they add and delete properties as the basis for categorization. If early categories are based on physical properties like size, shape and color, or functional equivalence, many of these properties are less important in adult classification (Clark, 1973). Therefore, dimensional properties cannot be innate.

Could we then say that the rules for category formation are innate? At least for prototypic categories the answer will be difficult to provide. If the child builds what seems to be a very heterogeneous category, we can always say the child is indeed consistent but uses more attributes and more unconventional attributes than the adult does. If the child builds or recognizes an equivalence class, it is difficult to determine whether the infant does so by deliberately abstracting only one common attribute or whether the child fails to discriminate other attributes that could be the basis for conceptual organization. However, even if we discard questionable instances of classification, we cannot deny there are instances where the infant does respond by treating new cases as if they were equivalent to old and somewhat dissimilar material. Assimilation involves some aspects similar to categorization. But is assimilation classification? We return to this point later.

Conceptual Development as the Translation of Natural into Conventional Categories

Palermo himself concedes in parts of his paper that semantic categories are not the only kind of category system individuals use. He proposes that although initial concepts are based on an innate set of dimensions and structures, which words are used to convey, the child, faced with the necessity of reducing information and making predictions, must develop logical categories and learn to distinguish between natural semantic concepts and the acquired conventions of logic.

This progression may explain some of the variability in children's performance on cognitive and linguistic tasks (see Rosch, 1973; C. L. Smith, 1979; Smith & Kemler, 1977, for the same arguments). Children appear to be most similar to adults in tasks of memorization and category recognition when they can use the prototype as a guide for performance (e.g., Carson & Abrahamson, 1976). They will be unlike adults when they must abstract criterial attributes to form equivalence classes or deal with peripheral class members.

The transition from semantic to logical categories may explain why the rules for category formation change during childhood. The young child's inconsistent sorting on equivalence classification tasks reflects a conceptualization of categories based on family resemblances or disjunctions. The older child differentiates the logical from the semantic class so as to produce consistent, exhaustive classes. All items in the class contain the criterial attribute, and every item containing the criterial attribute is in the class. Thus, the older child grasps the logic of intension and extension. Similarly, the semantic basis for categorization changes. The prototypes in most categories are defined by functions and parts, or what Inhelder and Piaget (1964) call *belongingness*. Whereas preschoolers explain their performance on object sorting tasks on the basis of functions, older children emphasize taxonomic relations or perceptual features. Young children inappropriately generalize from semantics to logic.

When during the course of their education children are exposed to demands for scientific inference, they transform semantic into taxonomic equivalence classes. A similar argument about memorization has been made by Paris (1978) and Flavell (Kreutzer, Leonard, & Flavell, 1975). Some of the ways children memorize events are not permitted in a school setting. At home a young child can use an external memory aid like a willing adult, but school rules do not allow copying from peers and from notes during testing. The young child memorizes meaningful material for his or her own purposes, but the older child has to learn by rote material such as geography or multiplication tables, which may seem useless. Therefore, the child has to acquire new methods of memorizing school material. Poor recall performance may reflect inappropriate transfer of illicit or inefficient tricks the child had employed previously. The child's problems with classification show up in other tasks and in other populations. Nonwestern uneducated adults often produce categories that resemble the preschooler's (e.g., Cole, Gay, Glick, & Sharp, 1971; Scribner, 1974). They do not know the narrow conventions of the categorization game, nor do they know when that game is to be played. Similarly, elderly adults who do not produce consistent taxonomic classes may have forgotten the context in which that mode of classification is appropriate (Denney & Cornelius, 1975; Smiley & Brown, 1979).

Palermo's explanation of the differences between logical and semantic classes could explain why semantic categorization appears much earlier in development than logical categorization. He also explains why children may appear to have difficulty even with semantic categories. A rule is not equally easy to apply in every context. In the past, situational variability in rule application has been discussed in terms of information-processing load (e.g., Pascual-Leone & Smith, 1969; Scardamalia, 1977), with rules being easier to apply when there are fewer instances to deal with. Palermo's view of rule application is more similar to Odom's (1978). Perceptual salience and cue validity determine ease of classification. We perform better with typical exemplars because they present multiple, overlapping cues that are regularly associated with category membership. Palermo also calls attention to context sensitivity as a determinant of classification. As concepts always contain some ambiguity, the child must learn which exemplars are more representative in certain contexts and how and when to apply concepts. Development is not simply the acquisition of knowledge but also the acquisition of sensitivity to the cues that enable us to tell when our knowledge is applicable.

By emphasizing the dual nature of classification strategies, acquisition, and utilization, Palermo's paper touches a weak spot in many developmental theories. A constructivist view of conceptual development often assumes that acquisition leads to immediate utilization, so the focus is almost exclusively on acquisition. Nativist views take acquisition for granted and often neglect the utilization process. Palermo's view, which describes a transformation of concepts from natural to conventional and from context insensitive to context sensitive, opens up the topic of utilization, but no details are provided. Palermo's theory must not only describe innate categories and why they are transformed but also how they are transformed. How does the child learn the mechanics of conventional classification or learn about context sensitivity? Flavell and Wellman (1977) discuss the transition between automatic and purposeful memorization in terms of metamemory, awareness of the repertoire of mnemonics and of the situation in which mnemonics need to be deployed. Palermo suggests that classes have an invariant set of core prototypes, but peripheral members shift in distance from the prototypes depending on situational contexts. But what is the basis of the way classes shift their organization depending on the context? How does the child acquire knowledge of the way in which classes shift? How does the child also learn that those shifts appropriate to semantic classes are not appropriate to logical classes? Despite all the advantages that the focus on prototypes offers, it does not solve the very problems of conceptual development that it raises. What is innate? What is acquired? How is it acquired? How does one go from semantic to logical categorization?

Conventional Categories Are not Simply a Later Version of Semantic Categories

Theories that point to other forms of categorization as precursors to conventional categorization may oversimplify the nature of conceptual development because conventional categorization as described by Piaget differs in many ways from semantic categorization. Some of these ways are crucial if we are to understand development. The difference between logical and semantic categories is not simply one of structure. There are additional requirements, which make the Piagetian description of classes very different from the application of a verbal label. If we were only to emphasize structural issues, the distinction between logical and semantic classes does not account for common difficulties children have in constructing either type of category. Finally, I am not sure that natural categories are innate and that there is such a discrepancy between semantic and logical development.

Whenever there are differences in the timing of acquisition of particular skills and procedures, it is wise to ask whether the procedures or skills are really very similar. This becomes particularly important in resolving the differences between Palermo and Piaget with respect to the temporal priority and naturalness of semantic as opposed to logical categories. I would like to paraphrase two discussions about the differences between logical and semantic categories. Each points out that the differences between class logic and semantic categories are not so much structural as conceptual. Class logic *as it is tested by Piaget* adds an important requirement often missing from tests of semantic concepts. Flavell (1970), in his chapter on concept development, made a distinction between classes as instruments and classes as objects. Children may use concepts instrumentally to give meaning to events, but they may not know what a class is. Certainly, one of the challenges for research on infant speech perception is that 1-month-olds show categorical perception of stop consonants, but we do not know how or even whether that knowledge guides their acquisition of articulatory control or their ability to segment spoken words into phonemes as they learn to read.

Lunzer (1964) states the issue elegantly:

> Even if overt classifications represent a somewhat artificial type of situation, their interest lies in the fact that they are intimately linked with the ability to "turn round on a schema" *to abstract the criteria of generalization.*

It is true that the simplest kinds of sorting, e.g., sorting a collection of cards which are similar in every respect except colour, into red, yellow and blue, may be carried out without mediation of an awareness of criteria of sorting. But such a test represents a special case, and its bearing on everyday intelligent behavior is almost notional. For in fact we are constantly interpreting new situations in the light of previous experience, and in the final analysis this means we are grouping or classifying these diverse situations under the same heading. Only rarely, if ever, can the determinants or the criteria of this grouping be wholly unambiguous. Often enough, the tendency to assimilate the new to the familiar will lead to false analogies . . . at variance with the facts. The question then arises whether we can detect the error, and in order to do so, we need to be aware of the initial criteria which determined the analogy. We have to be able to retrace our steps, to go back on our reasoning.

. . . Young children undoubtedly try to organize their experience after a fashion, and in the same way, they are willing enough to impose some kind of organization on an array of objects. But to begin with they fail to carry out the task in any coherent way because they deal with objects one at a time and the basis of their own behaviour eludes them. They cannot turn round on their own activity and abstract any single criterion to govern the entire sequence . . .

. . . If classificatory problems are somehow connected with the problems of inference in general, it is because classifications depend on the abstraction and retention of clear and unambiguous criteria. When this restriction is not attended to, the results of classificatory experiments can just as easily mislead as clarify the processes involved in reasoning [pp. xiv–xv].

The baby may recognize concepts, but it is not clear that the baby recognizes the concept of class. Perhaps the ability exists, but the correct tests, which would determine if the child both detects the concept of class and the violation of class logic, have not been performed. Thus, to establish that the child understands classification in the habituation paradigm, we might show the child slides with all slides depicting a class of objects, but with each representing a different class. If the infant could habituate to the idea of similarity, then one could present the child with the same objects, but this time the group depicted on each slide would be heterogeneous. Such a test would establish whether the child had an idea of class structure. The test of violation of class structure must necessarily focus on violation of intension. It might contrast rate of habituation to a set of objects all belonging to the same category with rate of habituation when only one or two instances in a habituation series did not belong to the same category but the rest did. We should expect that in the former group habituation would proceed more rapidly than in the latter group. If the infants habituated to a set of instances drawn from one category, then we would expect them to recover from habituation when the child sees instances of the old category mixed with instances from a new category. Thus, if the child saw slides of each depicting three stuffed animals, there should be recovery from habituation if a slide depicted two stuffed animals with an instance of another class.

Even then babies may work with concepts, but they may not work with them in the same way that older children do. There is a point in language development when children can step aside from their own productions to detect how they are constructing sentences (e.g., DeVilliers & DeVilliers, 1974; Gleitman, Gleitman, & Shipley, 1972), or when their sentences are ambiguous, and when they are punning. There is a parallel trend in cognition exemplified by another met metaconceptual skill, class logic. Thus, there is less of a discrepancy between semantic and logical categorization than we think. It could be that classification skills develop early, but we have not chosen the appropriate tests of infant classification to test the presence of logic. Nor have we demonstrated that when classification develops, categories based on family resemblance appear in the child's repertoire before equivalence categories. In fact, the literature on classification reviewed earlier shows as many instances of early equivalence classes as prototype construction. Most of the tests showing early acquisition make different response demands than tests of logical classification. They require less abstraction and less self-awareness. Palermo is quite right in saying that an important test of semantic development is metaphor. In metaphor as in classification, the individual must abstract and specify criteria. Therefore, there may be more parallels between performance on tasks of construction of metaphors and classes than between the use of labels and construction of logical categories. In summary, if demonstration of classification skills merely requires detection of similarities, these skills are evident early in development. But if we redefine classification in terms of the knowledge that similarity dictates a rule for grouping which cannot be violated and the knowledge of which similarity is important, then we lack evidence one way or the other that infants possess the concept of a class and that such awareness is more likely to occur for natural than conventional categories.

So far I have argued that recognition of a class is not the sole criterion for understanding classification. Children's use of categories does not guarantee that they know what categories are and when the rules have been violated. Tests of semantic development that fail to examine groupings in this light do not address the same issues as tests of equivalence concepts. If tests of semantic development are passed earlier, it may not be because semantic concepts are simpler and more basic but because the test is less demanding.

But if the strucutre of semantic concepts is indeed simpler, in what respect is this the case? Palermo's theory of semantics refers to three properties of semantic classes—context sensitivity, fuzzy extension, and disjunctive intension. Some of these aspects of natural categories may actually pose more problems to the child than the formation of equivalence classes poses. None of these aspects of semantic categories is easily mastered by the child. Therefore, there is the need for developmental analysis.

Conventional equivalence classes require decontextualization as one abstracts a common property across objects. We all know that the abstraction required is difficult for the young child. Palermo suggests that a semantic category requires both decontextualization and context sensitivity. The core of the class is constant regardless of context, but the items at the periphery switch. It would seem that semantic concepts are therefore more complex than equivalence classes because the child must simultaneously deal with a stable core and shifting peripheral members or with abstraction and context sensitivity. It is questionable whether young children can do this as shown in the following experiment. As a preliminary to an investigation on the role of class logic is constructive memory, Johnson and I asked fourth graders, sixth graders, and college students to rate a list of nouns in terms of whether they were good examples of different categories. There were some striking age differences. "Doll" and "rattle" are prototypes of the adult *toy* category, but they are peripheral members for fourth grade boys. Similarly, "skirt" is a typical member of the adult *clothing* category but not for fourth grade boys. For sixth grade girls, "bra" was central. Whereas adults do not think that "refrigerator" is a good example of an item of *furniture,* it was rated highly by sixth grade boys. College students may take the view of the "generalized other" when they rate concepts, but children take their own personal perspective. As a consequence, even semantically organized classes pose problems in organization and decontextualization. Just as children have difficulty in shifting criteria for sorting, (e.g., Kofsky, 1966), young children also appear to have difficulties in shifting perspectives and in reorganizing semantic classes. Moreover, some shifts in context may be easier to handle than others.

Semantic classes have fuzzy boundaries, whereas equivalence classes have precise ones. The lack of clarity in boundaries may indeed pose obstacles for the child. There are numerous examples of children producing overextended or underextended classes during the course of early language and concept acquisition (e.g., Clark, 1973; Nelson & Bonvillian, 1978). But the examples persist well past the point when the child can sort diverse colored shapes by either dimension. For example, Kendler and Guenther (1980) asked children to classify faces and breeds of dogs, two classes with "natural semantic structure." There was a substantial proportion of errors in overextension before the age of 5 and persistent underextension below the age of 8 (see also Nelson, 1974; Rosner & Hayes, 1977; Saltz, Soller, & Sigel, 1972). Even in dealing with semantic classes, children have problems in finding equivalence whether we call the task synonymy or coextension and in constructing overlaps whether we call the task metaphor or class inclusion.

Recognition of intension may be the one domain where semantic classes could be easier to deal with than formal logical classes. Note that the recognition of intension is the focus of most tests of infant classification. If the members of a semantic class possess a large number of defining attributes, then the child need neither maintain focus on a single attribute nor cope with dimensions low in salience. Any of a number of attributes, some of which are bound to be salient to the child, will be available in constructing the category. Because semantic classes are based on disjunction, the class may be easy to form, but it may not be easy to define except in cases where the child has learned a class label.

However, even isolating the intension of semantic classes may pose obstacles, which in many ways parallel the child's travails with equivalence classes. Rosch (Rosch et al., 1976) does not claim that all semantic categories are accessible early in development. Instead she distinguishes three levels of categorization based on the degree to which objects in a class are similar to one another but different from nonexemplars. The most basic level is the intermediate one, where there is a high degree of overlap in intension among members, but the exemplars are still easy to discriminate from nonexemplars. An example is the class *cats*. Basic level categories should be the easiest to work with. Superordinate categories have too few common intensional cues to make the class psychologically coherent (as in the category of animals), whereas subordinate classes contain so many attributes in common with other categories that their exemplars are hard to discriminate from exemplars of other subordinate classes (as in discriminating Siamese from Persian cats). Rosch has claimed that for nonbiological categories children acquire labels first at the basic level (but they acquire superordinate names for biological categories). She also asked children to sort when the stimuli were all prototypes of basic categories (e.g., different pairs of socks or different male faces) or all members of a superordinate category (e.g., different items of clothing). Whereas most kindergarten children produced acceptable sorts of basic categories, it was not until third grade that children could form superordinate categories. Labeling of these superordinate categories was not correct until fifth grade. Thus, not all semantic categories are equally easy to form. Mervis and Mervis (1982) argue that even those initial basic categories may undergo reorganization because what is basic to the child may not be basic to the adult.

Inasmuch as even semantically organized superordinate categories with core members can be difficult to group, we are still left with the problem central to concept acquisition (Rosch et al., 1976): "specification of the complex processes by which environmental structure (and adult categorizations) become internalized in children [p. 422]." Those processes may be somewhat different for semantic and logical classes, but there are many similarities with respect to the very issues that Inhelder and Piaget (1964) called attention to: awareness of procedures for the formation of classes, coordination of intension and extension, and appreciation of the variable and stable properties of classes.

Palermo's paper makes an excellent case for two premises that I accept: (1) semantics is the imposition of the child's knowledge of the world upon language; (2) the resulting concepts are not homogeneous, resulting in both abstract equivalence classes and context-sensitive categories. But neither kind of concept is wholly innate, and the two kinds of concepts are not entirely distinct from one another. There are many problems that arise in the acquisition and utilization of semantic concepts, which have also been discussed in the literature on equivalence formation. Semantic concepts and the procedures by which they are constructed do not appear in mature form early in development. There is enormous reorganization as the child acquires knowledge of a semantic domain, and there is increasing awareness of logic as a procedure abstracted from any particular domain. To ignore those issues in classificatory development is to ignore the very nature of cognitive development.

REFERENCES

Bloom, L. *Language development: Form and function in emerging grammars.* Cambridge, Mass.: MIT Press, 1970.

Bowerman, M. Structural relationships in children's utterances: Syntactic or semantic? In T. E. Moore (Ed.), *Cognitive development and the acquisition of language.* New York: Academic Press, 1973.

Braine, M. D.S. Children's first word combinations. *Monographs of the Society for Research in Child Development,* 1976, *41*(Serial No. 164).

Braine, M. D. S. On the relation between natural logic of reasoning and standard logic. *Psychological Review,* 1978, *85,* 1–21.

Carey, S. *Are children fundamentally different kinds of thinkers and learners than adults?* Paper presented at the National Institute of Education conference on Thinking and Learning Skills. Pittsburgh, October 1980.

Carey, S., Diamond, R., & Woods, B. Development of face recognition: A maturational component? *Developmental Psychology,* 1980, *16,* 257–269.

Caron, A. J., Caron, R. F., & Carlson, V. R. Infant perception of the invariant shape of objects varying in slant. *Child Development,* 1979, *50,* 716–721.

Caron, R. F., Caron, A. J., & Myers, R. S. *Abstraction of invariant face expressions in infancy.* Paper presented at the biennial meeting of the Society for Research in Child Development. Boston, April 1981.

Carson, M. T., & Abrahamson, A. Some members are more equal than others: The effect of semantic typicality on class inclusion performance. *Child Development,* 1976, *47,* 1186–1190.

Clark, E. V. What's in a word? On the child's acquisition of semantics in his first language. In T. E. Moore (Ed.), *Cognitive development and the acquisition of language.* New York: Academic Press, 1973.

Cohen, L. B., & Strauss, M. S. Concept acquisition in the human infant. *Child Development,* 1979, *50,* 419–424.

Cohen, L. B., & Younger, B. A. Perceptual categorization in the infant. In E. K. Scholnick (Ed.), *New trends in conceptual representation.* Hillsdale, N.J.: Lawrence Erlbaum Associates, 1983.

Cole, M., Gay, J., Glick, J., & Sharp, D. *The cultural context of learning and thinking.* New York: Basic Books, 1971.

Denney, N. W., & Cornelius, S. W. Class inclusion and multiple classification in middle and old age. *Developmental Psychology,* 1975, *11,* 521–522.

DeVilliers, J. G., & DeVilliers, P. A. Competence and performance in child language: Are children really competent to judge? *Journal of Child Language,* 1974, *1,* 11–22.

Diamond, R., & Carey, S. Developmental changes in the representation of faces. *Journal of Experimental Child Psychology,* 1977, *23,* 1–22.

Donaldson, M. *Children's minds.* New York: Norton, 1978.

Ennis, R. H. An alternative to Piaget's theory of logical competence. *Child Development,* 1976, *47,* 903–919.

Flavell, J. H. Concept development. In P. H. Mussen (Ed.), *Carmichael's manual of child psychology* (Vol. 1) (3rd ed.). New York: Wiley, 1970.

Flavell, J. H., & Wellman, H. M. Metamemory. In R. V. Kail, Jr. & J. W. Hagen (Eds.), *Perspectives on the development of memory and cognition*. Hillsdale, N.J.: Lawrence Erlbaum Associates, 1977.

Gelman, R. Cognitive development. *Annual Review of Psychology, 1978, 29,* 297–332.

Gelman, R. Preschool thought. *American Psychologist, 1979, 34,* 900–905.

Gelman, R., & Gallistel, C. R. *The child's understanding of number.* Cambridge, Mass.: MIT Press, 1978.

Gleitman, L. R., Gleitman, H., & Shipley, E. F. The emergence of the child as grammarian. *Cognition.* 1972, *1,* 137–164.

Hill, S. A. *A study of logical abilities in children.* Unpublished doctoral dissertation, Stanford University, 1961.

Inhelder, B., & Piaget, J. *The early growth of logic in the child.* New York: Norton, 1964.

Kendler, H. H., & Guenther, K. Developmental changes in classificatory behavior. *Child Development, 1980, 51,* 339–348.

Kofsky, E. A scalogram study of classificatory development. *Child Development, 1966, 37,* 191–204.

Kreutzer, M. A., Leonard, C., & Flavell, J. H. An interview study of children's knowledge about memory. *Monographs of the Society for Research in Child Development, 1975, 40*(Serial No. 159).

Lunzer, E. A. Translator's introduction. In B. Inhelder & J. Piaget, *The early growth of logic in the child.* New York: Norton, 1964.

Lunzer, E. A., Harrison, C., & Davey, M. The four-card problem and the generality of formal reasoning. *Quarterly Journal of Experimental Psychology, 1972, 24,* 326–339.

Mandler, J. M., & Johnson, N. S. Remembrances of things parsed: Story structure and recall. *Cognitive Psychology, 1977, 9,* 111–151.

Markman, E. M., Cox, B., & Machida, S. The standard object-sorting task as a measure of conceptual organization. *Developmental Psychology, 1981, 17,* 115–117.

Markman, E. M., Horton, M. S., & McLanahan, A. G. Classes and collections: Principles of organization in the learning of hierarchical relations. *Cognition, 1980, 8,* 227–241.

Markman, E. M., & Seibert, R. J. Classes and collections: Internal organization and resulting wholistic properties. *Cognitive Psychology, 1976, 8,* 561–577.

Mervis, C. B., & Mervis, C. A. Leopards are kitty-cats: Object labeling by mothers for their 13-month-olds. *Child Development, 1982, 53,* 267–273.

Neimark, E. D. Development of comprehension of logical connectives: Understanding of "or," *Psychonomic Science, 1970, 21,* 217–219.

Neimark, E. D., & Chapman, R. H. Development of the comprehension of logical quantifiers. In R. J. Falmange (Ed.), *Reasoning: Representation and process.* Hillsdale, N.J.: Lawrence Erlbaum Associates, 1975.

Neimark, E. D., & Slotnick, N. S. Development of the understanding of logical connectives. *Journal of Educational Psychology, 1970, 61,* 451–460.

Nelson, K. E., & Bonvillian, J. D. Early language development: Conceptual growth and related processes between 2 and 4½ years of age. In K. E. Nelson (Ed.), *Children's language* (Vol. 1). New York: Gardner Press, 1978.

Nelson, K. J. Variation in children's concepts by age and category. *Child Development, 1974, 45,* 577–584.

Odom, R. D. A perceptual-salience account of decalage relations and developmental change. In L. S. Siegel & C. J. Brainerd (Eds.), *Alternatives to Piaget: Critical essays on the theory.* New York: Academic Press, 1978.

Paris, S. G. Coordination of means and goals in the development of mnemonic skills. In P. A.

Ornstein (Ed.), *Memory development in children*. Hillsdale, N.J.: Lawrence Erlbaum Associates, 1978.

Pascual-Leone, J., & Smith, J. The encoding and decoding of symbols by children: A new experimental paradigm and a neo-Piagetian model. *Journal of Experimental Child Psychology*, 1969, *8*, 328–355.

Revlis, R. Syllogistic reasoning: Logical decisions from a complex data base. In R. J. Falmage (Ed.), *Reasoning: Representation and process*. Hillsdale, N.J.: Lawrence Erlbaum Associates, 1975.

Rosch, E. On the internal structure of perceptual and semantic categories. In T. E. Moore (Ed.), *Cognitive development and the acquisition of language*. New York: Academic Press, 1973.

Rosch, E. Cognitive representations of semantic categories. *Journal of Experimental Psychology: General*, 1975, *104*, 192–233.

Rosch, E., & Mervis, C. B. Family resemblances: Studies in the internal structure of categories. *Cognitive Psychology*, 1975, *7*, 573–605.

Rosch, E., Mervis, C. B., Gray, E. D., Johnson, D. M., & Boyes-Braem, P. Basic subjects in natural categories. *Cognitive Psychology*, 1976, *8*, 382–439.

Rosner, S. R., & Hayes, D. S. A developmental study of category item production. *Child Development*, 1977, *48*, 1062–1065.

Ross, G. S. Categorization in 1- to 2-year-olds. *Developmental Psychology*, 1980, *16*, 391–396.

Saltz, E., Soller, E., & Sigel, I. E. The development of natural language concepts. *Child Development*, 1972, *43*, 1191–1202.

Scardamalia, M. Information processing capacity and the problems of horizontal decalage: A demonstration using combinatorial reasoning tasks. *Child Development*, 1977, *48*, 28–37.

Scholnick, E. K., & Wing, C. S. Evaluating propositions and presuppositions. *Journal of Child Language* (in press).

Scribner, S. Developmental aspects of categorized recall in a West African Society. *Cognitive Psychology*, 1974, *6*, 475–494.

Siegel, L. S., McCabe, A. E., Brand, J., & Matthews, J. Evidence for understanding of class inclusion in preschool children: Linguistic factors and training effects. *Child Development*, 1978, *49*, 688–693.

Smiley, S. S., & Brown, A. L. Conceptual preference for thematic or taxonomic relations: A nonmonotonic trend from preschool to old age. *Journal of Experimental Child Psychology*, 1979, *28*, 249–257.

Smith, C. L. Children's understanding of natural language hierarchies. *Journal of Experimental Child Psychology*, 1979, *27*, 437–458.

Smith, L. B. Perceptual development and category generalization. *Child Development*, 1979, *50*, 705–715.

Smith, L. B., & Kemler, D. G. Developmental trends in free classification: Evidence for a new conceptualization of perceptual development. *Journal of Experimental Child Psychology*, 1977, *24*, 279–298.

Strauss, M. S. Abstraction of prototypical information by adults and 10-month-old infants. *Journal of Experimental Psychology: Human Learning and Memory*, 1979, *5*, 618–632.

Taplin, J. E., Staudenmayer, H., & Taddonio, J. C. Developmental changes in conditional reasoning: Linguistic or logical. *Journal of Experimental Child Psychology*, 1974, *17*, 360–373.

Trabasso, T. Representation, memory and reasoning: How do we make transitive inferences? A. D. Pick (Ed.), *Minnesota Symposia on Child Psychology* (Vol. 9). Minneapolis: University of Minnesota Press, 1975.

Wason, P. C. Regression in reasoning. *British Journal of Psychology*, 1969, *60*, 471–480.

Winer, G. A. Class inclusion reasoning in children: A review of the empirical literature. *Child Development*, 1980, *51*, 309–328.

6 Structural Invariants in Development

Jean M. Mandler
University of California, San Diego

In Piaget's constructivist theory of cognitive development, knowledge is not something one passively takes from the environment, but a constructive enterprise, in which the child plays an active role in building the organized structures that govern mental life. Piaget promulgated this view in passionate opposition to the old empiricist, or associationist, position that knowledge develops solely through incorporating the contingencies provided by an independently organized environment. Piaget clearly won the battle; I think it safe to say that the old associationist view of development is dead. But there was more than one opponent to fight. Once the field moved beyond associationist principles, the way was cleared for many different ideas about how learning and development might proceed.

Piaget's view has been that the organism comes to its task equipped with a set of inherited modes of processing information. These ways of functioning are interactive, consisting of the tendency to organize information from the environment and to adapt to the environment through the twin processes of assimilation and accommodation. He considers these processes to be biological in nature and sufficient in themselves to account for the cognitive structures that are gradually formed. Hence, he has not stressed any biological constraints on the type of structures humans acquire, considering the interactive nature of the functional invariants sufficient as an explanatory principle. The emphasis on universal modes of processing rather than on universal mental structures freed him from being concerned with inborn structural constraints: he could thus stress qualitative changes in the structures that are constructed during the course of development.

However, the universality of various types of cognitive functioning has increasingly led many psychologists (as well as linguists and philosophers) to seek an alternate position. This new school of thought also disavows associationism as a theory of development but shifts instead toward a strongly nativist position, in which human intelligence is seen as the progressive unfolding of genetically determined cognitive structures. The nativist view emphasizes constraints on human development, not only on ways of processing information but also on the kinds of structures the human mind can form. These structures may or may not be unique to humans, but to the extent that they are universal to the species they are seen as another form of biological inheritance.

The nativist and constructivist schools seem to be in considerable opposition, a view that is reinforced by the apparently irreconcilable positions espoused in the debate between Piaget and Chomsky some years ago at Royaumont (Piattelli-Palmarini, 1980). Nevertheless, there are ways to bridge the gap between nativist and constructivist ideas. One of these is the notion that invariant modes of functioning lead to invariant cognitive structures. This is the view that I develop in this chapter. The notions outlined here are not meant to be complete; they only suggest some kinds of cognitive structures that seem to appear early in life and that do not show the stagelike properties one would expect to find when working within a Piagetian framework. The ideas expressed here cannot be more than suggestive, given our still woeful ignorance of many kinds of processing in infancy. The account skips over fundamental issues concerning the mechanisms for forming such cognitive structures. The mechanisms might be provided either by a nativist or a constructivist set of principles. Before seeking the mechanisms, however, it seems necessary to provide at least a rough description of what these structures are and to indicate the role they play in mental life.

Piaget includes in his system at least one kind of functioning that does not undergo major qualitative change, namely, perceptual functioning. But perception tends to be given short shrift in his theory; it is merely a source for the formation of the more important structures of the intelligence. The latter are said to undergo major qualitative shifts during their long, slow construction. However, there is increasing evidence that some cognitive structures that play an important role in thinking remain qualitatively invariant from their inception. Although there are undoubtedly many qualitative changes in development, nevertheless we seem to construct a knowledge base according to principles that do not vary greatly from infancy to adulthood. The constructive processes that form our representational system are not only functionally invariant, but they result in at least some structural invariants as well. It is thus possible to take a generally constructivist position and at the same time eschew a stage theory of the sort that Piaget has proposed.

I discuss five topics in this chapter, all concerned with the specification of one type of cognitive structure, the schema, which seems to qualify as one of the universal, basic forms of representation. In particular, I concentrate on those schemata that organize our understanding of common event sequences. In the first section, some defining characteristics of schemata are sketched out. The next section speculates on the course of acquisition of event schemata, a topic about which we still know very little. Third, some principles of processing associated with the schematic structuring of knowledge are presented. Fourth, some evidence is presented that this kind of structure tends to generate domain-specific performance. Finally, the implications of these views for stage theory are considered in relation to the concepts of qualitative and quantitative changes in development.

Before proceeding, I should briefly discuss what I mean by the term *representation* because it is used in several ways.[1] I use the term to mean the knowledge base a person has, the store of facts and procedures with which the person interprets the world and which govern his or her thinking and actions. Representation in this usage actually has two senses, one sense referring to *what* knowledge a person has, the other to the format or structure of that knowledge. The present, all-purpose use of the term covers both content and type of structure. It should be contrasted to the third and more traditional use of representation to mean some symbolic production used to stand for or to refer to an aspect of the world. I emphasize the distinction because confusion results when one person uses representation of an event to mean knowledge of an event or how the knowledge is structured, and another uses representation of an event to refer to one or more ways of symbolizing it (e.g., naming it, drawing a map, or painting a picture of it). Each of these uses is perfectly reasonable, but the generativity of our language occasionally trips us up, and it quite often does so in the case of this particular term.

The use of representation to refer to a knowledge base and how it is structured has become standard in the terminology of cognitive psychology. This usage reflects a major theoretical interest in the structure and properties of knowledge. Piaget, of course, has similar concerns, but the domains of knowledge studied in Genevan psychology and current cognitive psychology (sometimes called human information processing) have not always overlapped, and the conclusions reached by the two groups have tended to be somewhat different.

Two principal concerns in cognitive psychology are how comprehension and retrieval take place within the domain of everyday behavior. How do we use our representations of the world to direct the course of processing and to interpret incoming information in light of what we already know? Similarly, how do those representations, or the knowledge base, affect retrieval of information from memory? Thus, the interest in representation is intimately tied to the details of how it is used in various activities. It has even been stated, with a good deal of justification, that we must always consider representation-process pairs when we discuss the merits of various theories because what one theory places in a representation in order to account for a phenomenon, another places in a processing

---

[1] A fuller discussion of these issues, including Piaget's uses of the term, can be found in Mandler (1983).

mechanism to account for the same predicted result (Anderson, 1978). I consider both representations and processes in what follows.

SCHEMATA

Many workers in cognitive psychology center their thinking about representation on the concept of *schema,* but it is important to note that their use of the term varies somewhat from that of Piaget. The current concept of a schema is derived from the same historical sources as Piaget's, but it is a mixture of the notions of operative and figurative schemata. A schema is considered to be a cognitive structure (i.e., an organized body of knowledge) that controls various kinds of perceiving, thinking, or acting. A schema consists of a set of units connected by various spatial and/or temporal relationships, which have been learned by experiencing co-occurrences of things in time and space. This formulation may sound like a reversion to the principle of association by contiguity, but the concept of a schema is antithetic to the classic associationist views. The schema versus association arguments have been laid out by Piaget in many places (e.g., Piaget, 1952) and need not be detailed again here. We can note in passing the argument that a schema is a structure that controls intake of information from the environment as well as being formed by it. Of more importance is an aspect of the current notion of schema that not only differentiates it from the old associationist position but also perhaps from Piaget's view: There are constraints that limit the kinds of information that can be used to form a unit of a cognitive structure.

Association in some guise or other plays a role in all psychological theories. For Piaget, for example, the notion of reciprocal assimilation serves a role somewhat similar to the old empiricist view of association in that it allows the building of more complex structures from simpler ones. Inasmuch as our world consists of co-occurrences of things, and furthermore things that are more or less similar to each other, some principles accounting for responsivity of the organism to both similarity and proximity are necessary. What the old principle of contiguity does not account for, however, is *what* can be associated and how information is segmented into units. We understand as yet relatively little about these constraints, although we know that there is a pervasive tendency of organisms to segment the world in certain ways and to respond to some kinds of information in the environment rather than others. It is about this aspect of human functioning that the nativists have the strongest arguments.

A good deal of progress has been made in understanding the limits of associationism within the animal domain by the introduction of concepts such as preparedness (see Seligman & Hager, 1972). Within the human domain there is the emphasis on the biological foundations of language (e.g., Lenneberg, 1967). In addition, a great deal of recent perceptual research with infants has investigated the kinds of information to which infants selectively attend and the nature of the units that are thereby formed. To cite just a few examples, there is Eimas' work (1975) on categorical perception of speech sounds, Bertoncini and Mehler's work (1981) on segmentation of speech into syllables, Strauss' work (1979) on categorical perception of faces, and Gibson's chapter (this volume) on the detection of invariant patterns in visual stimuli. All of this work leads inescapably to the conclusion that the organism as much as the environment determines what will or will not be associated and the size and nature of the units that will be formed.

Assuming the kinds of constraints just discussed, all schemata are formed on the basis of experiencing regularities in the environment, such as objects that regularly appear together or events that regularly follow one another. One can have a schema for anything that has been experienced often enough to become familiar, whether it be what faces look like, what objects will be found in a kitchen, or the events that take place at bedtime. For purposes of this chapter, I assume an organism that has already learned to segregate and unitize objects and simple events, however that accomplishment is achieved. I am particularly interested here in how *aggregations* of objects and *sequences* of events come to be structured into what I have called scene and event schemata (Mandler, 1979). Our knowledge of individual objects (e.g., chairs or faces) or simple events (e.g., drinking from a glass or putting on a shirt) are also types of schemata (see Rumelhart & Ortony, 1977), but these are the building blocks for the larger structures that I deal with here.

Much of this knowledge is figurative in that it concerns the appearances of things; other aspects are more properly considered operative, including implicit knowledge of various physical laws and transformations of states. Both of these kinds of knowledge are tied together to form sets of expectations that guide understanding of what is taking place and create predictions about what will happen next. Schemata can thus be conceived as control procedures guiding processing. As such, they are complex mixtures of what we see and what we know. Within this framework it does not seem feasible to isolate perceptual and operative schemata as Piaget often does.

Because a schema is formed on the basis of encountering regularities in the environment, when a situation is met again expectations are aroused (normally unconsciously) about what things will look like and the order in which they will occur. The parts, or units, of this organized representation consist of sets of variables, which in any given instance can be filled by more or less probable values. You do not know exactly what you will see when visiting a friend's home for the first time, but you do have a surprising number of expectations about the types of rooms and their arrangements, the kinds of furniture the rooms will contain, let alone such basic facts as there will be walls, windows, and doors. Your expectations are even more precise for your own home. Similarly, when you visit a new restaurant you have many quite general expectations about the sequence of events that will occur there. One you have eaten in on many occasions will arouse a much more detailed set of expectations, perhaps even including the waiter's jokes.

The most important part of this kind of schematically organized knowledge of scenes and events is the intrusive role it plays in processing. The more invariant a sequence of events has been in the past, the more schematic knowledge of it will control the speed and accuracy of processing. The more expectations brought to an event, the more they control processing in what has been called a top-down, or conceptually driven, fashion (Bobrow & Norman, 1975). What you see is always partly determined by the knowledge base you have constructed from past experience, but it plays a more important role as a situation becomes more familiar. As Rumelhart (1980) puts it, a schema is an active computational device that evaluates its fit to the incoming data. It is procedural knowledge that determines how well current information can be accounted for. If the fit is good, relatively few processing resources need to be spent; if the fit is poor, other schemata must be called upon. If a situation is new and the knowledge base small, more processing must occur in a bottom-up, or data-given, fashion. If you have relatively few sets of expectations to draw upon, you must pay close attention to the details of a new experience to organize it sufficiently to comprehend and remember it.

To a Piagetian there is a familiar ring to some of these characteristics of schemata as they have been described in the recent literature. For example, the extent to which effortful work must be expended in a situation is a function of available schemata. If the situation is familiar, one need only assimilate the current data, with little accommodative work required. Further, what one attends to and assimilates is a function of the schemata that are activated. Clearly, then, this view of schemata is related to Piagetian conceptions. Nevertheless, it is exceedingly difficult to make precise contrasts, in part because of the broad-ranging use of the term schema in Piaget's writings. I do not refer here to the varying translation in the English and American literatures of schema and scheme. That issue can be, and usually is, clarified in translators' or text writers' introductory comments. I refer instead to the variety of uses of the terms schema and structure that Piaget has introduced over the years. Such variation is hardly surprising given the size of the corpus and the great span of years over which it has been produced. Nevertheless, it makes precise definition difficult.

First, there are the sensorimotor schemata. Piaget's earliest use of this term refers to groups of actions themselves (rather than the mental structures controlling them). They are contrasted with mental (sometimes called representational or conceptual) schemata. In later work, sensorimotor schemata appear to be classified as mental schemata, either as structures controlling action or as knowledge having to do with sensorimotor activity. Frequently, perceptual schemata are considered to be a subclass of the sensorimotor schemata. In still later writings, the phrase "figurative aspects of schemata" begins to appear, referring to perceptual aspects of the operative schemata (sometimes called operational structures, operations, or operational systems). In many of Piaget's writings the conception of operative schemata is a broad one, but when discussed in detail it usually comes down to certain concrete operational schemata such as classification and seriation or formal operational schemata such as combination of variables and proportions.

For purposes of arriving at an overarching conception of a schema, this is a mixed bag. It is true that the most general characteristics of all these types of schemata remain the same; they actively control the intake of information from the environment and regulate the kinds of mental processing in which the organism can engage. In this sense, Piaget's use of the term is similar to that of many current cognitive psychologists. But this characterization is very general and does not guarantee agreement about the details. Noting that cognitive psychology's use of the term (in what has come to be known as "schema theory") is also only very generally specified, I tentatively suggest some differences in emphasis.

First, the current use of schema does not make as sharp a distinction between figurative and operative knowledge as does Piaget's. Nevertheless, a scene or event schema is probably closer to what Piaget would call a figurative or perceptual schema than an operative one. Although a schema contains information both about what one sees and what one knows, and knowing includes operative aspects, the figurative component seems to loom larger. To take an example that Piaget himself addressed (Piaget & Inhelder, 1969), how should we characterize the knowledge an infant acquires about the fact that cats "miaow?" Piaget (Piaget & Inhelder, 1969) says the following about this kind of inference:

> . . . it is not at the first perceptual contact that "cat" implies "miaowing." The cat miaows and this is no more than a fact. But from the second contact, when the baby recognizes a cat, he can infer that it will miaow. Implication is thus subordinated to an act of assimilation. Assimilation means construction of schemata (implication in the broad sense is in fact the expression of these schemata) and it is this schematization which probably constitutes the point of departure of operational activities and of their structurizations [p. 149].

This example is ambiguous with respect to the figurative–operative distinction, yet because it concerns infancy we can presume that the learning occurring in this situation is not what Piaget would call operative knowledge, However, it is exactly this kind of learning, beginning in infancy, which I believe forms the basis of the schematic organization of knowledge that underlies much of our normal functioning and thinking both as children and as adults. The claim is that these schemata (which Piaget might call conceptual rather than perceptual schemata) play a larger role in determining the character of thinking, problem solving, and memory than Piaget's theory suggests.

Part of the difference in emphasis between schema theory and Piagetian theory lies in the particular schemata that have been chosen for study and the aspects of schemata that have been stressed. Both in current cognitive work and in Piagetian theory the schema is treated as a building block in a general theory of comprehension and memory (Rumelhart, 1980). Research on specific content areas (e.g., the current work on story schemata to be described in the following section) has been used in an attempt to explicate the general characteristics of this kind of mental structure. But very different content areas have been studied. The schemata of classification, seriation, proportions, and so on lie in quite a different domain from knowledge about stories, solving algebra "story problems," identifying a face, or eating a meal at a restaurant.

Because of the different contents that have been studied, different structural characteristics have been proposed. The characteristics of operative schemata as defined by Piaget involve the grouping properties of identity, reversibility, and so on and bear little resemblance to the characteristics of schemata being described in this chapter. As one example, consider the notion of reversibility. Even using a rough concept of empirical reversibility, in the sense of being able to "retrace one's steps," little is yet known about the extent to which a schema enables such an operation. Piaget would agree that a sensorimotor schema does not involve reversibility properties, but neither do the conceptual schemata that schema theory proposes. As far as logical reversibility is concerned, with its implications of opposing and canceling operations, the concept is probably not even applicable to the current conceptions of schemata.

Thus, in spite of a similar spirit in the uses of the term schema and mutual interest in the concept as a building block of cognition and as an active regulatory mechanism, the terms are not synonymous in Piaget's and other current theories. The closest point of contact actually comes in the current usage of the term and Piaget's early discussions of the sensorimotor schema. Processes of assimilation and accommodation play major roles in both conceptions, and both involve a complex mix of perception and action. In schema theory, however, the action is often mental.

ACQUISITION OF SCHEMATA

Piaget (1952) has extensively documented the acquisition in infancy of many sensorimotor schemata. This work concentrated on the development of action patterns and the gradual formation of the conceptual schema of the object. Other schemata, governing understanding of places and common event sequences, also begin to be formed early in infancy. For the most part, we still have only informal observation of the earliest development of knowledge of event sequences. We infer such knowledge, for example, from infants' distress when familiar routines are changed. Schank and Abelson (1977) and Nelson (1978) cite common examples that are familiar in kind to those that many parents report.

It is perfectly feasible (although surely not easy) to apply more detailed observational and experimental methods to very young children, but to date most work on the development of representation of event sequences has been carried out with somewhat older children.

There have been a few speculations about the uses to which infant construction of familiar event sequences might be put. For example, Kessen and Nelson (1978) suggest that the first instances of recall may occur within the context of familiar routines. They use as an example the routine arrival of a father at the time of a child's dinner or bedtime. Within this familiar context, if one day the father does not appear the child's "contextual structure" may lead him or her to notice the absence of the expected event. The implication is that the contextual support enables the child to retrieve at least some aspect of the missing part of the event sequence. This account is speculative indeed, but it is an interesting suggestion about an early use of a schematic organization to attain access to a representation of an object in its absence.

Although I will discuss the acquisition of event schemata will, it should be remembered that our knowledge of objects and places is governed by similar principles. Gibson (this volume) and Spelke (1979), among others, have demonstrated that from early infancy babies come to expect certain regularities between what they see and hear; they may become confused or distressed when those regularities are violated. Piaget (1951) cites a charming example from a slightly older child: Jacqueline cannot recognize her younger sister when she is wearing a bathing cap, which hides her hair. It seems likely that we will learn more about the construction of representations of larger contexts in which scenes and events are organized from the techniques currently in use in studies of infant perception.

Because of the paucity of data on event representation in the first few years of life, we must turn to slightly older children to examine this development. Nelson (1978) has provided us with information on how preschool children organize their knowledge of common event sequences, such as eating dinner at home, having lunch at a day-care center, and eating at a McDonald's restaurant. These familiar sequences, often called *scripts* (Schank & Abelson, 1977), are prime examples of concrete event schemata. Nelson found a surprising degree of commonality in how 4- and 5-year-old children describe these event sequences. Although the day is a continuous stream of activity, they tend to agree on where the lunch sequence starts and stops, on the order in which the various parts take place, and most impressively, on the chunking of information into "basic events" (i.e., events that are uniformly described at a specific level of detail and not further broken down into subparts). These data on young children show a great deal of qualitative similarity to descriptions that have been produced by adults for similar scriptlike situations (Bower, Black, & Turner, 1979).

More recently, there has been pilot work in Nelson's laboratory that suggests similar knowledge in even younger children (personal communication). When asked to arrange pictures representing events in the school day, even 3-year-old children rejected inappropriate pictures, noticed the absence of pictures showing central events, and arranged the pictures in the correct temporal sequence. In addition, children who have been in school longer have more complex scripts, with more interconnections between the basic events (Nelson, 1978).

The question arises as to whether the schematic structures that have been built up in these situations are inextricably linked to particular contents. This question concerns not only the limits of generalizability to new situations, but also whether or not any broadly applicable structures are being formed at the same time. As we see later, there are limits on the generalizability of schemata, but they are not totally bound to previously encountered content. From an early age, children can encode new material if it conforms to a structure with which they are already familiar. Brown (1976a) has shown that preschool children can use sensible or predictable orderings of new material to help them remember sequences and do better than on arbitrarily ordered material. Even when the order of events is not a predictable sequence, but is made meaningful by being fashioned into a narrative sequence, children of this age tend not to make mistakes when reconstructing the correct order. The young children in Brown's studies apparently did not do quite so well as those in Nelson's script studies, but in the latter case not only was the structure familiar but also the specific content of the sequences.

The degree of familiarity with both content and structure undoubtedly accounts for the discrepancy between these results and the earlier work of Piaget (1926). As you know, Piaget reported that children were poor at maintaining the correct sequence of events when retelling stories, and this characterization was accepted for many years.[2] When I first began to study children's recall of stories, I thought of using the three stories that Piaget had used. I began to worry about them, however, when I found that I had a great deal of difficulty in remembering one of them, particularly in getting the sequence of events right. Upon analysis, its plot structure seemed arbitrary, and the reason behind the sequence of events was obscure. The other two stories that Piaget used had clearer structure, but in one of them temporal connections between events were stressed rather than the causal connections one would ordinarily expect to find. In addition, the motivation for the characters' actions was unlikely to be understood by young children. So we rewrote two of the stories, making their temporal and causal connections clear, and added two other "well-formed" stories. Under these circumstances, we found that first grade children had no difficulty in retelling the stories in their correct sequence; in fact, they made no more temporal inversions than

---

[2]Piaget (1926) presents very little actual data, only samples from protocols. Stein and Trabasso (1982) point out that the protocols he does present are better ordered than Piaget indicates in the text. Apparently, however, the most inversions occurred on the story with the poorest structure (the Swan Story).

adults (Mandler & Johnson, 1977). Note that the content was new to the children in both Piaget's and our studies; what was unfamiliar in one case and familiar in the other was the stories' overall structure.

An illuminating incident in connection with our early work occurred at this time. By chance I discovered that Stein was also collecting data on children's recall of stories. I commented to her that it was interesting that first graders had no difficulty in telling stories in their proper order and did not show the inversions in sequencing that Piaget had described. She, on the other hand, was finding many inversions in first grade children's story recall. We argued back and forth about the matter in typically adult egocentric fashion, until we finally thought to ask about the story materials that each of us was using. She had taken her stories from a grade school primer! When we analyzed the stories in detail, the answer to the mystery became obvious. Those little primer stories, such as those commonly used, by the way, to test comprehension in the schools, had even *less* structure than the stories used by Piaget. (In her next study, she used well-structured stories and found the same result that Johnson and I had: very few inversions in sequence in first graders' recall, Stein & Glenn, 1979).

Children's ability to retell stories in their correct sequence, provided that the sequence is a meaningful one, develops earlier than the first grade. Johnson and Gandel (1980) have found that even many 4-year-olds can reproduce new fairy tales in the proper order. This is not to say that young children recall as much of stories as do older children and adults; there is quantitative improvement throughout the school years.

We have found other commonalities between young children's recall and that of adults. Very similar *patterns* of recall are found at least from the first grade onward. If one analyzes the structure of traditional stories, such as folk tales, fables, and myths, one finds regular constituent structures. Regardless of the content of the particular story, it can be divided into episodes, and these episodes have a highly predictable sequence. A story typically begins with a setting, in which the protagonist and other characters are introduced. The first episode then commences with a beginning, an event to which the protagonist responds. The response, called a complex reaction, consists of some emotional response or thought, followed by a formulation of a goal in response to the beginning. The goal is in turn followed by a goal path, which consists of an attempt to reach the goal and the outcome of that attempt. The episode closes with some kind of ending, a statement of the long-range consequences of the goal path or of the protagonist's or other character's reactions to the events that have taken place. Not only can traditional stories be divided quite cleanly into episodes, there are fairly limited numbers of ways in which episodes are connected to form longer stories (Johnson & Mandler, 1980).

Given that stories have constituent structures that can be uncovered, it is possible to score story recall in terms of how well each constituent is remembered. One can also score story productions, summaries, and so on. This technique enables a comparative analysis of recall and other measures from different populations, so that one can study developmental or cross-cultural differences in a theoretically principled way.

The commonalities that have been found among the various populations studied to date are quite striking. As mentioned earlier, children's recall is qualitatively similar to that of adults in that the patterns of amount recalled from each of the constituents remain almost the same, even though the overall quantity of recall is lower. Commonalities have been found cross-culturally as well. In conjunction with Scribner and Cole, we have tested the recall of the same stories we used in our earlier work (Mandler & Johnson, 1977) among the Vai in Liberia. We tested people from age 6 to 50, schooled and unschooled, literate and nonliterate. The patterning of recall was virtually the same from each group, whether American or Vai, regardless of schooling or literacy, although again there were quantitative differences between the children and adults (Mandler, Scribner, Cole, & DeForest, 1980). Similar qualitative commonalities have been reported for a variety of other populations, such as learning disabled adults (Worden, Malmgrem, & Gabourie, 1982), dyslexic children (Weaver, 1978), and deaf children (Gaines, Mandler, & Bryant, 1981). Not surprisingly, other characteristics of recall differ in deviant populations such as dyslexic children; however, the nature of the underlying representation of stories appears to be quite similar in all these cases.

Considering the developmental and cross-cultural differences in recall that have so often been reported, I find these commonalities remarkable and their implications worth pondering. They are especially remarkable when we consider the abstractness of the knowledge involved. Note that many different stories, varying widely in content and cultural origin, have been used in these studies, so the commalities in performance cannot be due to familiarity with the particulars of the individual stories themselves. The child listening to a new story cannot use his or her knowledge of a familiar sequence of events such as the routines involved in waking up in the morning, the events of the school day, and so on. The only knowledge the child can have is of the general, expected structure of a story, the kinds of things that are likely to happen in fairy tales, and the sequence in which they are likely to occur. This kind of knowledge does not involve memory for specific details; it represents a much more general schema for stories. Abstracting this kind of a schema is similar in kind to the picking up of perceptual invariances that Gibson describes (this volume).

Because of its abstractness, one would not expect a story schema to be formed as early as some of the scriptlike knowledge of common event sequences described earlier. In addition, listening to stories begins later in life than does experiencing many common script situations. Indeed, the limited amount of available evidence suggests that a story schema only begins to be formed around the age of 2 or 3 years. Some information abou the growth of a story schema has been obtained from children's self-generated stories, but one must be cautious in the conclusions drawn from this work because the labor of production probably masks some underlying competence. The young child who generates a story consisting of "Once upon a time there was a lion, the end" may actually know considerably more about story structure than this production indicates. Nevertheless, a number of studies of children's self-generated stories indicate increasing sophistication in the use of a story schema to guide production (Botvin & Sutton-Smith, 1977; Glenn & Stein, 1980).

THE USE OF SCHEMATA IN PROCESSING

To describe how knowledge is represented is to tell only half the story. Even if knowledge is organized similarly by children and adults, the obviously more complex schemata of older children and adults might result in qualitative as well as quantitative differences in processing. There are still relatively few studies carried out to study developmental trends in processing scenes and events, but those that have been conducted have found remarkably similar patterns. The common patterns of story recall just described are one example; common patterns in the recognition of various kinds of information in complex scenes are another (Mandler & Robinson, 1978).

I describe some general principles of encoding and retrieval of information that seem to follow from a schematic form of organization and mention a few experiments that have studied these phenomena developmentally. Let me repeat that I am considering processing in situations in which people have a good many expectations about what is going on, that is, the kind of situation in which top-down processing plays a major role. I am not considering here situations in which we have relatively few prior expectations. When we encounter a situation that is new, we must engage in much more bottom-up processing and depend heavily on new structuring activity to make sense of it. There are few occasions in which adults encounter something totally new. As an example, consider yourself as an adult watching a soccer game for the first time. Even in this case, although you may not be able to understand much that is happening, you have a great deal of knowledge about other team sports, which you can apply to get some overall sense of how the game is played and what it is about. Typically, you will assimilate what you are seeing to your schemata of various team sports (consequently making some wrong assumptions) and will have to work hard if you are to accommodate the differences and accurately encode what is happening. Similarly, when we are asked to memorize verbatim arbitrary lists of materials, if we are to make sense of and remember them we must impose some kind of organization on them. This kind of processing takes effort, close attention, and skill at analysis, which is probably the reason that young children (and not a few adults!) are so poor at it. Of course, very young children encounter many more experiences that are new, but from an early age there are familiar schemata that can be used to aid the encoding of new situations, and in principle the type of processing involved should not differ.

Even in familiar situations, the extent to which you have detailed expectations to guide your processing will vary. Reading a fairy tale, for example, is not the same as reading a modern short story. The genre of traditional stories, such as folk tales and fables, is a limited domain. Johnson and I have speculated that the small number of forms found in traditional stories may be the result of their having originated in an oral tradition. When one does not have recourse to the printed word, there are restrictions on what is memorable, and if a story was not memorable in an oral tradition, presumably it did not survive. Whatever the reason for the limited formats of such stories, however, it is those very limits that account for the marked effects of our structural knowledge on the way we encode and retrieve them. On the other hand, in the modern short story, or in students' essays we are called upon to grade, we can have relatively little knowledge about the overall format or what will come next as we turn the page. Our processing looks different in this case (and is often more time consuming and less success-ful). I stress this point because it has occasionally been misunderstood. A struc-tural analysis of traditional stories is useful for gleaning hypotheses about one kind of schematically organized knowledge, but that does not mean that all stories or other kinds of texts should be governed by the same principles.

The first principle of processing guided by schemata might be called *gist encoding*. We do not, in fact cannot, take in all of the overwhelming amount of information that is showered upon us. If we have few schemata to guide us in a situation, we may be somewhat haphazard about what we notice and remember. Perhaps as we try out various schemata to find a fit, we pick up bits and pieces of information appropriate to a variety of different organizations. But when an appropriate schema is activated, it guides our processing in a characteristic way. We glean the main ideas, the overall sense of the scene; irrelevant details, even if encoded at the time, tend to become quickly lost (Bransford & McCarrell, 1974). In studies of memory for stories, for example, from preschool to adulthood the same phenomenon is found: Everyone recalls the gist of the main events, omits irrelevant details, and falsely recognizes new material that is consistent with what was presented (Bower et al., 1979; Brown, 1976b). Loftus (e.g., 1975) has shown similar phenomena in memory for scenes. This kind of processing is quite different from verbatim memorizing; the latter is a specialized situation rarely encountered in daily life.

The second principle, *default processing,* is closely related to gist encoding. It is the other side of the coin of the economy afforded by ready-made knowledge, namely, the loss of accuracy about the precise details of expected things. A schema enables us to encode expected objects and events very rapidly, but often without careful inspection. Default processing refers to encoding and retrieving what should have been there or what should have happened, that is, the most likely values of the variables in the schema. Because the default values are those that usually *do* occur, we can afford to give expected events scant attention. We are rarely called upon to remember more than gist, so this mode of processing is a sensible way of proceeding (although it is surely one of the major causes of marital disputes when consensus about the details of some event must be reached; it is so natural that we are typically unaware that we have engaged in it). This kind of processing frees our limited resources to concentrate on the new and unusual. Thus, we should predict that people will be more accurate about the details of the unexpected in a familiar scene than about the expected. This is exactly what happens, and it is true for children as well as for adults. Friedman (1979) showed adults pictures of common scenes such as a kitchen and a schoolroom. Each object in each scene had been ranked according to its likelihood of occurrence. Recognition of changes made on the objects was an inverse function of their probability of occurrence. If the kitchen scene contained a refrigerator, its details were poorly processed, but if the kitchen had a fireplace, people noticed it and processed it more thoroughly. Goodman (1980) reports the same phenomenon in children's recognition of scenes.

It might seem from the foregoing that there is a conflict between gist encoding and default processing. On the one hand, I have said that relevant material is processed better than irrelevant detail and, on the other, that expected (relevant) things are more poorly processed than the unexpected. Exactly how these processes dovetail needs further work (see Mandler, 1979), but I do not think they conflict. To get the gist or overall meaning is one thing, and you will not even get the main idea if you cannot find relevant knowledge structures; to get detail is another matter. The unexpected can be quite relevant in the sense that we may need to figure out why an odd thing is happening, what its implications are, and how it can fit into our understanding. To use an example of Loftus and Mackworth (1978), we must expend a good deal of processing to understand why there is an octopus in the farmyard. Irrelevant details are those that are incidental to the overall meaning of a scene or story; they are not necessarily expected, but typically they don't matter and are not well attended.

The third principle of schematic processing is that it provides a specific kind of retrieval search plan for remembering. This characteristic of schematic organization is more obvious for events than for scenes, but aspects of it are common to both. In the case of remembering a scriptlike event sequence or a story, the schema provides an automatic start point, a temporally organized series of units to guide retrieval step by step, and a clear-cut stop point for the search. This kind of memory search is characteristically different from searching a categorical (taxonomic) organization, in which so many developmental differences have been found (Mandler, 1979).

I have already indicated some of the evidence showing that schematic search through memory is organized in the same way for children as for adults. Other evidence of control of the retrieval process by a schema can be seen in the tendency to retell irregular stories in more regular form. For example, in two studies we told children and adults stories consisting of two episodes, each one about a different character's adventures. For some subjects, the two episodes were told sequentially in the way they would normally be told. For other subjects, the two episodes were told in an "interleaved" fashion; that is, the story moved back and forth between the adventures of the two characters. The interleaved stories were sensible, and no one had trouble following what was going on. Nevertheless, both children and adults tended to recall the interleaved stories in their schematic, canonical form as two separate episodes, rather than in the form in which they had heard them (Mandler, 1978). In the second experiment, (Mandler & DeForest, 1979), instead of letting subjects merely follow their own preferences in how they retold the stories, we explicitly instructed them to recall the interleaved stories in the order in which they had been presented. Even in this case, subjects tended to revert to the canonical order in their recall. Interestingly enough, children in both experiments were more prone to follow the schematic order than were adults, suggesting an even greater control over retrieval by schematically organized knowledge for children.

It seems likely that one important developmental difference lies not in how knowledge is structured or typically used in processing but in a greater flexibility in imposing new organizational schemes on materials on demand and in a generally greater flexibility of access to different organizational schemes. This point is not a new one, of course; lack of flexibility in processing has been observed by many developmental researchers and extensively documented by Piaget, for example, in his studies of classification.

A fourth principle is that a schema provides a major source for the reconstructive aspects of memory. Reconstructive activity is linked to default processing. If we cannot remember exactly what happened at a certain point in a story, for example, our schemata tell us approximately what *should* have happened, and we can invent material that will be reasonable in terms of the overall structure, even though it may be wrong in detail. This phenomenon has been reported by several investigators for both children and adults (e.g., Mandler & Johnson, 1977; Stein & Glenn, 1979). In addition, a schema provides a mechanism by which so-called "natural" or "incidental" memory occurs. Inasmuch as the whole process of comprehension of familiar scenes and events is structured by our schematic knowledge, it is not surprising that a schema is activated when remembering them. Because a schema runs off automatically, no particular strategic activity is required, yet good recall can result. "Good" recall does not necessarily mean verbatim recall, however, a state that we hardly ever achieve or even try to achieve unless forced into elaborate memorizing activity. We sometimes forget that our recall is usually of the gist of things, full of normalization and default processing—in short, a rough reconstruction rather than a fading reflection of reality.

In a similar vein, our schematic knowledge is the source of many of our everyday inferences. Perhaps beginning with familiar event sequences such as the examples cited earlier of a father's typical appearance at bedtime or a cat meowing for food, these clusters of objects and events provide the expectations necessary to infer what might happen next, what might have happened when you were not looking, or what is missing from a familiar situation. Such inferences are not the same as the logical inferences of transitive reasoning and other aspects of formal logic, yet presumably our understanding of the latter has its roots in the schema-driven, inference-saturated character of our daily lives.

SCHEMATA
AND DOMAIN-SPECIFIC KNOWLEDGE

I have suggested that much of our thinking about the world is controlled by schematic organizations. Further, schemata appear to be constructed around specific content areas, even though they can be flexibly applied to varying content within a given area. These considerations suggest two implications for development. First, behavior in familiar circumstances will differ from that displayed in new ones. Familiar situations are those for which schemata have already been formed and in which top-down processes play a larger role. A major difference between the child and the adult, of course, is in just how many situations are new. Not only have adults learned to cope with many more situations than have children, it is my distinct impression that much of adult life is spent in managing to avoid new situations or at least situations that are profoundly new. A little novelty is titilating, to be sure, but for the adult as for the child, too much novelty is often incomprehensible and occasionally frightening. Children, however, have very little to say about whether they encounter totally new situations. In their own milieu they can control the extent of the novelty they choose to explore, but they are frequently carted around at adult whim, start school by legislative fiat, and so on.

The implication of this view for the study of development is obvious and has been stated by several investigators in recent years; a different picture of children's knowledge emerges when they are tested in familiar situations instead of new ones. Part of the difference is due to a lack of familiar procedures in new situations, accompanied by differences in ease of processing and in the details of what is processed. Another difference in old and new situations arises from the sheer amount of knowledge the child has that is relevant to the required tasks. Many well-known developmental trends decrease or disappear altogether when the size of the knowledge base is controlled. If the size of the knowledge base is actually reversed from the usual case, children show superior performance to adults. Chi (1978) has given us an elegant demonstration of this principle in her work with 10-year-old chess experts, who learned chess positions faster and remembered them better than did adult chess amateurs, although the same adults remembered more digits from a list than did the children.

The second implication for development follows closely from the first. If performance in a given domain depends on how well our knowledge of that domain is structured, marked décalages must appear in performance across various domains, even within a single individual. These décalages are so numerous that the concept of stages in thinking is in danger of becoming lost in a territory full of rifts and chasms. A stage theory may still be recoverable, but if it is, I suspect that it will have fewer principles and lesser generality than have been ascribed to it in Piagetian theory.

Décalages can be found whenever any body of knowledge is unusually well-known but, because of the way in which schemata govern the details of processing, they are particularly evident in activities controlled by schematically organized knowledge. As mentioned earlier, schemata act as sets of procedures that govern our behavior in a given domain. They act like a series of route maps that tell us how to get to work, remember a story, or recognize a face. We have all had the experience of seeing people who are familiar to us, yet not being able to remember who they are or where we have seen them before. We know many faces only in the context of particular routines; when they are seen outside that context they may seem familiar, but no further information is retrievable (Mandler, 1980).

Such dependency of recognition on familiar procedures can even trip us up in very familiar environments. A few months ago, I took an elevator that is at the opposite end of my office building to my accustomed entrance. As I stepped off, I absent-mindedly turned in my usual direction only to find myself in front of an unrecognizable scene. More than momentary panic ensued as I tried to figure out who could have stolen my lab and built a new one in its place. It took an inordinate amount of time and inspection to realize what had happened—that I was merely at the opposite end of the building from where I thought I was. At once the scene became familiar; I was standing in front of a colleague's lab, although a moment earlier it was as if I had never seen it before.

There is a great deal more than anecdotal evidence about the specificity of knowledge to procedures carried out within particular contexts, although events such as the one just described can have dramatic impact on one's thinking. There are many examples in the literature, but one of the most cogent demonstrations was invented by Wason (1968) and has since been studied by a number of investigators (see D'Andrade, 1980, for a history and analysis of the problem). The example concerns conditional reasoning, and the responses are so consistent that I have used it for several years as a classroom demonstration. In the D'Andrade version, adults are asked to solve a conditional reasoning problem in one of two contexts. The first is in the framework of checking charge slips at Sears. The instructions to the subject (adapted from D'Andrade's) are as follows:

> As part of your job as assistant section manager at Sears, you have to check sales receipts efficiently according to the following rule, so that you check no more than is absolutely necessary. The rule for the checking of receipts is that all sales of $50

or more must be approved by the section manager, Mr. Sluggo. The amount of the sale is written on the front of the form, while the space for Mr. Sluggo's approval is on the reverse side. Which of the following forms would you have to turn over to make sure that this rule has been followed?

The subjects are then given the slips shown in the left panel of Fig. 6.1 and asked to circle those that they would turn over. Typically, about 70–75% of the students in my college classes find the correct solution. They know they must turn over the $75 slip to check for the signature on the back. They also realize that the slip with the unsigned side showing must be turned over to make sure that the purchase was not for some exorbitant amount. They correctly ignore the slip for only $35 because it is too small to matter, and they also correctly ignore the slip that has already been signed because Mr. Sluggo is responsible for whatever amount may be there.

So far so good. But if the identical problem is couched in the form of checking labels in a label factory, in which the job is to determine that all slips with a vowel on one side have an odd number on the other, only about 15–20% of the students in my college classes solve it. The instructions are as follows:

All labels made at the Pica Custom Label Factory have a letter printed on one side and a number printed on the other. As part of your job as chief label inspector, you

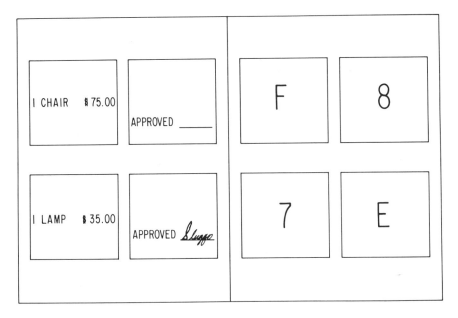

FIG. 6.1   Materials for two reasoning problems. The left panel contains materials for a problem couched in a familiar framework; the right panel contains materials for a problem in an unfamiliar setting.

have to check labels efficiently according to the following rule, so that you check no more than is absolutely necessary. The rule for checking labels is that all labels with a vowel on one side must have an odd number on the other side. Which of the following labels would you have to turn over to make sure that this rule has been followed?

The subjects are given the slips shown in the right panel of Fig. 6.1. As an exercise I suggest you answer the problem before reading further. Now that you have made your choices, note that the structure of the two problems is identical, and the solution is also the same. If you see a vowel (equivalent to $50 or more) you must check to be sure it has an odd number (signature) on the back. If you see an even number (no signature) you had better check to make sure there isn't a vowel ($50 or more) on the other side because if there is the rule has been violated. If you see a consonant (under $50) there is no reason to look at the other side because it is irrelevant to the rule you are checking, and if there is an odd number (a signature) it is not necessary to check because the rule cannot have been violated in that case.

Only the context has been changed in the two structurally identical problems, but performance varies dramatically. The most likely reason for the difference is that in the Sears problem you can use your knowledge about what matters in the world to tell you how to proceed. Your performance looks like a general understanding of conditional reasoning, but in fact it is only knowledge of what matters in a familiar setting. When you do not have such knowledge and must decide whether to turn over a card to check an arbitrary rule, your mastery of abstract principles of conditional reasoning is shown to be illusory. As Rumelhart (1979) has pointed out, this is exactly the result we would expect if our knowledge of reasoning is embedded in task-specific procedures rather than in general rules of inference.[3] It is also of interest to note that these data look much like those reported by Kuhn (1977) in her studies of conditional reasoning in children. Putting the problems into familiar contexts increased the likelihood of their being solved.

Similar contextual effects have been widely noted in psychological processing in general and in developmental investigations in particular. A typical observation is that of Sigel (1974). He observed that 2-year-old children entering nursery school frequently failed the Bayley Concept of One test, yet showed ample understanding of 1, and often of 2, in the context of their daily routines of sharing cookies and other school activities. Examples from even younger ages can be found in language acquisition; the earliest comprehension of words often seems bound to particular contexts (e.g., Huttenlocher, 1974).

These context-dependent kinds of behavior are to be expected to the extent that our knowledge is couched in the form of schemata. Schemata are formed in

---

[3] D'Andrade (1980) comments on other aspects of the problem that may influence performance, but the familiarity factor seems to play the major role.

the first instance around specific, concrete experiences. We know relatively little as yet about either the circumstances or the possible developmental changes that encourage their generalization. The 2-year-old's understanding of the number 1 rapidly generalizes beyond the initial context in which it was learned, but the concept itself is both discrete and concrete. Event sequences are more complex, consisting of many discrete items, but they also can be quite concrete. "Eating a hamburger at McDonald's" is a concrete schema, whereas "eating food at a restaurant" is a more abstract schema applicable to many similar instances within a domain. We have relatively little information as to how and when more abstract schemata are formed, although the information we do have about learning scripts and story schemata suggests that generalization at this level of abstraction occurs quite early.

Even in the case of abstract knowledge about the structure of stories, however, the schema is not necessarily easily applicable to other types of materials. It may only be at a low level of generality that application of a schema to new situations is a universal accomplishment. To learn to find common underlying structures for even more complex experiences or to apply a schema from one domain to an entirely new one may require formal instruction (or an act of genius). For example, to learn to hear the sonata form in music usually requires instruction, in part because of the great complexity and length of symphonies. In this case, only one domain (music) is involved. To learn to apply the sonata form by analogy to literature would be an example of schema abstraction at an even higher level because the domains themselves differ. This kind of activity seems far removed from the automatic structuring of experience that a schema usually provides. Without specific training, it may well be that the level of schema generalization, for either the child or the adult, tends not to extend beyond relatively limited domains, even though within a given content area the knowledge is at a general level.

These considerations suggest that truly abstract thought, that is, thought concerned only with formal relationships and not with content, should be a rarity. Indeed, the evidence suggests that this is the case. Without formal schooling, adults are often unable to engage in purely theoretical approaches to problems, or what Scribner (1979) calls thinking in the "logical genre." Furthermore, even schooled adults frequently do not use the logical genre in their thinking, or if they do they are unsuccessful when the problem is posed in an unfamiliar domain. The conditional reasoning problem discussed earlier is one example of such failure.

From the information available, then, it seems that abstract thought is unusual, and if it appears at all it is due to specialized training (although exactly which aspects of schooling give rise to this mode of functioning are not known). The more common situation is for people to think and solve problems within the context of familiar domains and on the basis of the knowledge they have accumulated in those domains in the past. Without specialized training, adults show encoding failures similar to those that are found when children try to solve problems in a new domain (Siegler, 1978). Scribner (1979) reports that the nonschooled adults who failed her reasoning problems had not accurately encoded the premises; in some cases they had assimilated the problem to a narrative form and in others to their personal knowledge about the "true" facts in the domain. It is possible that the college students who fail the conditional reasoning problems described earlier are having similar encoding difficulties. In any case, these differences in problem solving do not seem to be so much developmental phenomena (in the sense of being age related) as phenomena related to schooling in a particular mode of thought.

CONCLUSIONS

In the kinds of knowledge and ways of processing that I have described in this chapter, it is difficult to discern qualitative developmental changes, let alone anything that might qualify as a stage. Quantitative improvement abounds, but we will need principles to explain quantitative change other than those that have been offered to account for qualitative differences. There are a number of factors that bear on the explanation of quantitative change. Some of these have to do with attention and processing capacity, factors that may be independent of the way in which knowledge is structured. Others have to do with motivation and interests, which are not themselves developmental parameters but factors rooted in the nature of the task and the materials and how well they fit the subject's state. Possibly the most important factor affecting quantitative change in performance is the richness and complexity of the units and their interrelationships in the knowledge base. This kind of quantitative difference between adults and children can be found in almost any developmental study that has explored this issue (bearing in mind, of course, that it is not always older folk who have the richer structures in a given domain).

These statements about qualitative versus quantitative differences are broad and not easy to document without a comprehensive theory of development, which includes specification of both the underlying representations and the processes that range over them. Qualitative differences in performance could stem from either representational or processing differences. I have taken the position here that two representations are qualitatively similar if they have the same overall form of organization. To take an example from the classificatory domain, Keil (1979) has presented evidence that the tree structures underlying the predications people ascribe to various ontological categories of things in the world (e.g., animals, plants, nonliving objects, etc.) have similar forms for both children and adults. The adults' trees are more complex in that they have more nodes and branches. But in general the structures can be said to have the same organization; not only can they both be described as trees (e.g., as opposed to matrices or networks), but also the categories they have in common are located in the same relative places in the tree in terms of superordinate and subordinate relationships.

Comparable similarities in structure occur in the schematic organizations described in this chapter. Some differences in performance must follow, of course, from quantitative differences. For example, what a child and adult will encode and retain from a trip to a restaurant will differ if the child's representation does not contain information about paying the bill. I would term such omissions a quantitative difference. Yet, in spite of the differences in complexity of the child's and adult's knowledge, the format of the representations and the manner in which processing takes place appear to be similar in the two cases.

We can also ask whether *qualitative* differences in performance can result even when the structures are similar or whether qualitative differences always imply different structuring of the underlying representations. Again, this query can be addressed by considering the classificatory domain. Inhelder and Piaget (1964) have amply shown that young children have more difficulty with some aspects of hierarchical classification than do older children and adults. It has sometimes been assumed, therefore, that the underlying knowledge base must be differently organized. However, a good deal of recent work, such as the Keil studies just discussed, indicates that even young children have a hierarchically organized representation of taxonomic categories similar in character to that of adults (see Gelman & Baillargeon, 1983; Mandler, 1983, for reviews).

Inhelder and Piaget recognized that children form hierarchically based classifications before they understand all their implications, such as class inclusion. However, Piagetian theory does not always make a sharp distinction between knowledge and how it is used (i.e., between representation and process). The theory implies that because children have difficulty with problems involving class inclusion they do not have this information represented. Such a lack would appear to be a qualitative difference in the representation of classes between children and adults. However, it has been shown that even quite young children have some understanding of class inclusion (Smith, 1979). Therefore, it appears that class-inclusion relations are indeed represented and that the difficulty children have with class-inclusion problems has to do with processing limitations instead. They seem to have difficulty in accessing and using information that they have. In short, the fact that children have a strong tendency to compare two subordinate classes when you have asked them to compare a subordinate class with a superordinate one does not by itself imply that class-inclusion relations are lacking in their representational system (see Trabasso, Isen, Dolecki, McLanahan, Riley, & Tucker, 1978, for further discussion of processing difficulties in class-inclusion problems).

In general, many of the developmental differences that we observe may be due to processing differences rather than to changes in the basic organization of knowledge. One of the most important changes is growth in flexibility in using the representational system, including "multiple access" (Pylyshyn, 1978), or the ability to access concepts from many different contexts. Another change is the gradual development of what Pylyshyn calls "reflective access," or the ability to think about one's representations in addition to using them (see also Brown & Campione, 1980; Piaget, 1976; Rozin, 1976). To answer the typical class-inclusion questions may require the ability to reflect on the implications of one's knowledge. The ability to carry out this kind of reflection may or may not be considered a qualitative change in development, but in any case it does not seem to be a structural change in the way that knowledge is organized.

I do not wish to minimize the importance of qualitative changes in development because many certainly do occur. Further, some qualitative changes can probably best be described as structural ones. The acquisition of algebraic reasoning, for example, seems to involve a qualitatively different understanding of numerical principles than the earlier understanding of numerosity (Gelman & Gallistel, 1978). Nevertheless, there are broad areas of human functioning that seem to show relatively little qualitative change. In the research I have been describing, the commonalities between children's and adult's functioning seem to outweigh the differences, and the commonalities begin to appear at a young age. A little reflection suggests that this conclusion should not be surprising. After all, for the most part we understand and communicate with children quite well. We do not tell them how to structure their knowledge of objects, scenes, and events—we don't need to. We instruct them on bodies of fact, on society's rules, and the procedures for solving particular tasks, such as cooking or doing long division.

The kinds of knowledge that guide much of our daily behavior and understanding should not be dismissed as being low level or unimportant to the grander flights of human reasoning; they are intimately involved in much of our thought. As we saw earlier, even formal problem solving is usually strongly influenced by our daily routines, and this is true of adults as well as children (Tschirgi, 1980). The commonalities between children's and adults' functioning that I have described here are particularly evident when one looks at such prosaic activities as telling a story or noticing what is in a room, but they also underlie more "formal" tasks, such as reasoning and problem solving.

We are particularly likely to see major qualitative developmental differences in tasks in which the situation can be interpreted in more than one way, not automatically organized in terms of a particular schema. Thus, in a sorting task or in memorizing a list of words there is no single method of organizing the material because more than one principle of similarity is available. Here preferences for grouping things in various ways may differ considerably depending on current life styles, culture, and so forth. As an example, Smiley and Brown (1979) found that preferences for sorting items into thematic or taxonomic groupings showed a curvilinear relationship with age; young children and older people preferred to form thematic groups, whereas school-age children and college students preferred taxonomic groups. One would not want to use such data to suggest that the knowledge base is changing curvilinearly. The data might be explained on the basis of cohort differences in the organization of knowledge, but a more likely explanation is that the task permits more than one preference to be exhibited.[4]

We have relatively little choice as to how we structure many of our daily activities. There are certain steps we must go through to make an omelet or get to school, and these steps are repeated on a regular basis. Our knowledge is organized around such routines, and we interpret the world through the structures that develop from them. Even our taxonomic categories are developed in the contexts of these daily episodes, a process that must begin at or near birth. To the extent that we carry out the same routines, our knowledge is apt to be structured in similar ways, whether we be young or old.

In this view of development, not only are there functional invariants in the way that we take in information, there are also structural invariants that result from them. In Piagetian theory, only the tendency to organize information and to build schemata through the process of accommodation and assimilation are considered to be functionally invariant, that is, to characterize processing throughout life. The structures that result from these modes of processing are thought to differ qualitatively at different stages. But as we look more closely at the schemata that are formed by these processes, it appears that at least some of them remain structurally invariant as well. As yet, we know relatively little about the constraints that govern the type and size of the units that are formed from the universal modes of processing or about the variety of structures that may result. Nevertheless, even those structural invariants that we have discovered provide more continuity from childhood to adulthood than we have often admitted.

ACKNOWLEDGMENTS

Support for the preparation of this chapter came from National Institute of Health research grant MH–24492.

REFERENCES

Anderson, J. R. Arguments concerning representations for mental imagery. *Psychological Review*, 1978, *85*, 249–277.

Bertoncini, J., & Mehler, J. Syllables as units in infants' speech perception. *Infant Behavior and Development*, 1981, *4*, 225–246.

---

[4]Rabinowitz and Mandler (1981) found that even college students, when sorting items that could be used to create event sequences or taxonomic categories, tended to form schematic rather than taxonomic groups. Thus, even in sorting tasks, some materials are more apt to activate our routine schematic organizations than others.

Bobrow, D. G., & Norman, D. A. Some principles of memory schemata. In D. G. Bobrow & A. Collins (Eds.), *Representation and understanding: Studies in cognitive science.* New York: Academic Press, 1975.

Botvin, G. J., & Sutton-Smith, B. The development of complexity in children's fantasy narratives. *Developmental Psychology,* 1977, *13,* 377–388.

Bower, G. H., Black, J. B., & Turner, T. J. Scripts in memory for text. *Cognitive Psychology,* 1979, *11,* 177–220.

Bransford, J. D., & McCarrell, N. S. A sketch of a cognitive approach to comprehension. In W. Weimer & D. Palermo (Eds.), *Cognition and the symbolic processes.* Hillsdale, N.J.: Lawrence Erlbaum Associates, 1974.

Brown, A. L. The construction of temporal succession by preoperational children. In A. D. Pick (Ed.), *Minnesota Symposia on Child Psychology* (Vol. 10). Minneapolis: University of Minnesota Press, 1976. (a)

Brown, A. L. Semantic integration in children's reconstruction of narrative sequences. *Cognitive Psychology,* 1976, *8,* 247–262. (b)

Brown, A. L., & Campione, J. C. Inducing flexible thinking: The problem of access. In M. Friedman, J. D. Das, & N. O'Connor (Eds.), *Intelligence and learning.* New York: Plenum, 1980.

Chi, M. T. H. Knowledge structures and memory development. In R. S. Siegler (Ed.), *Children's thinking: What develops?* Hillsdale, N.J.: Lawrence Erlbaum Associates, 1978.

D'Andrade, R. G. *Reasoning and the Wason problem.* Unpublished manuscript, University of California, San Diego, 1980.

Eimas, P. D. Speech perception in early infancy. In L. B. Cohen & P. Salapatek (Eds.), *Infant perception: From sensation to cognition* (Vol. II). New York: Academic Press, 1975.

Friedman, A. Framing pictures: The role of knowledge in automatized encoding and memory for gist. *Journal of Experimental Psychology: General,* 1979, *108,* 316–355.

Gaines, R., Mandler, J. M., & Bryant, P. Immediate and delayed story recall by hearing and deaf children. *Journal of Speech and Hearing Research,* 1981, *24,* 116–122.

Gelman, R., & Baillargeon, R. A review of Piagetian concepts. In J. H. Flavell & E. M. Markman (Eds.), *Cognitive development,* Vol. 3 of P. Mussen (Ed.), *Manual of child psychology.* New York: Wiley, 1983.

Gelman, R., & Gallistel, C. R. *The child's understanding of number.* Cambridge, Mass.: Harvard University Press, 1978.

Glenn, C. G., & Stein, N. L. *Syntactic structures and real world themes in stories generated by children* (Center for the Study of Reading Tech. Rep.). Urbana: University of Illinois, 1980.

Goodman, G. S. Picture memory: How the action schema affects retention. *Cognitive Psychology,* 1980, *12,* 473–495.

Huttenlocher, J. The origins of language comprehension. In R. L. Solso (Ed.), *Theories in cognitive psychology: The Loyola Symposium.* Hillsdale, N.J.: Lawrence Erlbaum Associates, 1974.

Inhelder, B., & Piaget, J. *The early growth of logic in the child.* London: Routledge & Kegan Paul, 1964.

Johnson, N. S., & Gandel, R. *Preschool children's story recall: Effects of story organization.* Unpublished manuscript, State University of New York, Buffalo, 1980.

Johnson, N. S., & Mandler, J. M. A tale of two structures: Underlying and surface forms in stories. *Poetics,* 1980, *9,* 51–86.

Keil, F. C. *Semantic and conceptual development: An ontological perspective.* Cambridge, Mass.: Harvard University Press, 1979.

Kessen, W., & Nelson, K. What the child brings to language. In B. Z. Presseisen, D. Goldstein, & M. H. Appel (Eds.), *Topics in cognitive development* (Vol. 2), *Language and operational thought.* New York, Plenum, 1978.

Kuhn, D. Conditional reasoning in children. *Developmental Psychology,* 1977, *13,* 342–353.

Lenneberg, E. *The biological foundations of language.* New York: Wiley, 1967.

Loftus, E. F. Leading questions and the eyewitness report. *Cognitive Psychology,* 1975, *7,* 560–572.

Loftus, G. E., & Mackworth, N. H. Cognitive determinants of fixation location during picture viewing. *Journal of Experimental Psychology: Human Performance and Perception,* 1978, *4,* 565–572.

Mandler, G. Recognizing: The judgment of previous occurrence. *Psychological Review,* 1980, *87,* 252–271.

Mandler, J. M. A code in the node: The use of a story schema in retrieval. *Discourse Processes,* 1978, *1,* 14–35.

Mandler, J. M. Categorical and schematic organization in memory. In C. R. Puff (Ed.), *Memory organization and structure.* New York: Academic Press, 1979.

Mandler, J. M. Representation. In J. H. Flavell & E. M. Markman (Eds.), *Cognitive development,* Vol. 3 of P. Mussen (Ed.), *Manual of child psychology.* New York: Wiley, 1983.

Mandler, J. M., & DeForest, M. Is there more than one way to recall a story? *Child Development,* 1979, *50,* 886–889.

Mandler, J. M., & Johnson, N. S. Remembrance of things parsed: Story structure and recall. *Cognitive Psychology,* 1977, *9,* 111–151.

Mandler, J. M., & Robinson, C. A. Developmental changes in picture recognition. *Journal of Experimental Child Psychology,* 1978, *26,* 122–136.

Mandler, J. M., Scribner, S., Cole, M., & DeForest, M. Cross-cultural invariance in story recall. *Child Development,* 1980, *51,* 19–26.

Nelson, K. How children represent knowledge of their world in and out of language: A preliminary report. In R. S. Siegler (Ed.), *Children's thinking: What develops?* Hillsdale, N.J.: Lawrence Erlbaum Associates, 1978.

Piaget, J. *The language and thought of the child.* New York: Harcourt Brace, 1926.

Piaget, J. *Play, dreams and imitation in childhood.* New York: Norton, 1951.

Piaget, J. *The origins of intelligence in children.* New York: International Universities Press, 1952.

Piaget, J. *The grasp of consciousness: Action and concept in the young child.* Cambridge, Mass.: Harvard University Press, 1976.

Piaget, J., & Inhelder, B. Intellectual operations and their development. In P. Oleron, J. Piaget, B. Inhelder, & P. Greco (Eds.), *Intelligence,* Vol. VII of P. Fraisse & J. Piaget (Eds.), *Experimental psychology: Its scope and method.* London: Routledge & Kegan Paul, 1969.

Piattelli-Palmarini, M. (Ed.). *Language and learning: The debate between Jean Piaget and Noam Chomsky.* Cambridge, Mass.: Harvard University Press, 1980.

Pylyshyn, Z. W. When is attribution of beliefs justified? *The Behavioral and Brain Sciences,* 1978, *1,* 592–593.

Rabinowitz, M., & Mandler, J. M. *Schematic and taxonomic organization in free recall.* Paper presented at the meetings of the American Educational Research Association, Los Angeles, April 1981.

Rozin, P. The evolution of intelligence and access to the cognitive unconscious. *Progress in psychobiology and physiological psychology* 1976, *6,* 245–280.

Rumelhart, D. E. *Analogical processes and procedural representation* (Center for Human Information Processing Tech. Rep. No. 81). La Jolla, Cal.: University of California, San Diego, 1979.

Rumelhart, D. E. Schemata: The building blocks of cognition. In R. Spiro, B. Bruce, & W. Brewer (Eds.), *Theoretical issues in reading comprehension.* Hillsdale, N.J.: Lawrence Erlbaum Associates, 1980.

Rumelhart, D. E., & Ortony, A. The representation of knowledge in memory. In R. C. Anderson, R. J. Spiro, & W. E. Montague (Eds.), *Schooling and the acquisition of knowledge.* Hillsdale, N.J.: Lawrence Erlbaum Associates, 1977.

Schank, R. C., & Abelson, R. *Scripts, plans, goals and understanding.* Hillsdale, N.J.: Lawrence Erlbaum Associates, 1977.

Scribner, S. Modes of thinking and ways of speaking: Culture and logic reconsidered. In R. C. Freedle (Ed.), *New directions in discourse processing* (Vol. II). Norwood, N.J.: Ablex, 1979.

Seligman, M. E. P., & Hager, J. L. (Eds.). *Biological boundaries of learning.* New York: Appleton-Century-Crofts, 1972.

Siegler, R. S. The origins of scientific thinking. In R. S. Siegler (Ed.), *Children's thinking: What develops?* Hillsdale, N.J.: Lawrence Erlbaum Associates, 1978.

Sigel, I. E. When do we know what a child knows? *Human Development,* 1974, *17,* 201–217.

Smiley, S. S., & Brown, A. L. Conceptual preference for thematic or taxonomic relations: A nonmonotonic trend from preschool to old age. *Journal of Experimental Child Psychology,* 1979, *28,* 249–257.

Smith, C. L. Children's understanding of natural language hierarchies. *Journal of Experimental Child Psychology,* 1979, *27,* 437–458.

Spelke, E. Perceiving bimodally specified events in infancy. *Developmental Psychology,* 1979, *15,* 626–636.

Stein, N. L., & Glenn, C. G. An analysis of story comprehension in elementary school children. In R. C. Freedle (Ed.), *New directions in discourse processing* (Vol. II). Norwood, N.J.: Ablex, 1979.

Stein, N. S., & Trabasso, T. What's in a story: Critical issues in comprehension and instruction. In R. Glaser (Ed.), *Advances in the psychology of instruction* (Vol. 2). Norwood, N.J.: Ablex, 1982.

Strauss, M. S. Abstraction of prototypical information by adults and 10-month-old infants. *Journal of Experimental Psychology: Human Learning and Memory,* 1979, *5,* 618–632.

Trabasso, T., Isen, A. M., Dolecki, P., McLanahan, A. G., Riley, C. A., & Tucker, T. How do children solve class inclusion problems? In R. S. Siegler (Ed.), *Children's thinking: What develops?* Hillsdale, N.J.: Lawrence Erlbaum Associates, 1978.

Tschirgi, J. E. Sensible reasoning: A hypothesis about hypotheses. *Child Development,* 1980, *51,* 1–10.

Wason, P. C. Reasoning about a rule. *Quarterly Journal of Experimental Psychology,* 1968, *20,* 273–281.

Weaver, P. A. Comprehension, recall, and dyslexia: A proposal for the application of schema theory. *Bulletin of the Orton Society,* 1978, *28,* 92–113.

Worden, P. E., Malmgren, I., & Gabourie, P. *Memory for stories in learning disabled adults. Journal of Learning Disabilities,* 1982, *15,* 145–152.

7 Cognitive Development Is Structural and Transformational—Therefore Variant

Irving E. Sigel
Educational Testing Service

The structural construct has become a popular concept, especially for those interested in cognitive development and functioning. Mandler entitles her essay (this volume), for example, "Structural Invariants in Development." The assumption no doubt is that the use of the term *structure* conveys a precise meaning and so establishes a common frame of reference for the readership.

In this chapter, I address the issues and conceptualization implied in Mandler's title to argue that the structural concept is ambiguous. Furthermore, the assertion that structural invariance in cognitive development occurs (the core of Mandler's interest) is, from a Piagetian perspective, a contradiction in terms.

Before proceeding to present my case, let me provide a brief synopsis of Mandler's position so that readers know just what aspects of her interesting and provocative paper I am addressing.

Mandler's Thesis

Mandler's definition of cognitive structure is most clearly presented in a previous essay where she quotes Puff (1979) and states that cognitive structure can be defined as "an organized set of concepts and procedures [p. 260]," and further, that the terms structures and organization are interchangeable concepts. The particular type of structure of interest to Mandler in this volume is the *schema,* "which seems to qualify as one of the universal, basic forms of representation" Schema functions as an organizer enabling the understanding of common events. Her thesis (this volume) is that: "the constructive processes that form our representational system are not only functionally invariant, but they result in at least

125

some structural invariants as well.'' She concludes that children and adults construct their knowledge base by employing processes that do not differ greatly from childhood to adulthood. The particular knowledge base that is used to test this nondevelopmental proposition is the understanding of common event sequences. The schema is the structure involved.

Mandler's argument raises a number of critical issues in theory and method, which form the basis of my essay. The issues that are paramount deal with the concepts of *structure, schema, representation,* and *development.* I address each of these serially but, of necessity, veer back and forth among the concepts because they form an interlocking system. For example, as a function of developmental transformations, the form by which knowledge can be represented will differ. But, more about this later.

Let me digress a bit here before proceeding to the heart of my discussion to address an underlying argument Mandler uses, to wit, that the nativist and constructivist schools are in considerable opposition. Mandler's objective in her paper is to bridge the gap, or perhaps to reconcile these positions, by contending that invariant modes of functioning lead to invariant cognitive structures. The argument is that there is a gap between nativism and constructivism and that this gap is reconcilable.

It seems to me that there is no necessary argument, unless nativism denies subsequent development or learning. A nativist argument need not eschew constructivism because it refers to the organism's construction of knowledge as described by Piaget (1977): ''It is from . . . dialectic interaction ⇄ that the object is bit by bit discovered in its objective properties by a 'decentration' which frees knowledge of its subjective illusions. It is from this same interaction that the subject, by discovering and conquering the object, organizes his actions into a coherent system that constitutes the operations of his intelligence and his thought [p. 31].'' To accomplish such actions the child's biological structure has to be considered (e.g., the ability to reach). To act on objects is a necessary precondition for the construction of knowledge, and such an ability is inherent in the child's biological structure.

Emphasis on the organism-environment interaction provides a framework that avoids the extreme positions of either ignoring the biological givens or the converse argument for a biological performance, allowing no room for experience. Thus, as is shown in the subsequent section, the interactionist approach (consistent with the basic position of Piaget) forms the context within which the conceptions of structure, schema, representation, and development can be discussed.

Mandler's conclusion that structures are or can be invariant contrasts with my conception of cognitive development, as well as those held by Piaget, Werner, and others. These latter views hold that children are by their very nature developing cognitively through a series of transformations at various levels, irrespective of the contents involved. The differences in these two perspectives are especially evident in the interpretation given to the concepts of structure, representation, schema, and development. These definitional issues are discussed later, and in a subsequent section of the essay, I discuss the implication of these concepts for further research.

Specifically, the issues are as follows: Are there some structures that are invariant, manifesting no developmental changes? And in those structures in which change *is* evident, is it quantitative, derived from experience? Mandler argues for affirmative answers to both. I disagree.

STRUCTURE

The use of structure as a concept implies that one is working within the theoretical form of structuralism, hence definitions of structure and structuralism are needed. However, there is considerable disagreement. Let me illustrate by quoting Piaget (1970b) and Puff (1979), two theorists who are far apart in their perspective but who share the conviction that terminological differences exist and are difficult to reconcile. Piaget (1970b), for example, holds that: "Structuralism is often said to be hard to define because it has taken too many different forms for a common denominator to be in evidence: the structures invoked by the several 'structuralists' have acquired increasingly diverse significations [p. 3]."

This statement does reflect a general concern with the structure concept—a concern shared by others from very different theoretical perspectives. Puff (1979), for example, in a volume on memory, organization, and structure writes: "The variety of uses of these terms ['structure' and 'organization'] has expanded rapidly over the years until there is now no single, generally accepted referent of either organization or structure. A partial list of the usages of these terms . . . includes clustering, subjective organization, . . . schematic organization . . . [p. 4]." In spite of such acknowledged lack of common referents for the term structure, it is still used with little if any effort to define its meaning or place it in a historical or conceptual context.

Using the schema as the cornerstone of her conception of structure, Mandler (this volume) proceeds to develop her argument as follows:

> Although there are undoubtedly many qualitative changes in development, nevertheless we seem to construct a knowledge base according to principles that do not vary greatly from infancy to adulthood. The constructive processes that form our representational system are not only functionally invariant, but they result in at least some structural invariants as well. It is thus possible to take a generally constructivist position and at the same time eschew a stage theory of the sort that Piaget has proposed.

Although Mandler and other cognitive theorists employ the term structure, it is not clear whether they recognize that the term implies a mode of analysis called *structuralism*. There are explicit and implicit considerations regarding the notions of structure. Whether structure is synonymous with organization is not the only issue. Whether one uses the term organization or structure, the implication is that wholeness, relatedness, and transformation are intrinsic characteristics of structure. If these are not incorporated into the structure concept, how can a structure be said to exist? Thus, before we can address the issue of structural invariants (i.e., nondevelopmental processes), let me clarify the structural notions in more detail.

According to Lane (1970), part of the difficulty in definition is due to the fact that structuralism is a mode of analysis and a "mode of thought common to disciplines as widely separated as mathematics and literary criticism. Next, its debts to the past and its relations to the present are highly eclectic. Again, none of those who call themselves or are called "structuralist' has explicitly formulated the fundamentals of structuralism, except in the most allusive or partial way [p. 11]." Among the structuralists, however, Piaget has devoted an entire volume to clarifying and elaborating structuralism. For Piaget (1970b), "a structure is a system of transformation [that involves] the idea of wholeness, the idea of transformation, and the idea of self-regulation [p. 5]." The implications of this definition for developmental cognitive theory are profound because they set the stage for his system. Structuralist analysis focuses on relations within time, rather than across time. A structure is conceptualized as an atemporal whole, composed of synchronous elements, which co-exist in relation to each other. Changes in the relationship among elements result in changing configurations and the emergence of new patterns, in effect, *transformation*, the second idea of structure. Lane (1970) holds that laws of transformation are: "law-like regularities that can be observed, or derived from observation by which one particular structural configuration changes into another [p. 17]."

The third aspect of structure is *regulation*, a process of reinforcement and corrective feedback. These processes are endemic to the formation of structures. According to Piaget (1977), regulation varies in complexity from simple regulations ". . . to self-regulations with self-organization which are capable of modifying and enriching the initial program by differentiation, multiplication, coordination of the goals, and integration of subsystems into a whole system [p. 21]." Regulation is a pervasive human activity that may be automatic (e.g., when one grasps an object) or may involve active adjustments (e.g., when the individual must change an approach to a problem).

But, the critical feature in the structure concept is the idea of transformation. A structure is transformed with the assimilation of new knowledge and subsequent accommodation to this new experience. Mandler, it can be recalled, holds that structural invariance is evident, basing this conclusion on the empirical finding that no qualitative differences are found between adults and children in story recall. From a Piagetian perspective, a structure is invariant when already developed, but to contend that structural invariance in development exists is a contradiction in terms.

REPRESENTATION

Mandler accurately portrays the confusion regarding the idea of representation in her discussion. Although it is true that the term has multiple meanings both in its technical use as well as its everyday use, it is important to establish a consistent definition. Mandler (this volume) is clear on her usage. Representation is defined as:

> The knowledge base a person has, the store of facts and procedures with which the person interprets the world and which govern his or her thinking and actions. Representation in this usage actually has two senses, one sense referring to *what* knowledge a person has, the other to the format or structure of that knowledge. The present, all-purpose use of the term covers both content and type of structure.

I cannot argue this point. What I would contend is that combining content (i.e., *what* is known) with the mode or medium in which the knowledge is used poses both a conceptual and a methodological problem. To clarify why the combining of content and mode poses problems, let me review how Piaget uses the term as a prelude to the difficulty I foresee based on my own research.

In his seminal book, *Play, Dreams and Imitation, in Childhood* Piaget (1951) describes in some detail his conceptualization of representation. One definition Piaget (1951) offers is that representation is characterized by the fact that "it goes beyond the present, extending the field of adaptation both in space and time [p. 273]." However, there are qualitative differences from infancy (sensorimotor-representational schema) to adulthood (formal operational-representational schema). Thus, there are different representational mechanisms, which are operative at each developmental level.

All of the references Mandler makes to representation refer to internal mental activities. But representation also refers to external phenomena such as language systems, pictures, drawings, and so forth. Understanding these external representations requires cognitive processing. My argument (Sigel, 1978) is that understanding these external representations requires having "the awareness that items can be represented in various media [p. 105]." In fact, in some of my own work, children did not respond to representations of objects (i.e., pictures) equivalent to their behavior with objects (Sigel, 1970). Preschool children would label pictorial items in the same way as adults. Pictures of a notebook, a cup, and a pencil, for example, were all properly labeled. However, when asked to classify these pictures along with others (all properly labeled) in any way they wished, the children had difficulty generating categories. But when presented with three-dimensional representations or with replicas of the pictures, the children had no difficulty finding common bases for grouping. Employing the label accurately was no guarantee that the child understood the class membership or other basis of relationship of the item (Sigel, Anderson, & Shapiro, 1966). Thus, no quantitative differences were found in the labeling activity, but differences were found when the task demand required grouping or classification.

These data suggest that the lack of understanding of the representational significance of the picture precluded the employment of relevant cognitive operations. But, the fact the child could group objects suggests that the understanding of "grouping" was present. Therefore, I concluded that although the children grasped principles of grouping, they could not employ them when the representational significance of the item was not within their repertoire. These results suggest that relying solely on the lack of quantitative differences (no differences in labeling) as an indication of similarity between young and older children would be misleading. The differences between the groups are in their knowledge base, and this can only be discussed when the method employed seeks to inquire about the child's understanding of the phenomenon. I believe that such an approach is necessary in studies of memory, where the data gathered are only children's ability to recall items in a story. I would like to know if the understanding of relations in the story is similar for young and older subjects because understanding relationships would reflect a structural analysis.

SCHEMA

The use of the term schema has been utilized for many years by a number of writers (e.g., Kant, Piaget, Neisser, to name but a few). In addition, other writers use analogous terms such as frame (e.g., Goffman, 1974; Minsky, 1975). All these uses share a common feature: a concern for ways of organizing knowledge. The variety of definitions, however, does pose problems in communication and in conceptualization. Although each author may use the term to label a relatively similar set of events, the attributes inherent in the definition of schema may vary (e.g., some include operations, others just content). However, even though definitions may vary, there is also some commonality because each refers to what is essentially cognitive, in structural terms, with reference to the organization of knowledge. Further, this core idea is generally accepted by investigators who eschew an associationist orientation. But nonassociationists are not necessarily all of one cloth. There are important differences both in emphasis and function.

Piaget (1970b) distinguishes between the nonoperational characteristic of schema and the operational characteristic of scheme, particularly in terms of memory in the widest sense. According to Ross and Kerst (1978): "This is simply the conservation of knowledge schemes . . . [where] schemes embody generalized knowledge such as practical actions and logical and mathematical concepts rather than reference to a specific post occurrence, therefore they are part of intelligence and so not subject to forgetting in the ordinary course of affairs [p. 196]." Ross and Kerst (1978) continue that a schema, on the other hand is "the regulatory mechanism governing the mental or graphic expression of the image—develops only slightly with age [p. 198]." Developmentally earlier schemes combine to form new and more comprehensive schemes.

The distinction is an important one from a structural perspective. Schemata change slowly in contrast to schemes, which are essentially cognitive operations and hence change with increasing age. In effect, Piaget presents an operational cognitive approach, distinguishing between figurative (schema) and operational (scheme) memory.

What this distinction accomplishes is to provide one type of classification of cognitive structures and functions. Mandler, however, does not deal with the Piagetian distinction. Her position is closer to that of Neisser (1976) in that schema refers not only to structure but also to functions. Schema operations and content are not differentiated. Neisser (1976) writes: "A schema is that portion of the entire perceptual cycle which is internal to the perceiver, modifiable by experience and somehow specific to what is being perceived. The schema accepts information as it becomes available at sensory surfaces and is changed by that information. It directs movements and exploratory activities that make more information available by which it is further modified [p. 54]."

Mandler and Neisser do not distinguish between the figurative and operative aspects of memory. By not making the distinction and not seeking to identify "operative" differences between children and adults, it is conceivable that differences in structures are not found. It can be recalled that schemata are the aspects of structure that interest Mandler. For Piaget, it is the schemes that show stagelike changes, not the schemata, so that from a Piagetian definition it is only the operations that manifest developmental change.

If, then, investigations into children's memory for everyday events seek to establish their knowledge base in terms of schema, it is not surprising that no differences are found, even from a Piagetian perspective, because it is the schemata that are involved and not the schemes. Liben (in press), in a review of memory research with story grammars and with scripts, concludes: ". . . developmental data do not suggest radical qualitative changes in the nature of this knowledge and as children get older (at least within the age range tested), data do suggest that older children's structural knowledge is more detailed and more complex than younger children's, changes that may support older children's better performance on a variety of memory tasks [p. 276]."

Both Mandler's report and Liben's conclusion would suggest that structural changes in knowledge of everyday events is but an increase in complexity (i.e., in quantity but not in quality). I am not convinced that the data presented address this issue, for two reasons: (1) recall of stories or scripts provides only figurative knowledge akin to recognitory memory without attending to relationships among elements of the whole; (2) the nature of increasing complexity or number of details is not specified, nor do the criteria presented preclude a qualitative change. Let me address each of these issues briefly here in the context of structuralism.

The children asked to recall the stories, the chess moves, or whatever may have already developed the necessary structures for that type of performance. If, for example, the children are concrete operational, as children in the Chi study probably are (Chi, 1978) they obviously have the schema and schemes necessary for that type of performance. The same is true for children's recall of story grammars or scripts. The cognitive demands for such mnemonics may tap into competencies already established. Thus, the conclusions regarding invariance in structural development may be a function of the fact that the children have already arrived at the level necessary for the cognitive demands of the task. Similarly, Liben (1982) has also suggested that the interesting developmental changes in story and event memory have probably occurred prior to the age tested because, by first grade, "children (at least the middle-class children typically tested) have already had extensive exposure to formal stories. In addition, many first graders are likely to have the concrete operations needed to understand and recall the causal and temporal relations found in these stories [p. 275]."

Second, I would not reject offhand the fact that the number of details or complexities older children include in their recollections are just "quantitative" change. What does quantitative change mean? Are there just more? Can the fact that more details are presented mean that the children are employing different processes to incorporate such additional knowledge into an already existing structure? Essentially, I have to know *what* processes are involved in the older child's or adult's organization of the additional knowledge. Do the older children employ different schemes to accomplish this increased quantity of material in recall? The design of such research requires additional data regarding the child's operational level to determine the relationship between operational level and recall, be it of story grammar or scripts.

Lest it be said that I am a skeptic because of my bias, I can only state that the evidence for the changes being solely quantitative and not qualitative must come from the methods of study. In effect, I ask if the design of the study and the analysis of the data provide incontrovertible evidence allowing one to argue that there must be some type of operation that mediates the perceptual experiencing of objects and incorporation of objects into a schema. The mechanisms in question are the operational schemes. Liben (1981), in a thorough review of the literature on this point, concludes: ". . . individual's operative schemes and knowledge influence memory not only for stimuli directly derived from Piaget's tasks, but also for a wide range of verbal and pictorial material [p. 141]." There are mechanisms employed in constructions that function in two directions: (1) to create new schemata; (2) to help the individual cope with additional and/or novel experience to alter schema. How, for example, does the child come to integrate "snake" into the schema *animal* when snakes share only *some* attributes of four-legged creatures organized as animals?

That schemata are repositories of knowledge is accepted as a given. Objects and events are defined not only from the perspective of the child, but they are also defined from the perspective of the culture of the adult world. "Tennis shoes" are in the schema *shoe* or *wearing apparel,* but the culture defines when it is appropriate to wear them. They are not worn to a formal dinner party. If a child does see a guest at a dinner party wearing tennis shoes, and if the child has learned that tennis shoes are inappropriate, then he or she experiences an obvious *discrepancy*. This inconsistency, I maintain, generates some tension that needs resolution of some kind. Efforts at discrepancy resolution can be described as quasi-motivational because they serve to activate the child cognitively. Discrepancies between the expected and the actual are bound to occur in everyday life, and our theories must explain them. But, again, our theories must explain how and by what mechanisms individuals are activated to acquire knowledge at various developmental levels. It seems reasonable to propose that the discrepancy construct is a major source activating or energizing the individual, but resolution (equilibration) will depend on what repertoire children possess to accomplish this. I submit that it is necessary to postulate mechanisms for such an achievement. This argument may then lead to proposing some kind of stage or level construct because children show age differences in how such resolutions are achieved (Sigel & Cocking, 1977).

Mandler, like many cognitive theorists, raises doubts regarding Piagetian stage theory. In recent years, much evidence has been accumulated to cast doubt on Piaget's formulation of stages. It may well be that even though stages as described by Piaget may be domain specific, and even then not correct, there is still a body of data reported by Piaget that demonstrates there are qualitative and quantitative differences between the thought of children and adults. Thus, for some of the areas Mandler describes, the difference between children and adults occurs, but the difference is quantitative rather than qualitative. However, Mandler does not report whether the process employed by the children or their awareness of their rules of organization does in fact distinguish child performance from adult performance.

One of the distinctions between adults and children not addressed by Mandler refers to the difference in understanding schema organization. If a schema is an organized body of knowledge, then there is reason to suppose that the criteria for the organization are known to the child. From my own research and that of others (Piaget, 1971; Sigel, 1971), it has become apparent that children do not necessarily have an awareness of the organizational principles they employ. The organizational criteria are not conceptual, but rather are based on physical features of the objects. To be sure, actions with the objects are often consistent with the characteristics of the objects (e.g., children wear the shoes, ride the bike, sit in the chair, etc.). But if asked to identify the organizing principles or the strategies that are used to combine different shoes into one schema, the principles will differ in quality between children and adults. The limited ability to articulate or to provide an organizing principle suggests a qualitative difference (Sigel & Cocking, 1977).

In some areas of knowledge, differences in quantity do exist. There may be cases where children, by virtue of limited experience, do not have the necessary knowledge. On the other hand, there are also areas where qualitative differences do in fact exist. Some of the areas Piaget studied (e.g., spatial relations, conservation, etc.) exemplify qualitative differences. In other words, it might be argued that generalization about schema origins will vary with the context domain. Will they also vary with the developmental level? The answer again seems to be yes because the differences between adults' and children's mnemonic performance may still be subject to differences in operative skills available to the individual.

Evidence for this assertion is extensive in the literature on cognitive development. First, Piaget's research on memory is a case in point, thus enabling Piaget to hold that the child's operative level influences the ways objects, pictures, and events are recalled. Liben (1975), working with kindergarten, first, second, and third grade children, asked them to copy a seriated array of 10 sticks. She (1981) reports: "Perfectly seriated drawings were produced by 38, 69, 79, and 92% of the children in each grade respectively [p. 137]." Assessing operative level directly instead of relying on age, Liben (1978) reported that children's accuracy to copy was related to operative level. She (1981) concludes that: "the findings from these studies all demonstrate that children have difficulty even in copying— and by implication, in perceiving—stimuli that are more advanced than their own conceptual levels [p. 138]."

Thus, there is a clear-cut difference between Mandler, who holds that structural invariants of development do in fact exist, and me, who argues that the data reported in her paper are insufficient for concluding structural invariance. Some of the reasons for the difference may, as indicated previously, be due to methodological as well as conceptual differences (e.g., the studies she reports may involve children who have already established the structures necessary for the tasks employed). Thus, her conclusion is a function of the maturity level of the subjects relative to the tasks used in the study. On the conceptual level, by using the schema concept as incorporating both figurative and operative knowledge, there is no reason to search for the operations that might be involved.

In the next section I would like to address some of the implications of my previous comments in the context of broader issues of theory and method. Thus, I address the following concepts: basic organization of knowledge, context, scripts, and task selection. Each of these are, of course, central to Mandler's chapter. By providing the two positions, the reader can perceive the discrepancy and decide how to deal with it. So, let me turn to the first issue, basic organization of knowledge.

IMPLICATIONS
OF DEFINITIONAL DIFFERENCES

The question is whether these definitional differences affect the way we interpret children's responses to problems such as story recall, class-inclusion tasks, and so forth. Mandler (this volume) contends that processing differences in the acquisition of knowledge may not reflect changes in basic organization of knowledge. This brings us back to how we conceptualize "basic organization of knowledge." I contend that children's organization or structuring of knowledge is a function of the meanings they extract from events. For example, although they may be able to use words in a way comparable to adults, they relate the meanings of materials differently. Children are more literal in their comprehension of fairy tales, they have difficulty in understanding causal connections, and they have difficulty differentiating fantasy from reality. It seems that even though children can recite the correct order of a story it does not mean they understand the connections between events. In effect, I accept the idea that young children do not engage in reflective abstractions and have difficulty in emancipating themselves from the concrete "pull" of actions and events, which precludes their dealing with experiences conceptually. This analysis, of course, may be viewed as an underestimation of children's ability. We are all familiar with the extraordinary memory of young children as well as their ability to differentiate certain events or anticipate others. Perhaps, Mandler's assertion is that all I am referring to is process, not organizational issues. However, I would like to present Werner's concept of analogous process, which may help clarify the issue.

Werner (1948) argues that analogous process is a concept derived from biology, which holds "that there need not be any identity of organ and the functions performed by that organ [pp. 213–214]." Werner (1948) translates the concept for developmental psychology as follows: Analogous processes are defined "as processes at different genetic levels directed toward the same achievement but involving different function patterns. . . . [p. 214]." In applying this principle to tasks such as story or event recall, we may ask if the child's achievement is reached by different processes than those used by the adult. The question is: What is the relationship between the structures and the functions relative to the achievement?

Good illustrations supporting Werner's notion of analogous process or functioning can be found in children's grouping behavior. Children select attributes of arrays and form groupings (Sigel, 1953). Although the same items are placed in the groups by children of different ages, rationales for the groupings vary with age. The productions look similar, but the bases vary (Sigel, 1954).

To argue, on the other hand, that developmental differences may be due to processing differences, not to basic organization, raises the critical question of whether processing differences can exist independently of structure of knowledge. This distinction suggests that two types of knowledge exist, process knowledge and structure knowledge, which for me correspond to Piaget's notion of figurative knowledge (schema) and operational knowledge (schemes) (Piaget, 1970a). This distinction is testable, even with story recall, if the rationale and meaning (i.e., the *understanding* of the story) are incorporated into the design of the study.

Issue of Context

There is no doubt that context is important. Having made this assertion, where do we go from here? If psychological research is to result in discovering generalizations about behavior, then it behooves us to strive to find conceptual and methodological ways of dealing with the issue. Context should be an integral part of our conceptualization, that is, a detailed formulation of contextual dimensions that interact with an individual's performance as implied in Lewin's (1936) classic statement that behavior is a function of the person and the environment ($B = F[P \times E]$). Hunt and Sullivan (1974) note: "*B-P-E* is *not* in itself a formula to explain behavior but a means of classification; it is *meta*theoretical—a way of thinking about and considering theories—rather than theoretical [p. 11]." The formula provides a perspective for designing and analyzing psychological experiments; it provides no solution. By contrast, Lewin's (1936) topological field theory did incorporate field factors in his formulations and experimental designs (Lewin, 1954). Today, we still need to decide how context is to be used, either as intrinsic to our theories or as a perspective.

To be sure, our current awareness of the significance context is commonplace. That is to the good. But the solution to the problem is not so common. Perhaps going back to Lewin's field theory may help because his conceptualization was not tied to particulars, but rather to field forces and vectors, which when incorporated with dimensions such as press (Murray, 1938) or the constraint-facilitation dimensions of Chein (1954) might move us beyond rhetoric.

Issue of Scripts

I would like to use Mandler's discussion of scripts as a point of departure in raising some questions. There is no doubt that psychologists have tended to assume that the analysis of behavior in an experimental context would yield generic knowledge about basic process and behavior. Findings from such procedures are assumed to produce generalizable statements regarding the behavior in question. Examination of research reports will reveal that the researcher will discuss the findings as not contingent on the tasks and methods employed, but rather in general terms. Children's logical thinking, for example, is diagnosed on the basis of a conservation task (Piaget, 1970a), or children's origins of scientific reasoning are described in terms of children's balance scale, projection of shadows, and probability task (Siegler, 1978). We are becoming aware that what we know about children's cognitive development is contingent on the tasks employed. To understand how children learn and adapt to everyday experience cannot be understood from our experimental paradigm. Thus, the "script" concept should help us because it is close to the reality of daily existence. This approach is analogous to the dramaturgical approach (Brissett & Edgley, 1975) of "life is theater" as used by sociologists. Each of us employs scripts in our everyday functioning, *but* we are often not aware of the scriptlike quality of our daily actions. When queried about our routines, however, we are able to reflect on them. The issue is how are these learned? It seems that events are learned almost incidentally. Children are often programmed by adults. For example, the trip to McDonald's described so elegantly by Nelson (1978) is controlled by adults. It is difficult not to assume that this learning is associative. The cognitive components may be minimal if we think of cognition as involving judgment, reasoning, and so on. It is when the unexpected happens in the everyday world (i.e., a discrepancy between the habitual and the novel) that cognitive processing gets activated. If the individual still wants to complete the habituated routine (e.g., go to McDonald's) and if some barrier (physical or psychological) intervenes, then it is necessary to engage in problem-solving behavior. This paradigm is the one Lewin used to study children's coping with field forces that prevent achieving a goal (Lewin, 1954).

I suppose the issue for me is what general questions are being asked and answered in studying script behavior of children, and further, what we learn about how children come to *know* about everyday events.

Issue of Task Selection

I have discussed the issue of task used in experimental and naturalistic studies in children's cognitive development. Mandler discusses this issue relative to the structure of the story in her recall experiments. In this section, I would like to address the more general question of task selection. It is obvious that the tasks selected in our research are to be considered exemplars of a class of phenomena. Consequently, the task selected is presumed to tap the phenomena under study. Responses, therefore, are samples of behavior transcending the particular task in a particular study. However, as we are all aware, no task is a pure measure of any variable because every task is multidimensional—even geometric forms varying only in color and form. Some children associate meaningful attributes to what adults describe as nonmeaningful. For example, triangles are at times perceived as tents, or circles, as balls. If children are not asked what their interpretation of a task is, and if they are asked only to act on the materials, then the knowledge base involved is unknown. On the other hand, it is difficult if not impossible to get young children in particular to verbalize meanings. Does all this preclude our getting children's understanding? Does my discussion of understanding and meaning of tasks preclude a psychological science that will provide generalization? My answer is an unequivocal *no*. I believe some of the following suggestions might be helpful.

First, I believe we have to develop a taxonomy of tasks categorized in terms of the cognitive demands a task makes as well as the content or format. If the task is solely categorized on the basis of cognitive demands, the nature of the stimuli confounds the results. For example, studies of color-form preference among young elementary school-age black children varied with the tasks employed.

Using geometric form tasks and an object and picture categorization task, Olmsted and Sigel (1970) found that frequency of color and form usage varied with type of material. A similar result was found by Bearison and Sigel (1968) when they investigated middle-class elementary school children's preference for color, form, or meaningfulness among items in a forced-choice paradigm. Meaningfulness was the dominant choice among all age groups (6–11), and form was the next most frequent. Color was rarely used. Extrapolating from these results (color-form preference is no longer a popular research topic), it is clear that generality of color or form preference is a function of materials and test format.

Second, more than one task has to be administered in order to test for reliability (Laosa, 1980), particularly in developmental psychology. Test-retest reliability poses a problem in developmental psychology because the length of time between assessments is more likely to assess stability than task reliability. Children are maturing at a rapid rate, especially in the early years. Hence, it seems more reasonable to employ more than one task assumed to tap particular competencies.

Third, efforts should be made to assess the child in settings where psychological characteristics are identified. For example, in assessing classification skills, we found that children performed differently on free sort tasks as compared to structured matrix tasks. In each case, classification was involved; the materials were the same, but the task requirements were different. The context in which classification was to be performed differed.

I am sure numerous examples can be generated to illustrate differences in performance in different settings. Data of this type will be useful in contributing to generalizability as well as in indicating limits for generalization.

Fourth, a concerted effort should be made whenever possible to use tasks reported in the literature instead of inventing new ones. Of course, this is not a new suggestion, and we all have reasons why no one else's tasks are acceptable. All I can say here is that, understandable as this situation is, it precludes comparing results from the various studies. There are notable exceptions to my assertion (e.g., the use of the Piagetian conservation task). But, regretably, this is an exception rather than the rule.

SUMMARY AND CONCLUSIONS

The purpose of this essay was not to critique Mandler's excellent paper. Rather, it was to point out differences in the conceptualization and interpretation of such basic concepts as structure, representation, schema, and development. My own preference is to continue thinking within a Piagetian framework and interpret research accordingly. The central core of Piagetian theory has yet to be clearly and systematically articulated. The breadth and depth of his conceptualization warrants continued study. This is not to say that his is the only position to take.

But for now, it is the position I find most compatible with my observations and reading of the literature. Consequently, I interpret Mandler's study within that framework.

The fundamental and heretofore unspoken question is: Do we really want to reconcile conceptual differences? My answer is, not necessarily. Let each system evolve on its own and make contact where relevant. Reconciliation or at least modification would be possible when and only when there is agreement on the questions to be asked. If the questions posed by the various researchers are different, movement toward conceptual revision is not possible. There has to be closer agreement on method as well as on appropriate questions for reconciliation to become possible. At this stage of the game, this seems unlikely. Consequently, we each define our territory, plough the field, sow our seeds, and harvest our crops. As long as we invite each other for dinner, we can continue to learn from each other.

REFERENCES

Bearison, D. J., & Sigel, I. E. Hierarchical attributes for categorization. *Perceptual and Motor Skills,* 1968, *27,* 147–153.

Brissett, D. C., & Edgley, C. (Eds.), *Life as theater: A dramaturgical sourcebook.* Chicago: Aldine, 1975.

Chein. I. The environment as a determinant of behavior. *Journal of Social Psychology,* 1954, *39,* 115–127.

Chi. M. T. H. Knowledge structures and memory development. In R. S. Siegler (Ed.), *Children's thinking: What develops?* Hillsdale, N.J.: Lawrence Erlbaum Associates, 1978.

Goffman, E. *Frame analysis: Essay on the organization of experience.* New York: Harper & Row, 1974.

Hunt, D. E., & Sullivan, E. B. *Between psychology and education.* Hinsdale, Ill.: Dryden Press, 1974.

Lane, M. (Ed.). *An introduction to structuralism.* New York: Basic Books, 1970.

Laosa, L. Measures for the study of maternal teaching strategies. *Applied Psychological Measurement,* 1980, *4,* 355–366.

Lewin, K. *Principles of topological psychology.* New York: McGraw-Hill, 1936.

Lewin, K. Behavior and development as a function of the total situation. In L. Carmichael (Ed.), *Manual of child psychology.* New York: Wiley, 1954.

Liben, L. S. Evidence for developmental differences in spontaneous seriation and its implications for past research in long term memory improvement. *Developmental Psychology,* 1975, *11,* 121–125.

Liben, L. S. *Children's reproductions of operative stimuli: Perceptual or mnemonic distortion.* Paper presented at the 86th Annual Convention of the American Psychological Association, Toronto, August 1978.

Liben, L. S. Individuals' contributions to their own development during childhood: A Piagetian perspective. In R. M. Lerner & N. Busch-Rossnagel (Eds.), *Individuals as producers of their development.* New York: Academic Press, 1981.

Liben, L. S. The developmental study of children's memory. In T. M. Field, A. Huston, H. C. Quay, L. Troll, & G. E. Finley (Eds.), *Review of human development.* New York: Wiley, 1982.

Minsky, M. A framework for representing knowledge. In P. Winston (Ed.), *The psychology of computer vision.* New York: McGraw-Hill, 1975.

Murray, H. A. *Explorations in personality.* New York: Oxford, 1938.

Neisser, U. *Cognition and reality: Principles and implications of cognitive psychology.* San Francisco: Freeman, 1976.

Nelson, K. How children represent knowledge of the world in and out of language: A preliminary report. In R. Siegler (Ed.), *Children's thinking: What develops?* Hillsdale, N.J.: Lawrence Erlbaum Associates, 1978.

Olmsted, P. P., & Sigel, I. E. The generality of color-form preference as a function of materials and task requirements among lower-class Negro children. *Child Development,* 1970, *41,* 1025–1032.

Piaget, J. *Play, dreams and imitation in childhood.* New York: Norton, 1951.

Piaget, J. Piaget's theory. In P. H. Mussen (Ed.), *Carmichael's manual of child psychology* (Vol. 2) (3rd ed.). New York: Wiley, 1970. (a)

Piaget, J. *Structuralism.* New York: Basic Books, 1970. (b)

Piaget, J. *Biology and knowledge.* Chicago: University of Chicago Press, 1971.

Piaget, J. *The development of thought.* New York: Viking Press, 1977.

Puff, C. R. (Ed.). *Memory organization and structure.* New York: Academic Press, 1979.

Ross, B. M., & Kerst, S. M. Developmental memory theories: Baldwin and Piaget. In H. W. Reece & L. P. Litsett (Eds.), *Advances in child development and behavior* (Vol. 12). New York: Academic Press, 1978.

Siegler, R. S. The origins of scientific reasoning. In R. S. Siegler (Ed.), *Children's thinking: What develops?* Hillsdale, N.J.: Lawrence Erlbaum Associates, 1978.

Sigel, I. E. Developmental trends in the abstraction ability of children. *Child Development,* 1953, *24,* 131–144.

Sigel, I. E. The dominance of meaning. *Journal of Genetic Psychology,* 1954, *85,* 201–207.

Sigel, I. E. The distancing hypothesis: A causal hypothesis for the acquisition of representational thought. In M. R. Jones (Ed.), *Miami Symposium on the Prediction of Behavior, 1968: Effect of early experience.* Coral Gables, Fla.: University of Miami Press, 1970.

Sigel, I. E. The development of classificatory skills in young children: A training program. *Young Children,* 1971, *26*(3), 170–184.

Sigel, I. E. The development of pictorial comprehension. In B. S. Randhawa & W. E. Coffman (Eds.), *Visual learning, thinking, and communication.* New York: Academic Press, 1978.

Sigel, I. E., Anderson, L. M., & Shapiro, H. Categorization behavior of lower and middle class Negro preschool children: Differences in dealing with representation of familiar objects. *Journal of Negro Education,* 1966, *35*(3), 218–229.

Sigel, I. E., & Cocking, R. R. Cognition and communication: A dialectic paradigm for development. In M. Lewis & L. A. Rosenblum (Eds.), *Interaction, conversation, and the development of language: The origins of behavior* (Vol. 5). New York: Wiley, 1977.

Werner, H. *Comparative psychology of mental development.* Chicago: Follett, 1948.

8

Newton, Einstein, Piaget, and the Concept of Self: The Role of the Self in the Process of Knowing

Michael Lewis
Rutgers Medical School

This essay is concerned with the relationship of the knower to the known. It is particularly useful for developmental study to consider three aspects of the problem: (1) the knower, something that I refer to as the self; (2) the known, that is, information about the world; (3) the relationship between the knower and the known. Such a distinction does not imply that these aspects are separate; to the contrary, they are inseparable by their very nature. The advantage in focusing selectively on these three aspects is heuristic. The various sections of this chapter, although concerned with a set of diverse problems, should lead toward a more focused frame in which to consider this relationship both from a general epistemological view and from a developmental perspective.

The problem of the relationship between the known and knower can be viewed in a variety of ways with each aspect focusing on a distinct issue. In what follows, seven views are presented that demonstrate the interdependence of the known and knower. Little attention has been paid to the interconnections between these issues; instead, each is dealt with separately as it applies to some aspect of the role of the self in knowing.

First, the common-sense view of this relationship is considered in a set of three examples. Such examples remind us that this epistemological problem expresses itself often and in everyday terms. Second, the initial developments in the child's construction of a self are described. Using self-recognition tasks, Lewis and Brooks-Gunn (1979a) have demonstrated that during infancy self-knowledge emerges with and facilitates knowledge of both objects and people. This demonstration of the existence of a ''knower'' so early in life establishes the problem of the relationship between knowing and knower at the start of the developmental process.

141

In the third section, the role of self is discussed within the context of the history of science. In particular, the relevance of the self in knowing for the study of both quantum mechanics and relativity theory demonstrates the need to consider both the scientist and the science. By altering the Baconian and Newtonian views of science and the universe, contemporary physicists shook the foundations of past models of epistemology. Specific ways of knowing (e.g., through classification) may depend on aspects of the knower. Specifically, the fourth section presents the results of a life-span study indicating that age classifications depend on the age of the beholder. This consideration leads to a definition of social cognition in the fifth section in which one's internal feelings and perceptions distinguish social and nonsocial cognition rather than external characteristics of the stimuli. In the sixth section, the role of self is considered in the understanding of "private acts" such as feeling and thinking of others. Finally, the seventh section offers the conclusion that even the scientific method is not free of the knower–known relationship and that even in the higher forms of knowing the role of the knower must be considered.

The relationship between the knower and the known presents itself whenever knowledge is constructed. In a paper entitled "The Meaning of a Response or Why Developmental Psychologists Should Be Oriental Metaphysicians" (Lewis, 1967), I concluded that the meaning of a behavioral act, both for the child and experimenter, not only was a construction based on behavior but was, by the very nature of its construction, relative to the "constructor." That is, the construction of meaning is embedded in a larger network of previously accepted meaning systems. It is impossible to understand the development of the child until one appreciates this interconnection. Behavior in general and any single behavior in particular cannot be used to construct meaning in an absolute sense. Thus, for example, the meaning of words can only be understood as they are embedded in other words, sentences, and paragraphs, or as they are embedded in the actions of self or others (Bloom, 1973).

Lest we think we can take refuge in a biological outlook where behavior and meaning are thought to share a common thread, we have only to be reminded that meaning must be constructed by those who study it, and therefore meaning is always relative. For example, postural behaviors are often used to give meaning to a feeling state. Tail wagging is such a behavior in that it reflects friendliness in dogs. However, this simple motor response may be misleading. Although tail wagging reflects a friendly, approachable attitude in dogs, tail wagging in cats indicates a disturbed, "stay away" state. Even within the same species, a particular behavior may take on a different meaning when embedded in a different context (Lewis & Starr, 1979). For example, preening in ducks can be regarded either as a cleaning behavior or as a displacement behavior exhibited during sex or aggression. Another example is head bobbing, which in ducks is an aggressive act in a male–male interaction but a courtship behavior in a male–female interaction (Tinbergen, 1951). Thus, the dependence of behavior on context for meaning suggests that the study of behavior is ambiguous. Any particular behavior possesses little meaning in and of itself. Therefore, the meaning given to an event can never be absolute but must be considered relative, not only to the beholder (whether child or adult, subject or experimenter) but also to concurrent events.

The problems in the construction of meaning are problems shared by the developing child and the scientist. Throughout the chapter, this parallelism appears in discussing the relationship between the knower and known. If the enterprise is profitable, we can see that the meaning of scientific facts—accepted as "true" representations of some collective reality—is constructed through their relationship to other facts and to the scientist. Indeed, scientists studying quantum mechanics have reached similar conclusions about the physical world. According to Strapp (in Zukav, 1979), the physical world is: "not a structure built out of independently existing unanalyzable entities, but rather a web of relationships between elements whose meanings arise wholly from their relationships to the whole [p. 103]." Although it appears to be a tautology, facts are considered facts primarily because they are related to other events we call facts. For example, scores on a personality inventory (or measures of any set of behaviors) are validated against other scales or sets of behaviors, which are themselves validated against still other behaviors. Thus, as Kuhn (1970) argues, science is not so much the heroic pitting of one paradigm against another as the more mundane task of collecting information that is accepted or rejected as fact within the current zeitgeist.

MAKING SENSE OF THE WORLD

My exploration of the relationship between the knower and known was influenced by three occurrences that provide a convenient starting point in the analysis of this problem. First, I suggested to a young man deliberating about possible career choices that he consider the discipline of psychology. After some thought and further conversations, he said that he did not want to be a psychologist but would rather be a physicist because "anyone can be a psychologist, but not everyone can be a physicist."

This statement seems to reflect perceived differences in the intellectual (and other) skills necessary to be successful in each career. Yet it is not clear that physics requires more intellectual ability than psychology, and the little data that exist on the subject do not show that physicists score higher than psychologists on standard intelligence tests. However, upon more reflection it seems that the young man may have been right. Indeed, anyone can be a psychologist because all human beings are psychologists. To live and interact with other people and objects necessitates knowledge of both oneself and the external world. Inasmuch as the study of psychology has, in fact, the task of making explicit our implicit knowledge, the statement that "anyone can be a psychologist" is not altogether incorrect. However, a more accurate form of the statement would be "we are all psychologists."

This same issue is raised when the amusing but disturbing phrase "Buba psychology" is applied to some areas of study. *Buba* is the Russian word for grandmother, and Buba psychology refers to the wisdom that can only be acquired through a lifetime of experience. Buba psychology, then, cannot be taught in a classroom; rather, it is learned by living. As discussed by Lewin in the early 1900s, the relatively lower esteem of psychology may derive in part from the knower already having some knowledge about the known. Thus, it may be the case that the degree of esteem accorded to a discipline is determined by the extent to which what is to be discovered is already known. The history of science seems to support this claim in that the various scientific disciplines have evolved in an inverse relationship to their proximity to day-to-day human activity, starting first with investigations of the heavens and moving slowly into this century's concern for the study of human behavior.

The view that the status of a science is related to its complexity receives some support from a recent report by Armstrong (1981). An experimenter had faculty members rate 10 management journals on their prestige and concluded these ratings with measures of readability of the articles contained in the journals. The results showed that low scores on readability were positively correlated (.67) with high prestige. That is, journals with hard-to-read articles were rated higher in prestige than journels with articles that were easier to read. This had nothing to do with the complexity of the articles in the various journals because the experimenter also found that easy-to-read versions were rated lower in competence than more difficult versions of the same article.

My second example comes from religion. In Christianity there are several texts that are not considered part of the core of the religion, such as the Greek *Gospel of Thomas* and the *Apocryphon* ("secret book") *of John.* Pagels (1979) has published a book called *The Gnostic Gospels* in which she recalls the discovery in 1945 of a large set of texts or gospels reported to be written around the same time as the four New Testament gospels, which are accepted as the basis of Christianity. These other texts were banned, and those who believed them were excommunicated from the church and declared heretics. The explanation of this event is related both to the issue of the relationship between the knower and known and to the meaning of *gnosis.*

The Greek word *gnosis* is usually translated as knowledge. The Greek language, however, distinguishes between scientific and reflective knowledge (e.g., "she knows historical facts" vs. "she knows me" or knowing through observation or experience). It is this latter form of knowing that is *gnosis.* From the Gospel of Truth, one of the recently discovered texts, it is clear that one group of early Christians believed that to know God required that they also know themselves. This was the heresy of these believers. According to Pagels (1979), while the group now considered orthodox Christians "insisted that a chasm separates humanity from its creator: God is wholly other . . . the gnostics contradicted this. They held that self-knowledge is knowledge of God; the self and the divine are identical [p. xx]."

In short, this gnostic view broke down the barrier between what was to be known and the knower. The orthodox view held that what was to be known, God, could only be known through some intermediary. The intermediaries were the true disciples, those to whom God had given authority. Thus, the gnostics posed a threat to the structure of the church and to clerical authority. Consequently, this form of gnosis was declared heretical.

In this example the issue of the knower and the known is again central. For orthodox Christians, knowing is a process of distancing oneself from the known, thereby creating a chasm that separates the two. For the gnostics, knowing was to be found in the process of knowing oneself: Through the use of oneself, the barrier separating the knower from the known could be broken.

In the third example, the nature of the scientist and science are considered directly. In thinking about the scientific enterprise or, for that matter, any intellectual enterprise, I cannot help being struck by something almost too obvious to mention. On virtually any topic there are people who subscribe to very different views. Although it is not surprising to find disagreement between a learned and ignorant person, to find disagreement between two learned people is something of a surprise. These differences of opinion within a discipline cannot be accounted for by claiming that one side is more intelligent than the other (although this might be the case). Rather, such differences are more often explained by basic models or paradigmatic differences between the combatants (e.g., Reese & Overton, 1970). It is usually at this level that the consideration of difference is left.

This problem could be pursued further, however, by asking where and how these different paradigms arise. How is it that two highly intelligent scientists, each possessing similar information, can arrive at discrepant sets of conclusions? The answer to this question may lie in the parallelism between the scientific knowing and personal knowing of individuals. The answer again involves the relationship between the knower and known. In this example, one must move beyond the paradigmatic view and ask what it is about an individual that facilitates thinking about a problem in a particular way. It is important then to examine characteristics of the knower in order to understand what is known (or at least thought to be known). In particular, certain characteristics of scientists may affect the truth value they assign to an event as well as the inclination of the scientific community to accept an event as fact. Thus, the announcement of an unusual and unexpected discovery is more readily accepted when made by a well-known and respected scientist than by an unknown student. Indeed, pronouncements of eminent scholars often extend beyond their particular areas of expertise, yet they are listened by others because of their prestige. Thus, the acceptance of what is known goes well beyond mere statistical probability levels and involves the personal attributes of the scientist.

The scientist is related to science in other ways as well. As every sociology major is taught, one must be somewhat suspicious of an informant, especially when the informant is telling something that he or she wishes to be true. Are we more or less likely to believe a finding when it was predicted in advance by the investigator than when it was not? Predicted facts have a higher regard than nonpredicted ones, as is suggested by the difference between one- and two-tailed statistical tests. However, we would be much less likely to believe that smoking is injurious to health if the investigator is someone who does not smoke and believes smoking to be vile.

The scientific enterprise usually assumes that the characteristics of the scientist are orthogonal to the phenomenon investigated. A corollary to this is the belief that whenever a relationship exists between the knower and known, the facts discovered are likely to be suspect. For example, if we were to give a personality inventory to two groups of scientists who held different theories and found that the groups differed along some personality dimension, both theories might be challenged. Consequently, one of the primary goals of western science is to separate the scientist from the science, or the knower from the known.

Unfortunately, relatively little research on the characteristics of scientists have been conducted. Exceptions to this are provided by Roe (1951, 1953), Eiduson (1962), and Hudson (1972), all of whom have found significant and interesting scientist differences between and within various scientific disciplines. Thus, although much of the scientific enterprise since the time of Bacon has tried to separate, isolate, and distance the scientist from the phenomena being studied, this may be impossible.

In sum, the three examples highlight the thesis that what is known is not necessarily independent of the knower. However, before discussing the issue of the interaction between the knower and known, the nature of the knower, or the issue of the self, should be addressed. The following summary of the early origins of self-knowledge demonstrates in part that the study of even the earliest forms of knowing must consider the knower in relationship to the known.

THE KNOWER OR SELF

Many have written about the self, self-concept, and self-esteem (e.g., Epstein, 1980; Gergen, 1971; Rosenberg, 1965), but few scientists have focused on these issues from a developmental perspective. Recently, we initiated a series of studies aimed at finding measures that could be used with preverbal children to provide information about children's emerging concepts of self (Lewis & Brooks-Gunn, 1979a). In these studies, the self is viewed as subject or agent and also as object (Lewis & Brooks, 1975; Wylie, 1974). In particular, we have investigated three domains: (1) children's early knowledge about relationships with their social world; (2) children's early emotional development; (3) children's early control over the object (nonsocial) world. By the end of the first 2 years of life, children enjoy a rich knowledge of their social world and of the assorted people who inhabit it (Lewis, 1979). What is more important is that children form important, complex, and reciprocal relationships with a number of people usually including their mother, father, siblings, friends, and other caregivers. In fact, these relationships appear in their earliest forms within the first year of life (Ainsworth, Belhar, Waters, & Wall, 1978). Although more evidence is needed, there is reason to believe that children's early interactions with others contribute to the development of a general schema in the infant. These interactions may affect social relationships through their role in the development of a specific self–other schema. Indeed, it is difficult to imagine social relationships that do not have as a fundamental feature the ability of a dyadic member both to distinguish and to utilize knowledge about self and other. Relationships, by definition, require the negotiation of two or more selves (Mead, 1934; Sullivan, 1953).

Later in this chapter, the distinction between private and public acts is considered in some detail. For the moment, however, one class of private acts, feelings and emotions, can be considered in terms of its relationship to self. In considering the difference between emotional states and experiences the role of the self as object takes on some meaning. My colleagues and I (Lewis, 1980; Lewis & Brooks-Gunn, 1978; Lewis & Michalson, 1982) have tried to distinguish between signs of emotional states (e.g., changes in facial, vocal, postural, and physiological activity) and actual emotional experiences (which include the attending[1] to these behavioral and somatosensory changes and the accompanying thoughts or statements such as ''I am fearful'' or ''I am hungry''). The ability to reflect on a set of events that occur inside oneself rather than somewhere else suggests the importance of considering the development of self.

The demonstration of the control of behavior, such as in the case of an infant causing a mobile to move (Watson, 1966), leads us to consider the source of that control. Early in the child's life the source of the effect may be located in the stimulus itself or in some combinations of the stimulus with the discriminate stimuli surrounding it, but by the time the child is 5- or 6-months-old there is reason to believe that the effect is being caused by the child's intention (Piaget, 1954). Explanations that invoke sensorimotor schema (in particular, complex circular reactions) appear reasonable. However, these reactions and the development of a concept of means and ends also suggest that the self as agent is beginning to emerge. Means–ends behaviors and the ability to select different means to reach the same goal imply some type of planning on the part of the

---

[1]Attending here refers to the conscious level. However, it is possible that similar processes occur at some unconscious level as well.

child. Planning, however rudimentary, requires goals and subgoals, checking progress against such goals, and the changing of behavior that fails to meet the goals. Setting goals and executing motor acts imply the existence of intentions and agency in whatever way young children might conceptualize them. Indeed, whether children know of their agency or intention (i.e., whether they have a meta-intention) is not clear, and it is not necessary (nor reasonable) for us to infer it in our study of the self.

The confluence of such issues around the self as subject and object and the lack of inquiry into the development of self led to a series of studies (Lewis & Brooks-Gunn, 1979a) in which we used the term *development of self* to refer to children's construction of agency (self as subject), a me–other distinction, and self as an object that has attributes such as feelings, physical features, and a name.

We focused on self-development in the first 2 years of life because after this period children's language and their behaviors lead us to believe that a concept of self as subject is already operating. Undoubtedly, children continue to acquire self-knowledge after 2 years of age, but the origins seem to be located in this earlier period. In describing the development of self, one word of caution is in order: Self-recognition is measured by responses to reflected surfaces, TV monitors, and still and motion pictures. Although the ability to recognize oneself implies both a self–other distinction (self as subject) and a recognition of specific physical attributes of the self (self as object), the relationship between these measures of self-recognition and self-concept or other aspects of self-awareness has not been established.

The following description derives both from our work (Lewis & Brooks-Gunn, 1979a) and from others who are cited as we proceed. The periods presented are not fixed; rather, they represent a starting point for further inquiry and as such have heuristic value in providing a possible map for this unexplored area.

Period 1: Birth to 3 Months.   This period can be characterized chiefly by a biological determinism. There exist both simple and complex reflexes including responses to others that enhance interactions with the caregivers. Reflexive behavior, at first predominant, declines over this period as early schema and learning begin to predominate (Lewis & Brooks-Gunn, 1979a; Lipsitt, 1980; Papousek & Papousek, 1981). Infant's differentiation among social objects and simple circular reactions can be seen. Through both social and object interactions, the beginnings of a self–other differentiation may make its appearance at the end of this period.

Period 2: 3 to 8 Months.   During this period, active learning takes precedence over a waning reflex system. Object interactions and social behavior are facilitated by developing cognitive processes of memory, discriminability, and the development of a more elaborate schema. Complex action-outcome pairings occur along with means–ends relationships in both the social and object domains. Primary and secondary circular reactions are almost developed, and the child learns of its effect on the world; agency and intention can be inferred. The distinction between self and other is consolidated but cannot be conserved over changes in the nature of the interaction, either in terms of people or objects. Reflected surfaces become interesting due to the contingency between the child's action and the action in the mirror (Dixon, 1957; Rheingold, 1971). There is little evidence of self-recognition, but children are able to adjust their body position in regard to visual changes in spatial cues indicating an elaborate visual-body schema in spatial knowledge (Butterfield & Hicks, 1977; Lee & Aronson, 1974).

Period 3: 8 to 12 Months.   One of the most critical features of this period is the establishment of self–other differentiation, which takes place through the initial conservation of the self as distinct from the other across most situations. This conservation of self as subject represents the first important conservation task and has parallels to the child's growing understanding of object existence. Indeed, object permanence and self-permanence must be viewed as parallel processes (Lewis & Brooks-Gunn, 1979a). The self as unique and permanent across time and space emerges. Although feature recognition does not exist in any appreciable way, self-recognition can be demonstrated in contingent situations (Lewis & Brooks-Gunn, 1979a). The emergence of self as agent facilitates more complex means–ends relationships, and with growing cognitive ability more elaborate plans can be observed.

Period 4: 12 to 30 Months.   This might be divided into two periods: the 12- to 18-month period, or what Dixon (1957) calls the "coy" stage, and the 18- to 30-month period, or "self-recognition" stage (Amsterdam, 1972). There are several important markers in this period. During the earlier period, coyness in front of the mirror becomes increasingly apparent, and fear of the loss of the mother becomes intense. These appear to be additional markers in the self–other differentiation. Between 12 and 18 months, self-recognition becomes less dependent on contingency and increasingly more dependent on feature analysis. The self as object becomes more evident in this feature recognition. Pointing behavior emerges, and self-recognition is evidenced through pointing to pictures of the self and through pointing to marks on the nose seen in reflecting surfaces. After 18 months, simple language knowledge (i.e., the mapping of the lexicon on some features) emerges and allows children to demonstrate knowledge of features of social objects, including themselves. These include gender and age (Brooks-Gunn & Lewis, 1979; Lewis & Brooks-Gunn, 1979a; Lewis, Edwards, Weistuch, & Cortelyou, 1981). Such knowledge supports the belief that the self as object emerges at this time and possesses a number of attributes, including good or bad and efficacy along with age and gender.

This overview, although sketchy, nevertheless provides an outline for the early development of the self. From it we can tentatively conclude that the assumption of the existence of a knower, even in early childhood, has some empirical support. As to the nature of the known, the bulk of research in the last 2 decades attests to what is known (or what can be demonstrated as known) by young children. Having addressed the issue of the knower and known from a developmental perspective, we can now turn to the problem of the relationship between the knower and known using as a more general framework issues in the history of science.

NEWTON, EINSTEIN, AND QUANTUM MECHANICS

The scientific method is designed to generate theory and predict events. These goals appear to be achieved, in part, through the separation of the scientist from the phenomena being investigated. Thus, the experimenter's word and belief are replaced by a method. This distancing of the individual from the phenomena of study through a commonly accepted method of empirical proof, reliability of measures, and logic represents a major event in the development of the scientific method.

Indeed, on an individual level, intellectual abstraction serves to distance the individual from events or objects. One function of a symbol is to separate the thinker from that which the symbol has come to represent. This process of separation serves the same function for both the individual and the science. It is an attempt to know through the reification of the thing to be known and assumes, in a Platonic sense, that there exists a reality or ideal independent of the knower.

One founder of these ideas was Francis Bacon, who in the early 17th century offered the western mind one of the first strongly empirical views of a philosophy of science. In *Advancement of Learning,* Bacon (see Durant, 1954) urged more systematic experimentation and documentation: "They [the physicians] rely too much on mere haphazard, uncoordinated *individual experience;* let them experiment more widely, . . . and above all, let them construct an easily accessible and intelligible record of experiments and results [p. 121]." In his first book of the Novum Organum, Bacon (see Durant, 1954) challenged existing metaphysical views: "Man, as the minister and interpreter of nature, does and understands as much as his observations on the order of nature . . . permit him, and neither knows nor is capable of more [p. 129]." He argued (see Durant, 1954) that science must rid itself of the machinery established by Aristotle and must become as "little children, innocent of isms and abstractions, washed clear of prejudices and preconceptions [p. 129]." In a word, Bacon counseled scientists to separate themselves from that which they wished to study.

Toward this goal, Bacon outlined the famous set of errors. The first is the *idols of the tribe,* which are fallacies considered natural to all human beings. Bacon rejected Protagoras' assertion that "man is the measure of all things" and wished to substitute a logical method free from the distortions of the human mind. This need for the scientist to become objective also implied that passions or emotions (anything hinting of subjectivity) be removed (see Durant, 1954): "In general let every student of nature take this as a rule that whatever his mind seizes and dwells upon with peculiar satisfaction, is to be held in suspicion; and that so much the more care is to be taken, in dealing with such questions, to keep the understanding even and clear [p. 131]."

The second class of errors, *idols of the cave,* is caused by particular characteristics of the individual. They may be due to prejudices, personality traits, past history, or socialization. For Bacon (see Durant, 1954), such errors are a personal cave, "which refracts and discolors the light of nature [p. 131]."

The third type of errors, *idols of the marketplace,* arises between individuals as a result of differences in communication styles, in language usage, and imperfections caused by the commerce of ideas. Finally, there are *idols of the theatre,* which are caused by the errors of others. These are the errors of dogma, the errors of "-isms."

From this list of errors, Bacon proceeded to explicate his scientific method of inquiry with its hypothesis generation, empirical methodology, results, and conclusions. Bacon's view of science flourished, first in the founding of the Royal Society in 1660 and then in the work of Newton who articulated a particular view of the universe and the role of science in comprehending that universe.

This view of science and the role of the scientist were carried into modern times, infusing the entire scientific enterprise. However, Bacon's view, along with the universe as constructed by Newton, were to be radically altered in the 20th century by modern physics. Einstein's revolutionary insight into the nature of relativity and Planck and Bohr's development of quantum mechanics profoundly altered our understanding of the relationship of knower to known, not only in physics but in other scientific domains as well. Before we apply these thoughts in developmental psychology to our own problems, a brief description of Newton's ideas and the emergence of modern physics is necessary.

Around the time of the founding of the Royal Society, Newton was ready to deliver his views, which became the foundation of contemporary science. With gravity as its center and the use of mathematical laws to explain planets, stars, small particles, and the actions of people, Newton constructed a simple but bold synthesis of the physical world and universe. The cornerstone of his entire system was the belief in the absolute nature of time and space. For Newton (see Clark, 1972):

Absolute time and mathematical time of itself and from its own nature, flows equally, without relations to anything external, and by another name is called duration . . .

Space could be absolute space, in its own nature, without relation to anything external which remains always similar and immovable; or relative space which was some moveable dimension or measure of the absolute space [p. 103].

To the degree that Newton went beyond the merely observable and constructed these theories, he had acted contrary to both Bacon's prescription and his own stated intention of only investigating tangible facts.

Newton's conception of the universe as an absolute and orderly system stood for over 200 years. Indeed, his view held so strong a sway over the minds of the physicists (see Clark, 1972) that they could say: "In the beginning . . . God created Newton's laws of motion together with necessary masses and forces. This is all; everything beyond this follows the development of appropriate mathematical methods by means of deduction [p. 59]." In this view, a person could examine the workings of this orderly universe and extract general principles and laws that could further explain the observed relationships. Newton's theories represent the most powerful example of the separation between the role of the knower and the known. Scientific objectivity, for Newton, rested upon the belief that there is an external world "out there" as opposed to an internal world, the "I" which is "in here." Nature is "out there," and the task of the scientist is to study those phenomena "out there."

The Newtonian universe, however, was imperfect, and toward the end of the 19th and early part of the 20th century many scientists began to question its truths. The planet Mercury refused to conform to Newton's laws. Ernst Mach and Henri Poincare, among others, challenged Newton's notions of absolute space and time. However, a radically new vision of the universe was provided by Einstein and 20th century quantum mechanics, accompanied by a totally new view of the nature of the scientific enterprise. Moreover, the new view of the universe and science brought with it a new view of the relationship between the knower and the known.

Einstein produced in a single year three papers that were to change forever the cherished view of the universe. To trace Einstein's influences, or indeed to expound his theory, is beyond the scope of this chapter. Nevertheless, it is important to note that his contribution took the form of a statement of relativity. No longer was the notion of "absolute" to dominate our ideas of the universe. Instead, the terms "relativity" and "probability" entered our discussions. For Einstein, relativity meant that the existing laws of nature were only valid when all observers moved at rates uniformly relative to one another. Einstein described relativity in many forms (see Clark, 1972) such as one in which he speaks of simultaneity as the perceived relationship between two things: "So we see that we cannot attach any absolute significance to the concept of simultaneity, but that two events which, viewed from a system of coordinates, are simultaneous, can no longer be looked upon as simultaneous events when envisaged from a system which is in motion relatively to that system [p. 182]."

Einstein's views of time, speed, and space changed the view of an absolute universe. The properties of objects, time, and space were not independent but dependent and changing according to the particular system from which they were viewed. Events became dependent on probabilities rather than absolute certainties. The impact of these ideas was profound on all of our notions of what was "absolute" and what was "real."

For example, Arthur Eddington (see Clark, 1972), in talking about the changing notions regarding property of objects, included a statement that suggested the perspective of knower to the known was not only of interest but was a necessity for proper interpretations of the data: "When a rod is started from rest into uniform motion, nothing whatever happens to the rod. We say that it contracts; but length is not a property of the rod; it is a relation between the rod and the observer. Until the observer is specified, the length of the rod is quite indeterminate [p. 120]."

Such statements capture a profound change in our view of nature. Although this new view may have had little impact on the everyday lives of most people and their perceptions of the world of objects and people, the effect on philosophers was profound. In Eddington's statement, "Until the observer is specified, the length of the rod is quite indeterminate," the knower and known enter into a relationship unthought of in the Newtonian period.

Einstein's theory of relativity and the study of quantum mechanics changed the notion of what science is and the perceived relationship of the scientist to science. No longer could one think of either scientists or knowers studying a phenomenon without considering their relationship to that phenomenon. The phenomenon no longer was believed to possess absolute properties, as scientists once believed.

Modern physics soon went beyond even Einstein's conception. Born, Heisenberg, and Bohr, working within the discipline of quantum physics, conceptualized the universe in a way that leveled all remaining notions of absolute and certainty. No longer is anything certain; probabilities are all that govern. No longer could one say that at a certain time a particle will be found in a certain place with a certain amount of energy or momentum. Such statements of certainty had to be altered to statements of probabilities.

However, in the study of subatomic particles, quantum mechanics was to go beyond merely stating probabilities. Not only was the notion of certainty shown to be incorrect, but the belief in a reality unaffected by human action was undermined. To some degree, human observation and measurement actually create the phenomenon of study. Quantum physicists began to consider questions such as: "Did a particle with momentum exist before we measured its momentum?" Thus, the relationship of knower to known became one of the major questions of quantum mechanics. A statement by John Wheeler (see Zukav, 1979) illustrates this well:

May the universe in some strange sense be 'brought into being' by the participation of those who participate? . . . The vital act is the act of participation. 'Participator' is the incontrovertible new concept given by quantum mechanics. It strikes down the term 'observer' of classical theory, the man who stands safely behind the thick glass wall and watches what goes on without taking part. It can't be done, quantum mechanics says [p. 54].

The developments of quantum mechanics produced startling consequences. Not only was our view of the universe changed, but we found we could no longer describe the universe with physical models. The universe was no longer reflected in ordinary sensory perceptions. It no longer allowed for the description of things but only the relationship between things, a relationship that was probabilistic. Furthermore, the distinction between an "out there" and an "in here," or an objective reality independent of the observer, was not feasible because it was impossible to observe anything without distorting it. Finally, the new view of the universe destroyed our belief that we could measure absolute truth; rather, we learned we can only correlate experience.

Although it is beyond the scope of this essay to detail the more recent developments in quantum mechanics, it should be noted that theories, which go beyond the issue of participation and observation as causes of the phenomenon of study, continue to evolve. For example, Everett (1973) suggests that it is not the case that only one of many possibilities occurs at a given time. Instead, possible events happen but in different worlds that coexist with ours.

The reduction of the absolute was complete. This new world view went beyond Einstein's personal belief. Until the end of his life, Einstein resisted the notions of chance and probability and sought to find lawful absolute principles that could be used to predict events with certainty. His now famous statement, "God does not play dice," relected his displeasure with the new conception. The nature of movement and the properties of matter, time, and space were relative. Epistemology, too, was changed. Referring to this change in view of science and knowing, Born (see Clark, 1972) writes that we had been:

> taught that there exists an objective physical world, which unfolds itself according to immutable laws independent of us. We are watching this process like the audience watches a play in a theatre. . . . Quantum mechanics, however, interprets the experience gained in atomic physics in a different way. We may compare the observer of a physical phenomenon not unlike the audience of a theatrical performance, but with that of a football game where the act of watching, accompanied by applauding or hissing, has a marked influence on the speed and concentration of the players, and thus on what is watched. In fact, a better simile is life itself, where audience and actors are the same persons. It is the action of the experimentalist who designs the apparatus which determines the essential features of the observations. Hence, there is no objectively existing situation, as was supposed to exist in classical physics [p. 143].

In sum, under the influence of Bacon and Newton, the object of the scientist was to remain uninvolved with the phenomena being studied. Indeed, the entire scientific enterprise and its methods revolved around this goal. Accompanying these aims was the notion of a reality that was independent of the scientist. New developments in the study of relativity and quantum physics, however, denied us this belief. Bohr's notion of "complementarity" directly affects the knower: The common denominator of all experiences is "I." Zukav (1979) states that experience, then, does not mirror external reality but "our interaction with it [p. 116]." The effect of such a conclusion on our role in knowing is profound. Zukav (1979), speaking of quantum physics, has the final word:

> Transferring the properties that we usually ascribe to light to our interaction with light deprives light of an independent existence. Without us, or by implication, anything else to interact with, light does not exist. This remarkable conclusion is only half the story. The other half is that, in a similar manner, without light, or, by implication, anything else to interact with, we do not exist! As Bohr himself put it, '. . . an independent reality in the ordinary physical sense can be ascribed neither to the phenomena nor to the agencies of observation' [p. 118].

Properties belong to the interaction of the phenomena and observer. It is to the notion of this relationship that our developmental inquiries must turn.

THE RELATIONSHIP
BETWEEN KNOWER AND KNOWN

Many examples can be found to document the interrelatedness of what is known and the knower. For instance, Bower's demonstration that who you identify with in a story will affect and change the interpretation of the story (Owens, Bower, & Black, 1979) suggests that the role of the self has an important influence in constructing information. Even more central to our concern is the demonstration that memory is facilitated if what is to be remembered is made relevant to the self (Hyde & Jenkins, 1969; Kruper & Rogers, in press; Rogers, Kui er, & Kirker, 1977).

Language acquisition is another area in which the relationship between self and knowing can be demonstrated. In researching the acquisition of prepositions, we have found a developmental sequence: The prepositions *in* and *out, on* or *under,* and *in front of* or *behind* are learned in that order. Almost all 2-year-olds know the meanings of *in* and *out,* but far fewer know *on* or *under,* and almost none know *in front of* or *behind.* Although 2-year-olds could demonstrate "on–under" knowledge by manipulating two objects, they had far less difficulty when asked to "get *on* the table" or "get *under* the table." That is, when they were one of the two objects that was to be related to another, the children had far less difficulty in demonstrating their knowledge than when they had to manipulate two objects in the same way. In a similar vein, Huttenlocker (personal communication, 1980) reports that intentional verbals are applied to the self prior to being applied to others.

The foregoing examples indicate that there is a difference in cognitive activity when the self is engaged. The influence of self on the outcome is no proof that a "factual" existence independent of self does not exist, but it does point out that in some forms of knowing the self plays an important role. In the discussion that follows, the effect of self on classification behavior is explored in more detail. The purpose of this demonstration is to provide an example of how the self (knower) interacts with the ability to order or classify information.

Age is one particular social feature that young children appear to learn and which is relatively easy to study. Because age is usually considered in terms of number of years, the acquisition of age knowledge or classification has not been studied before children are able to use number concepts and seriation. However, covarying with numerical age are physical features of the face and body, which children and adults may use to determine age apart from number of years. Indeed, number concepts may be mapped upon these initial features at a latter time.

In our earlier work, we found that young children rarely make age errors; that is, when asked to point to a picture of their father's face, when father's picture is embedded in a set of pictures containing other people of varying ages and sex, children between 15 and 24 months almost never make an error on age. They may pick the wrong adult, but seldom do they point to a child. Gender errors are also quite rare (Brooks-Gunn & Lewis, 1979; Lewis & Weinraub, 1976).

In order to explore age knowledge in more detail, we showed two sets of pictures to 60 children, 12 at each of 18, 21, 24, 30, and 36 months of age. The first set contained pictures of male faces: a baby (1 year), a child (3 years), and an adult (over 20 years), which the subjects were asked to identify as baby, child, or adult. The second set was the same except the faces were female. Thus, each child was given six trials; the total possible correct score was 6.

Figure 8.1 presents the results of this study. Observe that there are three curves. The solid-line curve represents the percentage of correct response when all children were included in the analysis. Notice that even here the 18-month-olds answer 15% of the questions correctly, and by 24 months nearly 60% are answered correctly. The statistical analyses were significant for the 24-month-old and older infants indicating that this is not a function of the performance of one or two subjects.

The dotted-line curve represents the percentage correct if we eliminate those children who never pointed to a single picture in all six trials. Because "pointing toward" is a difficult task, which also follows a developmental path, we thought it wise to eliminate these subjects. Of the nine subjects who never pointed, most were in the 18- and 21-month-age groups. We see now that 18-month-olds answer nearly 35% of the questions correctly, and 24-month-olds respond correctly to 65% of the questions. From then on, age differences are not significant on this task.

The dashed-line curve represents only those subjects who pointed at some picture on all six trials. These subjects represent those children who clearly

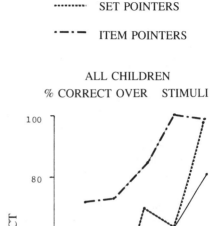

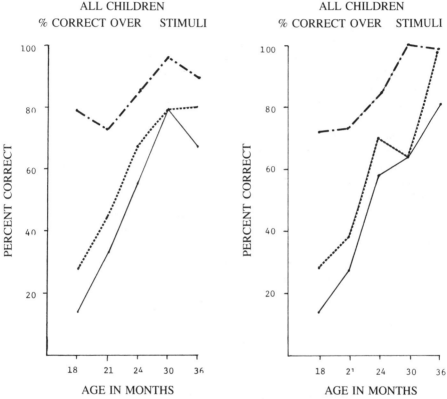

FIG. 8.1   Percentage of correct responses for all subjects, those who never pointed and those who pointed on each trial.

understood what was expected of them. As you can see, there is no developmental path for these subjects; if they understood what they were asked to do, they
could point to the correct picture. These results support our belief that even
young children have some knowledge of this feature of their social environment.

A study that can be used to exemplify the role of the knower in classification
extends this research (Lewis, Edwards, Weistuch & Cortelyou, 1981). Three- to
five-year-old children were asked to sort a set of pictures of faces. The faces
were of people aged 1 to 20 years in the first study and 1 to 70 years in the second

study. All children were given the same task; they were asked to sort the pictures into three piles (in the first study) and four piles (in the second study). The labels given to the piles were little girls and boys, big girls and boys, mothers and fathers, and, in the second study, grandmothers and grandfathers. The children were allowed to move pictures back and forth from one pile to another.

The results are depicted in Fig. 8.2. Notice that as the age of the person in the picture increases, the number of children who place that particular face in a particular pile changes. Of importance for our discussion is the age of transition. Notice that approximately 60% of the subjects place 5-year-old faces in the little girl and boy pile, whereas approximately 70% place the 7-year-old faces in the big girl and boy pile. We assume from this information that 6 years is the commonly preferred transition age between little and big children. Remember, no years are used in the study. Likewise, the transition age for children to parents appears to be 13 years and for parent to grandparent 40 years.

Adults (20- to 60-year-olds) also have little difficulty with the same task. However, the ages of transition have changed (Fig. 8.3). The age of transition between little and big children is now around 13 years, between big children and parents is between 17 and 20 years, and between parents and grandparents 40 years.

These results are not surprising. They show that the classification of age into groups, not by number of years old but by features, varies with the age of the respondent. For the 3-year-old child, the 7-year-old is big, whereas for the 20-year-old, the 7-year-old is little. Neither classification is incorrect; both use their own age to construct the classification system.

We gave a similar task to students in a graduate seminar by asking them to divide an imagined set of faces and ages into four groups. Inasmuch as the graduate students were not given any labels for the groups, they were free to select age ranges that fit their own classification system. Five of the students were in their early 20s, and two were in their late 30s. The younger students all considered the first group to contain ages 1 to 10 years, whereas the two older students created groups of 1 to 14 years and 1 to 20 years. Even more interesting was the final grouping. The younger students' oldest students both started at age 50 to 55 years and went to 70 years, whereas the older students both started at 65 years of age. Thus, using imaginary stimuli, the effect of one's own age on age classification is apparent.[2]

Before ending this discussion, two further results pertaining to age classification can be presented. In one study, 3-year-olds were asked to select from pictures of 3-, 7-, and 20-year-olds the picture that looked most like themselves. Male pictures were shown to boys and female pictures to girls. Of the 25 boys,

---

[2]We have since given this task to over 40 subjects varying in age from 31–65 years and have obtained similar results. Age classification appears to be dependent on the respondent's age.

15 chose the 7-year-old and 10 chose the 3-year-old face. Only 5 girls chose the 7-year-old face and 20 chose the 3-year-old face. This significant difference was also found to be related to children's choice of playmates. Children who thought they looked like the 7-year-old chose to play with a 7-year-old, whereas those who chose the 3-year-old face as like themselves chose to play with a 3-year-old (Edwards & Lewis, 1979; Lewis, Young, Brooks-Gunn, & Michalson, 1975). Though not directly related to the acquisition of knowledge, these findings illustrate the role of the self in social behavior (at least in social preference).

In sum, the rule on age classification (when age in years is not known) suggests that the classification system and its boundaries depend on the age of the classifier and that social preference also depends on the age of the participant. We can make use of this in our understanding of the acquisition of knowledge in general and social knowledge in particular.

SOCIAL COGNITION
AND THE ROLE OF THE SELF

Both the historical account that has been reviewed and the data on the role of the subject's age in age classification provide support for the proposition that the role of the knower cannot be overlooked in either the scientific enterprise or the study of knowing. The epistemological issue of the knower and known has been recognized by Piaget (1960) and other interactional psychologists (Polyani, 1958). For them, knowing involves the interaction of the knower with objects, events, or people. The structures of knowledge (e.g., schemata) are assumed to originate from this interaction; they are the structures of mind. The mind of the knower, although formed through interactions, is believed to exist independently of the knower. Indeed, it has been thought that the degree to which the knower remains involved in the known is a measure of the immaturity (egocentrism) of the knower.

Although it may be possible to separate the knower from the structures of knowledge for some forms of knowledge, there are structures of knowledge that, by necessity, depend on the knower. Rather than a dichotomy between two types of cognition, it is probably more useful to think of knowing as a continuum. Thus, the following discussion rests on the view that *cognition, in general, represents a continuum of involvement of the knower (or self) with what is known. Social cognition represents that part of the continuum where there is a marked relationship between the knower and the known.* In other words, without the use of the self, some things are impossible to know.[3]

---

[3]The distinction between hot and cold cognitions contains some of the same difference as stated here. Hot cognitions (emotions) appear to involve the self and as such may be different from those that do not.

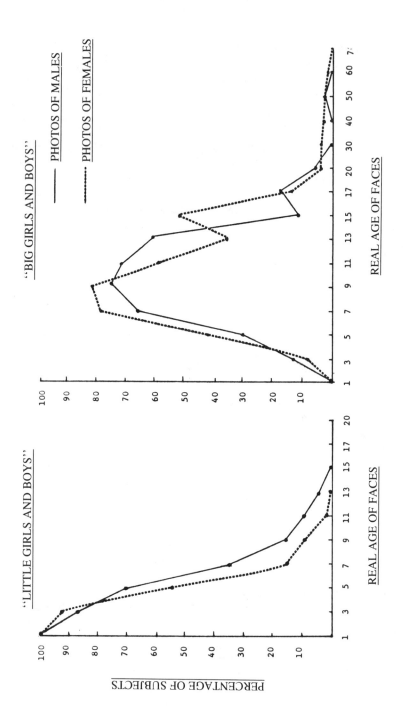

"BIG GIRLS AND BOYS"

—— PHOTOS OF MALES

······ PHOTOS OF FEMALES

REAL AGE OF FACES

"LITTLE GIRLS AND BOYS"

REAL AGE OF FACES

PERCENTAGE OF SUBJECTS

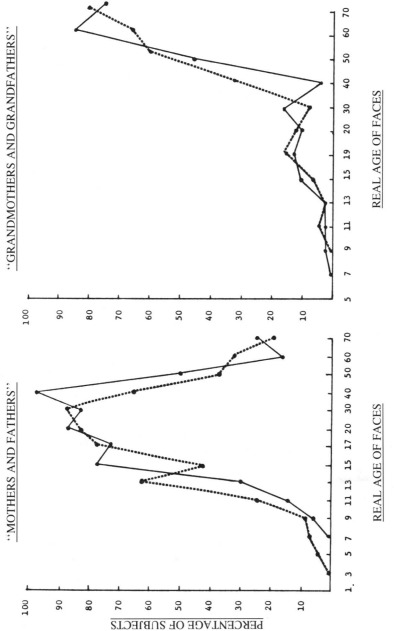

FIG. 8.2   Number of subjects classifying faces, 3–5 years old.

161

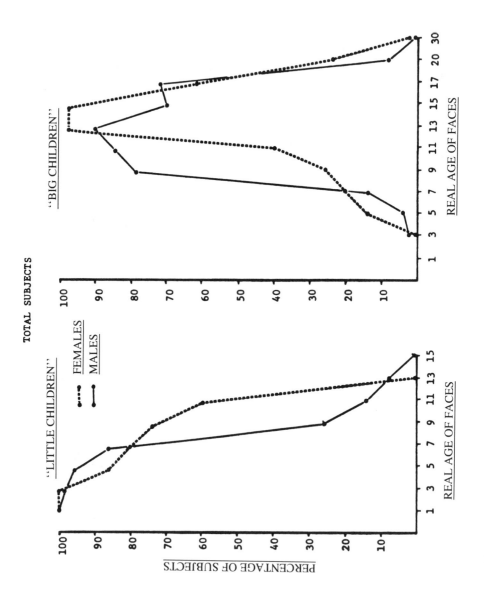

TOTAL SUBJECTS

"BIG CHILDREN"

REAL AGE OF FACES

"LITTLE CHILDREN"

FEMALES

MALES

REAL AGE OF FACES

PERCENTAGE OF SUBJECTS

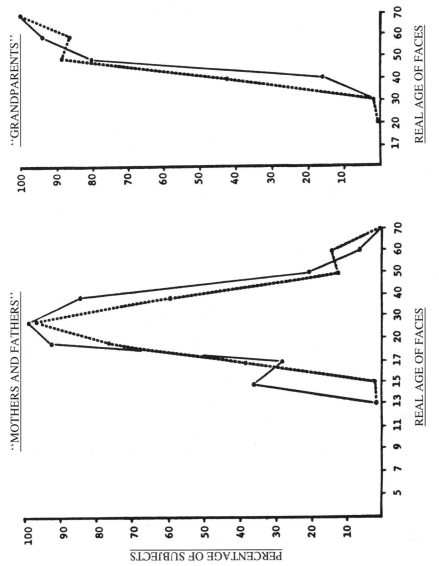

FIG. 8.3   Number of subjects classifying faces, 20–60 years old.

163

Social cognition has been defined as social perception (Bruner & Tagiuri, 1954), as the learning of social rules and obligations (Kohlberg, 1969), sex role knowledge (Mischel, 1970), and in terms of features such as age and gender (Edwards & Lewis, 1979). In each of these cases, the knowledge is considered social in that it applies to human beings, human attributes, and human products such as rules and obligations. To the degree that these pertain to features of human beings in some general sense, there is little reason to think that the knowledge formed and its developmental course should differ in any marked way from that already explicated by Piaget and others (Piaget, 1926, 1960; Piaget & Inhelder, 1956). So far as these features require little or no knowledge of the self, they are not relative and as such can be studied in a Newtonian fashion as other features, such as time, weight, and duration, have been studied. To the degree that these features do not involve the knower, they can be said to be absolute. Piaget has given careful attention to such features.

Social cognition has also been defined to include communicative competence (Krauss & Glucksberg, 1969), inferences about others (Flavell, 1974), role taking (Selman, 1971a, 1971b), and emotional experiences such as empathy (Hoffman, 1978). Tagiuri (1969) has offered a classification of social cognition involving events that are inside the person (e.g., intentions, attitudes, perceptions, consciousness, self-determination, etc.) and events between persons (e.g., friendship, love, etc.). These forms of knowledge are not independent of the knower, or self, because they pertain to knowledge that necessarily requires the use of the self. Role taking and empathy, for example, require that knowers put themselves in the place of another.

An example of the continuum of knowledge may help to demonstrate the features of social cognition. The child comes to understand the notion of weight by interacting with objects, lifting them, and receiving proprioceptive feedback at the same time as seeing them. Through development, the child learns to conserve the concept of weight independently of transformations of the object and, in general, is no longer fooled by experimental manipulations of some of the objects' properties. Having been schooled in gravitation fields, a person may learn that the weight of an object is relative to the mass on which it is weighed. Thus, *experience forms the cognition* about weight, and when one thinks about the weight of objects, the self is not involved.

Further along the social cognition continuum is our thought about another person. Depending on the cognitions involved, that person can be treated as an object: One can think about the features of the person independently of oneself, or one can think about the person in relation to oneself. Using features such as heavy or tall, young or strong, one may think about another apart from oneself. (Even here, however, we see that tall or short, young or old, and strong or weak can be features that are best considered in relationship to oneself.) If, however, one thinks of another person as kind or happy or if one thinks about how another person might feel "if he could see the sun setting behind the hill," the use of oneself as part of the cognition becomes essential.

Even more relative vis-à-vis the social cognition continuum is thinking about relationships. These cognitions involve the self in at least two ways: (1) when I think about relationships, by definition they involve me; (2) when I think about relationships, one of the things that I may think about is what the other thinks of me. Recursive cognitions can become quite complex, as for example, when I think of what others think that I think of them (Laing, 1970). Asch (1952), in his discussion of interpersonal relations, makes a similar point:

> The paramount fact about human interactions is that they are happenings that are psychologically represented in each of the participants. In our relationship to an object, perceiving, thinking and feeling take place on one side, whereas in relations between persons these processes take place on both sides and in dependence upon one another [p. 142].

Earlier, I considered social cognition as involving: (1) cognitions of others; (2) cognitions of self; (3) cognitions of the relationship of self and other. Cognitions about self and other are not separate processes but rather are part of a duality of knowledge. This view is shared by others. For example, Bannister and Agnew (1977) note: "The ways in which we elaborate our construing of self must be essentially those ways in which we elaborate our construing of others, for we have not a concept of self but a bipolar construct of self—not self or self-other [p. 99]." If this is the case, then social cognitions, as something different from cognitions in general, are not really content differences but differences based on the role of the self, or knower, in relationship to what is known. The definition of social cognitions involves the relationship between knower and known (they are relational cognitions) rather than features that apply to people.

By making social cognitions independent of human features, it becomes possible to talk about general cognitions that refer to people and social cognitions that refer to objects. That is, when cognitions about humans do not involve the knower or self they are not social cognitions; conversely, when cognitions about objects involve the knower or self they become social. As can be readily seen, the degree of the knower-to-known interaction becomes the definition of social cognition. The degree to which any cognition is so constructed is the degree to which social cognitions differ from nonsocial cognitions in their formal properties. One could say, then, that cognitions that do not involve the knower can be considered absolute and are Newtonian. Cognitions that rely upon the knower are relative and as such are Einsteinian. Inasmuch as the study of the known excludes the knower in genetic epistemology, it can be likened to a Newtonian study of absolute properties; when the self enters into the known, the study of the knower becomes relative.

Some have argued that in development recursive knowledge precedes nonegocentric thought (Piaget, 1960). Although development in general may take this form, not all cognitions do or can acquire a decentered form. Certainly the class of cognitions involving private acts, including the thoughts and the feelings of others or acts involving the relationship between people, must throughout development involve the self in the construction, maintenance, and form of cognition. Rather than arguing that the higher forms of intellectual development by definition are without self-involvement, it may be more profitable to conclude that only for some cognitions is self-involvement a less mature form. A different model allowing for multiple forms of cognition would enable us to replace the deficient model. To do so, however, requires at least two separate forms of cognition (general cognition and social cognition) and possibly two separate developmental tracks.

An examination of cultural differences in these different types of knowing is beyond the scope of this essay, but it should come as no surprise to find that cultural needs and values influence these differences. In fact, it may be a particular cultural requirement, a demand for abstraction and reification, that requires the knower be separated from the known. Thus, as Luria (1976) suggests, different developmental levels are not controlled by some genetic program but chiefly by cultural requirements. Similar arguments can be found in Polyani (1958) and Gratch (1979). Merleau-Ponty (1964) captures the spirit of social cognition in the following quote: "If I am a consciousness turned toward things, I can meet in things the actions of another and find in them a meaning because they are themes of possible activity for my own body [p. 113]."

Such a view is appealing, and it would be interesting to test whether the relationship of knower to known affects the nature of the cognition. What type of experimental conditions would be required to show that the introduction of the self into the acquisition or classification of knowledge affects the quality of that knowing? The examples given previously provide some answer, yet a more intriguing demonstration of the difference between social and nonsocial cognition would show that when the knower is "less involved" in the knowing, the knowledge acquired is (in the terms we have used previously) more featural; that is, being less recursive, the knowledge is less psychological and more feature-oriented. A demonstration using social stimuli (i.e., stimuli with human features) would offer further proof or evidence that an important aspect of social cognition is its recursive rather than featural nature.

Such evidence is provided, at least in part, in a recent experiment by Feldman (1979). Feldman was interested in person perception, or more precisely, the formation of inferences regarding the traits, motivations, and probable behavior of others in children younger than those characteristically thought to be able to form inferences about others. In this regard, the literature has indicated a strong developmental trend in person perception, with younger children's responses being restricted primarily to descriptions of others' physical appearance or possessions. In other words, children's descriptions are at first featural and do not acknowledge inner dimensions of the self. However, older children describe both physical appearances and traits or stable dispositions. Such descriptions are recursive in nature and are relational (Guttentag & Longfellow, 1977; Peevers &

Secord, 1973). Wellman (in press) has criticized the person-perception studies on methodological grounds, arguing that the language usage of differently aged children needs to be taken into account. For example, the response of an older child who says that another is intelligent is scored at a higher level than the response of a younger child who says that another is kooky. Discounting Wellman's criticism, it is apparent that rather than decreasing, the use of relational or recursive modes of thought may increase with age. Because of Feldman's concern for the effects of motivation on differently aged children's inference behavior, she introduced two experimental manipulations that bear directly on the issue of the self in the construction of knowledge. In one study, 5- to 6-year-old children and 9- to 10-year-olds observed on video tape four unknown peers who illustrated the traits of generosity, clingingness, physical coordination, and physical clumsiness. Different instructions were given to two groups. In one group, the instructions were "made personally relevant to" the subjects by informing them that they would meet the children in the video tape after the study. In the other group, this aspect of the instructions was eliminated. In a second study using only younger children, the instructions were varied in order to account for the possibility that making the video presentations personally relevant may have also made the children attend more. Therefore, instructions designed to increase attending were presented to one group, and the personally relevant instructions were presented to the other. This manipulation did not alter the results. In both studies, children who expected future interactions exhibited more inference about the actors. More important, the number of different traits used to describe the actions also increased when a future interaction was expected. Feldman (1979) states:

> It was predicted that subjects expecting future interaction would seek to learn as much as possible about the unknown other, and would, therfore, be likely to form inferences about predictable aspects of the action [p. 49].

> The expectation of future interaction . . . did not appear to be providing a more exhaustive information search. . . . Rather, subjects appeared to be formulating a search in which a criterion of personal relevance mediated a change in proposition of statement types . . . used in descriptions of the actions [p. 44].

The relevance of these findings to the notion of a continuum of involvement between the knower (or self) and what is known or constructed is clear. As the engagement of the self becomes more relevant to the task of knowing, as illustrated by the task of inferring, relational knowledge increases. Descriptions such as nice, friendly, and helpful are used more because they refer to the possible relationship the actor can have with *me*. Feldman's study also provides support for the converse, namely, that even with human stimuli, the absence of the usage of self results in a proportional decrease in the number of relational to featural descriptions. In light of these findings, it seems reasonable to believe that when the self is withdrawn from human stimuli, the interactions with these stimuli appear little different from those not possessing human features. This intrinsically appeals to our notion that people can be referred to and treated as objects and that objects can be referred to and treated as people. The independent variable or critical factor may be the degree of involvement of the self. Social knowledge and social action are dependent on the role of the knower. Like Asch (1952), Heider (1958) reflects this as a central theme when he states: "Social perceptions in general can best be described as a process between the center of one person and the center of another person, from life space to life space. . . . A, through psychological processes in himself, perceives psychological processes in B [p. 33]."

EGOCENTRISM AND PRIVATE ACTS

The concept of egocentrism needs to be reconsidered because the issue of the relationship of the knower to known brings the role of the knower back into consideration. In characterizing the differences between Mead and Piaget, Gratch (1978) asserts that one important difference was Mead's attempt to understand how children's actions with persons primarily resulted in learning about themselves, whereas Piaget: "focused less on the organization of nature and social life and more on describing the growth of mental structures that are responsible for the particular ways in which children order their acts and the world around them at different periods of life [p. 444]." In contrast to Piaget, for Mead the self remained an important part of the interaction. As Gratch points out, Mead's guiding metaphor was the "game" (i.e., the interaction between me and you), whereas Piaget's metaphor was the "construction of reality." The central difference, then, pertains to the role of the self.

Before examining the role of self and the nature of egocentrism in knowing, I should clarify what is meant by egocentrism because the definition varies with different investigators (Shantz, 1975). In the present discussion, egocentrism refers to reasoning that fails to appreciate that others have a perspective different from one's own. By this definition, nonegocentric behavior has been observed in children younger than expected by conventional theory. Although the data on role taking are less than clear (see Ford, 1979), it appears that when the role-taking task is simpler, is more related to perceptual cues, occurs more naturally, and involves more familiar people, the likelihood that young children (even as young as 18 months of age) can take the role of another is increased.

The construct of egocentrism, then, focuses on the knower's inability to separate personal feelings, thoughts, or perceptions from those of another. This is caused by an inability to understand that there is no logical necessity for what is felt, thought, or perceived by oneself to be felt, thought, or perceived by another. There is general support for the view that egocentrism as an attribute of the organism becomes less important with development and finally disappears as the adult knows that the other has feelings, thoughts, and perceptions different than oneself. However, to understand the role of the self it is necessary to separate the process of using the self to know from the necessity that what the self feels, sees, or thinks is the same as the other. I wish to consider the position that in some problems of knowing, feeling, or thinking about others, we utilize our own knowing, feeling, or thinking and assume that it is a fair approximation of how another might respond. In other words, for some types of knowing, especially the knowing of private acts, we know about the other through ourselves. Although we might recognize that the other does not *have to* think, feel, or perceive in our way (i.e., we know it does not logically follow that they think, feel, or perceive as we do), nevertheless we believe the other's private acts are similar to our own private acts under similar circumstances. In fact, as a initial proposition, I would state that with events that are public for which we know the cultural rules governing behavior, egocentrism is not necessary. However, with events that are private, mature behavior may require a form of *voluntary* egocentrism. In this case, voluntary indicates that the knower is aware of the logical constraints of his or her perception, feelings, or thoughts. For the sake of the following discussion, egocentrism refers to a process of knowing or feeling that involves the knower directly with the known but is not constrained by logical necessity.

This issue can be pursued by questioning how we come to know. It seems reasonable to assume that it is possible to know only in two broad ways. One can know general information. For example, one knows that the sun rises in the east and sets in the west. This piece of information is acquired through direct experience (i.e., watching the sunrise and sunset) or through indirect methods (i.e., accepting as valid the experiences of others in reading about it or being told). Let us now consider another example: the feelings of someone who has been hit by a car and is seriously hurt. One can know of the events that happened through reading the accident reports or seeing the accident. Both of these forms of knowing constitute public acts: Anyone can know of them by looking at or perceiving them directly. However, one can only know of the feelings of the accident victim through the use of the self. One can know how the victim feels by also having been in an automobile accident or by having cut one's finger with a knife and assuming that the pain resembles the pain of being hit by the car. It is impossible, however, to imagine the pain without ever experiencing pain. Thus, insofar as one is capable of using one's own past feelings and internal states, one can imagine the pain of another person. Likewise, one could see a mouth open and hear a scream, but without personal experience, the feelings of another are impossible to know. Any private act is by its nature known by another only through the use of the self in imagining what one would feel, think, or experience in a similar situation. This extension of the self into another, the process of social cognition, is egocentric.

From a developmental perspective, this form of egocentrism may not decrease with age. What may change is the child's belief that it necessarily follows that another feels x because I feel x; however, the use of self to feel the other's x does not change. Still, the issue is not settled. It has been repeatedly demonstrated that given certain tasks, very young children are not capable of assuming the perspective of another, whereas older children are, but the evidence does not indicate that the errors are egocentric. Rather, the children's mistakes are in considering what the other's perspective is rather than in giving their own. If these results are valid, the developmental nature of egocentrism needs to be reexamined. A more probable explanation for the results involves the child's inability to understand the task or the child's cognitive inability to find the other's perspective rather than the child's belief that there is no other perspective. Moreover, Ford (1979) has suggested that egocentrism is not a unitary construct because different egocentric tasks falling into categories such as visual/spatial, affective, and cognitive/communicative are minimally related (although visual/spatial and cognitive/communicative do show some relationship). Furthermore, Ford's finding that scores on affective egocentrism tasks are least related to the scores on visual/spatial or cognitive/communicative tasks supports the duality in the processes of knowing private versus public acts.

Another perspective is one that emphasizes individual or cultural differences in the use of self to understand private acts. Cultural values and personality characteristics may influence a person's judgment more than any cognitive construction of a logical reality. For example, employing the self to understand another may be avoided when we assume the other is "not like me." This can be seen in the case of war where the other (another soldier) ceases to be "another like me" and becomes "the enemy." Consequently, the enemy is labeled in a way that indicates they are not human "like me." Group labels such as pagan, Gentile, and so forth are all devices for separating self from other. If the culture holds to the belief that other creatures, such as birds or fish, are "like me," then members of the culture will attribute their feelings, thoughts, and perceptions to these creatures.

Personality differences also have been discussed in terms of egocentrism. People who are unwilling (or unable) to consider the other person are known to everyone. Such people are likely to treat other people as objects rather than people. Personality factors, then, as well as cultural factors may account for differences in egocentrism more than development. More research is needed before we can be satisfied with such a conclusion. Nonetheless, the role of the self and its utilization in knowing, especially about others, requires that some aspects of egocentrism be considered as mature and appropriate.

I have focused mostly on knowing in the everyday real world, learning facts, and understanding relationships. In addition, the role of the self in higher mental acts should be acknowledged. Forms of knowing such as creativity, scientific discovery, artistic creation, and those great intuitive leaps that appear infrequently in each generation have been neglected topics.

Perhaps the same processes that create the everyday world of each of us are also operative in such enterprises, but there are little data and almost no theories to support such a belief. What is the role of the knower in such acts? There are no answers. Yet, the enormous amounts of affective energy involved in these actions should alert us to the possiblity that the role of knower may be critical to these forms of knowing as well.

In a book entitled *The Eighth Day of Creation*, Judson (1979) touches upon this issue in talking about Linus Pauling and James Watson:

> To understand Pauling and Watson, you must remember that creativity is an ego drive, as much in science as anywhere else. I don't think there has ever been anybody doing great science whose ego has not been involved very, very deeply. . . . Only Linus showed the willingness to take the inductive leap. Then, once he had the idea, he pushed it. The history of science shows that that, in itself, is perfectly justified—yet it's the same egocentricity that led him to collect thousands of signatures of scientists on a petition to ban atomic testings [p. 86].

Although Pauling dismissed this intuitive difference, another contemporary scientist said, "But didn't Linus also tell you that he has got more imagination than other people?" Whatever the processes, great creative leaps of thought, whether in science, art, or any other endeavor, may involve the role of the knower in some way not found in our everyday actions and thoughts. Rather than following Bacon's advice to avoid "whatever the mind seizes and dwells upon with peculiar satisfaction," the history of science and the biographies of people who have made significant contributions advocate the reverse strategy: to seize and dwell with passion upon a problem and, perhaps, thereby find solution. One can think of no better example than Einstein's remark when asked what he wished to do with the remainder of his life. He replied that he could think of nothing more satisfactory than to spend the next 50 years thinking about light!

Thus, the aim of the scientific method is to separate the knower from the known (i.e., to allow for objectivity in thinking), but such a task may be difficult if not impossible. Even within the scientific enterprise the scientist is connected to the outcome. Although others have already recognized this (e.g., Eiduson, 1962; Hudson, 1972; Roe, 1961), one final example of this interconnection is in order. The point I am trying to demonstrate is that even within the scientific enterprise a relationship between knower and known exists. Rather than viewing this relationship as a failing of our task, knowledge of such a relationship might better enable us to understand both the process of thought and the scientific endeavor.

In order to study this problem, Wehren and I gathered every article ($N = 338$) published in *Child Development* and *Developmental Psychology* during 1977. (The year chosen was arbitrary.) Each article was coded on the following features: the sex of the principal investigator; whether sex or gender was mentioned in the title; whether sex differences were hypothesized; whether sex differences were analyzed; whether significant sex differences were found; the number of subjects used; and finally, whether the topic of study was social or nonsocial. Examples of social studies included studies of mother-infant interaction, communication, social competence, and sex role development, whereas nonsocial studies included studies of cognitive development, sensory integration, perception, and information processing.

Because the other features or characteristics of the scientist were not easily available, sex of the experimenter was chosen as the independent variable. Far better for our purposes would have been the personality, intellectual, attitudinal, or familial characteristics of the scientist. For the dependent variables, only information available in the scientific articles themselves was used. As such, our hypothesized relationship between scientist and scientific outcome was limited. As the investigation progressed, we were impressed by several facts. To begin with, if sex differences were hypothesized, it was more likely that the sample would be evenly divided between male and female subjects. Yet the nature of our statistical procedures is such that evenly divided samples require differences in mean values of smaller magnitude to be considered significant. Thus, by hypothesizing a difference and selecting samples of similar size, we increase the likelihood of finding that difference.

Other interesting results emerge from analyzing these types of data. For example, in 1977 there were more papers published by male than female experimenters (200 vs. 138). However, female experimenters tended to mention sex in the title more than did males, and studies with sex in the title were more likely to have a hypothesis about sex differences and were more likely to test that hypothesis than studies without sex in the title. Across all types of studies, female experimenters were more likely to have hypothesized a sex difference than males. The relationship, however, is more complex. Socially oriented studies were more likely to mention sex in the title than nonsocial studies, yet male experimenters were more likely to have a sex-difference hypothesis for social than for nonsocial studies, but female experimenters were not. In other words, male experimenters hypothesized sex differences for social studies but not nonsocial studies, whereas no study-type difference appears for female experimenters.[4]

Sample selection procedures also showed an interesting result. First, all studies reporting extreme sample selection (75–100% of one gender) were examined as a function of the sex of the experimenter. Seventeen extreme samples were located: Twelve samples were exclusively male, and five were exclusively female. When these were related to the sex of the experimenter, it was found that male experimenters chose more exclusively male than female samples, but no difference existed for female experimenters. This finding may be nothing more

---

[4]It cannot yet be determined if the nature of the problem influences the male experimenters' hypothesis or whether different types of males do social and nonsocial studies.

than the result of an unusually small sample size. However, it does follow one of the more important socialization rules found for sex role behavior. In our culture, boys are pressured more into male stereotypes than girls are into female stereotypes. For example, females can dress in either a feminine or masculine fashion, but males can dress only in a masculine fashion. It is possible, then, that extreme sample selection for adult scientists followed these same socialization rules. The interconnectedness of the processes of thought and socialization in the scientific enterprise may be apparent in examples such as this.

More directly related to these reported socialization differences between the sexes in the following example. The number of studies where the sex-difference hypothesis was confirmed—either a hypothesis of no sex difference and none was found or a hypothesis of sex differences where differences were found—was tabulated. It was found that male experimenters were correct at least three times more often than female experimenters. Several possibilities are available to explain these results. For example, male experimenters may be smarter than female experimenters, but this is unlikely. Alternatively, male experimenters may be more likely than females to report a hypothesis only after the results are tabulated. As hypothesis formulation supposedly should precede testing, female rather than male experimenters were following the rules. Similar sex differences in rule-governing behavior have been found by others using more naive subjects (Maccoby & Jacklin, 1974).

These preliminary findings serve to alert us to the interaction between the the characteristics of the scientist and the scientific facts that are discovered. Born's quote takes on further import: "It is the action of the experimentalist who designs the apparatus which determines the essential features of the observation." Here, however, it is not only the *action* of the scientist but the personal characteristics, including belief systems, that affect the outcome of the experiment.

This is not necessarily bad science. The notion that one can transcend oneself to reach for and attain a higher goal, to attain truth through a process of separating oneself from the action of knowing, has always been open to question. Modern physics has forced us to deny the existence of an objective, external reality independent of ourselves. Consequently, powerful models of Newtonian physics are no longer available, and we must now consider new models in which self and other in interaction become the units of inquiry. Perhaps rather than ignoring such a relationship, it is better that we try to understand it through the specification of its nature.

Our attempt throughout this chapter has been to call attention to the role of the self in knowing, not only the interaction of the self in the construction of knowledge but in its content. The various aspects of this role give witness to the complex influence of the self. The seven views that I have presented—the self in everyday knowing, the origins of self-recognition in infancy, the role of the scientist in knowing, the self and cognition, the self in social cognition, egocentrism, and the self and the scientific method—are examples of the ways in which the self appears to play a role in our actions, thoughts, feelings, and relationships. These examples illustrate different aspects of the problem; more could probably be generated. These views offer less than a complete and integrated theory about the self. Rather, I hope that when considered together they focus the problem and offer sufficient argument to make valid the study of the role of the self in knowing.

ACKNOWLEDGMENTS

The research described in this paper was supported in part by a NICHD Grant #N01HD–82849 and BEH Grant #300–77–0307.

REFERENCES

Ainsworth, M. D. S., Belhar, M. C., Waters, E., & Wall, S. *Patterns of attachment: A psychological study of the strange situation.* Hillsdale, N.J.: Lawrence Erlbaum Associates, 1978.

Amsterdam, B. K. Mirror self-image reactions before age two. *Developmental Psychology,* 1972, *5,* 297–305.

Armstrong, J. S. Prestige and poppycock. *Pediatrics,* 1981, *67,* 284 (A research note reprinted from *Glimpse*; September, 1980).

Asch, S. E. *Social psychology.* Englewood Cliffs, N.J.: Prentice-Hall, 1952.

Bannister, D., & Agnew, J. The child's construing of self. In J. Cole (Ed.), *Nebraska Symposium on Motivation* (Vol. 25). Lincoln: University of Nebraska Press, 1977.

Bloom, L. *One word at a time: The use of single-word utterances before syntax.* The Hague: Mouton, 1973.

Brooks-Gunn, J., & Lewis, M. "Why mama and papa?" The development of social labels. *Child Development,* 1979, *50,* 1203–1206.

Bruner, J. S., & Tagiuri, R. The perception of people. In G. Lindzey (Ed.), *Handbook of social psychology* (Vol. 2). Cambridge, Mass.: Addison-Wesley, 1954.

Butterfield, G., & Hicks, L. Visual proprioception and postural stability in infancy: A developmental study. *Perception,* 1977, *6,* 255–262.

Clark, R. W. *Einstein: The life and times.* New York: Avon, 1972.

Dixon, J. C. Development of self recognition. *Journal of Genetic Psychology,* 1957, *91,* 251–256.

Durant, W. *The story of philosophy.* New York: Pocket Books, 1954.

Edwards, C. P., & Lewis, M. Young children's concepts of social relations: Social functions and social objects. In M. Lewis & L. Rosenblum (Eds.), *The child and its family: The genesis of behavior* (Vol. 2). New York: Plenum, 1979.

Eiduson, B. T. *Scientists: Their psychological world.* New York: Basic Books, 1962.

Epstein, S. The self-concept: A review and the proposal of an integrated theory of personality. In E. Staub (Ed.), *Personality: Basic issues and current research.* Englewood Cliffs, N.J.: Prentice-Hall, 1980.

Everett, H. (Ed.). *Many worlds of interpretations of quantum mechanics: A fundamental exposition.* Princeton, N.J.: Princeton University Press, 1973.

Feldman, N. S. *Children's impressions of their peers: Motivational factors and the use of inference.* Unpublished doctoral dissertation, Princeton University, 1979.

Flavell, J. H. The genesis of our understanding of persons: Psychological studies. In T. Mischel (Ed.), *Understanding other persons.* Totowa, N.J.: Rowman & Littlefield, 1974.

Flavell, J., Botkin, P., Fry, C., Wright, J., & Jarvis, P. *The development of role-taking and communication skills in children.* New York: Wiley, 1968.

Ford, M. E. The construct validity of egocentrism. *Psychological Bulletin,* 1979, *86,* 1169–1188.

Gergen, K. J. *The concept of self.* New York: Holt, Reinhart & Winston, 1971.

Gratch, G. The development of thought and language in infancy. In J. Osofsky (Ed.), *Handbook of infant development.* New York: Wiley, 1979.

Gruber, H. E., & Barrett, P. H. *Darwin on man: A psychological study of scientific creativity.* New York: E. P. Dutton, 1974.

Guttentag, M., & Longfellow, C. Children's social attributions: Development and change. In H. E. Howe, Jr. (Ed.), *Nebraska Symposium on Motivation* (Vol. 25). Lincoln: University of Nebraska Press, 1977.

Heider, F. *The psychology of interpersonal relations.* New York: Wiley, 1958.

Hinde, R. A. On describing relationships. *Journal of Child Psychology and Psychiatry,* 1976, *17,* 1–19.

Hoffman, M. L. Toward a theory of empathic arousal and development. In M. Lewis & L. Rosenblum (Eds.), *The development of affect: The genesis of behavior* (Vol. 1). New York: Plenum, 1978.

Hudson, L. *The cult of the fact.* London: Cape, 1972.

Hyde, T. S., & Jenkins, J. J. The differential effects of incidental tasks on the organization of recall of a list of highly associated words. *Journal of Experimental Psychology,* 1969, *82,* 472–481.

Judson, H. F. *The eighth day of creation.* New York: Simon & Schuster, 1979.

Kohlberg, L. Stage and sequence: The cognitive-developmental approach to socialization. In D. A. Goslin (Ed.), *Handbook of socialization theory and research.* Chicago: Rand McNally, 1969.

Krauss, R. M., & Glucksberg, S. The development of communication: Competence as a function of age. *Child Development,* 1969, *40,* 255–266.

Kruper, N. A., & Rogers, T. B. The encoding of self–other differences. *Journal of Personality and Social Psychology,* in press.

Kuhn, T. S. *The structure of scientific revolutions* (2nd ed.). Chicago: University of Chicago Press, 1970.

Laing, R. D. *Knots.* New York: Pantheon Books, 1970.

Lee, D. N., & Aronson, E. Visual proprioceptive control of standing in human infants. *Perception & Psychophysics,* 1974, *15,* 529–532.

Lewis, M. The meaning of a response or why researchers in infant behavior should be Oriental metaphysicians. *Merrill Palmer Quarterly,* 1967, *13*(1), 7–18.

Lewis, M. *The social network: Toward a theory of social development.* Fiftieth anniversary invited address at the meetings of the Eastern Psychological Association, Philadelphia, April 1979.

Lewis, M. Issues in the development of fear. In I. L. Kutash & L. B. Schlesinger (Eds.), *Pressure point: Perspective on stress and anxiety.* San Francisco: Jossey-Bass, 1980.

Lewis, M., & Brooks, J. Infants' social perception: A constructivist view. In L. Cohen & P. Salapatek (Eds.), *Infant perception: From sensation to cognition* (Vol. 2). New York: Academic Press, 1975.

Lewis, M., & Brooks-Gunn, J. Self knowledge and emotional development. In M. Lewis & L. Rosenblum (Eds.), *The development of affect: The genesis of behavior* (Vol. 1). New York: Plenum, 1978.

Lewis, M., & Brooks-Gunn, J. *Social cognition and the acquisition of self.* New York: Plenum, 1979. (a)

Lewis, M., & Brooks-Gunn, J. Toward a theory of social cognition: The development of self. In I. Uzgiris (Ed.), *New directions in child development: Social interaction and communication during infancy*. San Francisco: Jossey-Bass, 1979. (b)

Lewis, M., Edwards, C. P., Weistuch, L., & Cortelyou, S. *Age as a social cognition*. Unpublished manuscript, 1981.

Lewis, M., & Michalson, L. The measurement of emotional state. In C. Izard (Ed.), *Measurement of emotions in infants and children*. New York: Cambridge University Press, 1982.

Lewis, M., & Starr, M. D. Developmental continuity. In J. Osofsky (Ed.), *Handbook of infant development*. New York: Wiley, 1979.

Lewis, M., & Weinraub, M. The father's role in the infant's social network. In M. Lamb (Ed.), *The role of the father in child development* (Vol. 1). New York: Wiley, 1976.

Lewis, M., Weinraub, M., & Feiring, C. The father as a member of the child's social network. In M. Lamb (Ed.), *The role of the father in child development* (2nd ed.). New York: Wiley, 1980.

Lewis, M., Young, G., Brooks, J., & Michalson, L. The beginning of friendship. In M. Lewis & L. Rosenblum (Eds.), *Friendship and peer relations: The origins of behavior* (Vol. 4). New York: Wiley, 1975.

Lipsitt, L. *The enduring significance of reflexes in human infancy: Developmental shifts in the first month of life*. Paper presented at the meetings of the Eastern Psychological Association, Hartford, Conn., April 1980.

Luria, A. R. *Cognitive development: Its cultural and social foundations*. Cambridge, Mass.: Harvard University Press, 1976.

Maccoby, E. E. & Jacklin, C. N. *The psychology of sex differences*. Stanford: Stanford University Press, 1974.

Mead, G. H. *Mind, Self, and society*. Chicago: University of Chicago Press, 1934.

Merleau-Ponty, M. *Primacy of perception* (J. Eddie, Ed. and W. Cobb, trans.). Evanston, Ill.: Northwestern University Press, 1964.

Mischel, W. Sex-typing and socialization. In P. Mussen (Ed.), *Carmichael's manual of child psychology* (Vol. 2). New York: Wiley, 1970.

Owens, J., Bower, G. H., & Black, J. B. The soap opera effect in story recall. *Memory & Cognition*, 1979, *1*, 185–191.

Pagels, E. *The gnostic gospels*. New York: Random House, 1979.

Papousek, H., & Papousek, M. The common in the uncommon children: Comments on the child's integrative capacities and on initiative parenting. In M. Lewis & L. Rosenblum (Eds.), *The uncommon child: The genesis of behavior* (Vol. 3). New York: Plenum, 1981.

Peevers, B., & Secord, P. Developmental changes in attribution of descriptive concepts of persons. *Journal of Personality and Social Psychology*, 1973, *27*, 120–128.

Piaget, J. *The language and thought of the child*. New York: Harcourt, Brace, 1926.

Piaget, J. *The construction of reality in the child*. New York: Basic, 1954 (Originally published 1937).

Piaget, J. *The psychology of intelligence*. New York: Littlefield Adams, 1960.

Piaget, J., & Inhelder, B. *The child's cognition of space*. New York: Humanities Press, 1956.

Polyani, M. *Personal language: Toward a post-critical philosophy*. London: Routledge & Kegan Paul, 1958.

Reese, H., & Overton, W. Models of development and theories of development. In L. R. Goulet & P. B. Baltes (Eds.), *Life span developmental psychology: Research and theory*. New York: Academic Press, 1970.

Rheingold, H. L. *Some visual determinants of smiling infants*. Unpublished manuscript, 1971.

Roe, A. A psychological study of eminent physical scientists. *General Psychology Monographs*, 1951, *43*, 121–135.

Roe, A. *The making of a scientist*. New York: Dodd/Mead, 1953.

Roe, A. The psychology of the scientist. *Science*, 1961, *134*, 456–459.

Rogers, T. B., Kuiper, N. A., & Kirker, W. S. Self-reference and the encoding of personal information. *Journal of Personality and Social Psychology,* 1977, *35,* 677–688.

Rosenberg, M. *Society and the adolescent self-image.* Princeton, N.J.: Princeton University Press, 1965.

Selman, R. The relation of role-taking ability to the development of moral judgment in children. *Child Development,* 1971, *42,* 79–91. (a)

Selman, R. Taking another's perspective: Role taking development in early childhood. *Child Development,* 1971, *42,* 1721–1734. (b)

Shantz, C. The development of social cognition. In E. M. Hetherington (Ed.), *Review of child development research* (Vol. 5). Chicago: University of Chicago Press, 1975.

Strapp, H. S-matrix interpretation of quantum theory. *Physical Review,* 1971, *D3,* 1303.

Sullivan, H. S. *The interpersonal theory of psychiatry.* New York: Norton, 1953.

Synonds, P. M. *Ego and the self.* Westport, Conn.: Greenwood, 1968. (Originally published, 1951.)

Tagiuri, R. Person perception. In G. Lindzey & E. Aronson (Eds.), *The handbook of social psychology.* Reading, Mass.: Addison-Wesley, 1969.

Tinbergen, U. *The study of instinct.* Oxford: Oxford University Press, 1951.

Watson, J. S. The development and generalization of "contingency awareness" in infancy. *Merrill-Palmer Quarterly,* 1966, *12,* 123–135.

Weinraub, M., Brooks, J., & Lewis, M. The social network: A reconsideration of the concept of attachment. *Human Development,* 1977, *20,* 31–47.

Wellman, H. M. A child's theory of mind: The development of conceptions of cognition. In S. Yussen (Ed.), *The growth of insight in the child.* New York: Academic Press, in press.

Wylie, R. *The self-concept* (Vol. 1). Lincoln: University of Nebraska Press, 1974.

Youniss, J. Another perspective on social cognition. In A. D. Pick (Ed.), *Minnesota Symposium on Child Psychology* (Vol. 9). Minneapolis: University of Minnesota Press, 1975.

Zukav, G. *The dancing Wu Li masters.* New York: Morrow, 1979.

9 Infant Social Cognition: Self, People, and Objects

Roberta Michnick Golinkoff
University of Delaware

What do infants know about their social and nonsocial worlds and when do they know it? Until recently, research on infant development, as in the rest of developmental psychology, was skewed in the direction of infant's cognitive appreciation of the world of inanimate objects and events. This chapter will address this imbalance by focusing on the infant's understanding of the self and of the properties and capabilities of people.

Specifically, the purpose of this chapter is to extend our understanding of social-cognitive development in infancy by drawing upon research in the development of communication and language. Researchers who study the development of communication in the first 2 years of life have been collectively engaged in a large enterprise, whose emphasis is social-cognitive development. The study of the development of communication may be uniquely suited to understanding two distinctions that the infant constructs, at least in a primitive way, in the first year of life, namely, the distinctions between the self and others, and between social and nonsocial objects. These basic concepts in infant social cognition develop sequentially in a three-step process: (1) the infant recognizes the existential or private self in the guise of its feelings and efficacious actions; (2) soon after, the infant distinguishes between the self and others; and (3) the infant divides "others" into social and nonsocial objects in the world. After a theoretical discussion of these three aspects of infant social cognition, this paper reviews and critiques some of the communication and language research that bears on their emergence in development.

THE NATURE OF THE SELF: EXISTENTIAL AND CATEGORICAL

Definitions of the "self" abound in the psychological literature (see Bannister & Agnew, 1976). Clearly, the notion of self that an infant evolves by the end of the first year of life will not be the same as a 5-year-old's or an adult's concept of the self. Epstein (1973) argued that the mature self-concept is a self-theory and, in so doing, described some of the components of the self:

> What is it that consists of concepts that are hierarchically organized and internally consistent; that assimilates knowledge, yet, itself, is an object of knowledge; that is dynamic, but must maintain a degree of stability; that is unified and differentiated at the same time; that is necessary for solving problems in the real world; and that is subject to sudden collapse, producing total disorganization when this occurs? The answer, by now, should be evident. In case it is not, I submit that the self-concept is a self-theory. . . . The most fundamental purpose of the self-theory is *to optimize the pleasure/pain balance of the individual over the course* of a lifetime [p. 407; Epstein's emphasis].

To the extent that the person begins this optimization of the pleasure/pain ratio in infancy, the infant may become dimly and inarticulately aware of some of the self's capabilities and limitations as an *agent*. The research in early communication bears on the self as an agent, as the self attempts to interact with and appeal to something outside the self for social ends or instrumental assistance. This component of the self is the same as the "existential self" discussed by Lewis and Brooks-Gunn (1979).

The Existential Self

Lewis and Brooks-Gunn (1979) have argued that the concept of self is characterized by the same duality that Epstein alludes to in the foregoing quotation, namely, the self as subject (the "existential self") and the self as object (the "categorical self"). Knowledge of the existential self comes for the infant through its proprioceptive feedback and its developing awareness of its thoughts, intentions, and feelings. Thus, the existential self emerges from the *processes* that take place within the organism, which only the subject can observe. The existential self comes to view itself as an agent in causing and evaluating its own actions. As Lewis and Brooks-Gunn (1979) have written:

> 'Agency' refers to that aspect of action that makes reference to the cause of action, that is, not only who or what is causing this stimulus change, but who is evaluating it . . . the ability of the organism to cause events to occur would seem to require some notion of self. If infants can cause an outcome to occur repeatedly through a behavior, as by secondary circular reactions (Piaget 1937/1954), then they have learned some of the causes and consequences of that behavior. For certain associations between events, the infant has learned the notion of his own agency; e.g., "I", cause something to happen. "I" has a location, although "I" also moves in space, two processes underlying the sense of permanence. This "I", which is different from other, has an internal location, and is permanent across time and space, is the beginning of self. As infants learn to affect their world, they also learn to evaluate themselves [pp. 188–189].

The infant's society can observe the outcomes of some of those internal processes in the form of behavior. Different attributions will be made about the resulting behaviors depending on existing cultural beliefs. Lock (1980) has discussed, for example, how the mother's interpretations of the infant's behaviors, in the context of the culture, will mirror back to the child what his or her self should be like. Such thinking is akin to the views of Mead (1934) and Cooley (1912), the oft-cited sociologists, who emphasized the role of social interaction for the construction of self. As Lock (1980) put it: "Different social realities imply different conceptions of self [p. 193]." However, even before the infant may be said to have a concept of the self, the way in which the animate environment responds to the infant may well condition the feelings and feedback the existential self experiences. For example, Suomi (1981) and Lamb (1981) believe that depending on the degree to which the infant's environment is responsive to him, the infant will develop either a sense of a powerful or a powerless existential self.

The Categorical Self

The other aspect of self is the self as object, or the categorical self. This aspect is defined more by *state* than by process variables. Whether the self is male or female, old or young, big or little, and so on are the sorts of categories the individual belongs to, although membership in some obviously changes. This self, the self the outside world can know, is also circumscribed by cultural beliefs. For example, my image of myself as a child will depend on how my particular culture views children's abilities. American preschool children are socialized to believe they are incapable of performing certain household tasks. However, among the Kaluli of New Guinea (Schieffelin & Ochs, in press) 2-year-olds are permitted to handle sharp knives, start fires, and perform other "dangerous" tasks. The socialization of males and females into the culturally acceptable sex roles is another well-known example of how culture shapes the person's view of the self.

The categorical self is manifest first in infants' recognition that the reflection they see in the mirror is *their* reflection and no one else's. Lewis and Brooks-Gunn (1979) have conducted experiments on this aspect of the self. Because experience with reflective surfaces must surely be much less frequent than experience with one's own actions and feelings (one's internal processes), the existential self would seem to emerge earlier than the categorical self.

This paper focuses on the infant's awareness of the existential self and the way in which selected achievements in the development of communication illuminate its growth. I believe the existential self is constructed by the infant in a social context because many (although not all) of the internal processes the infant experiences are triggered by relations with the social world. Piaget (1936/1952) may well have underestimated how much knowledge of the self in the sensorimotor period depends on the infants' interactions with others in a particular cultural frame. Differential treatment of the same infant behaviors by mothers in different cultures may well cause different internal responses in the infant, which in turn will lead to a different sense of the existential self once infants become aware of their feelings and agency.

THE DISTINCTION BETWEEN SOCIAL
AND NONSOCIAL OBJECTS

After infants have some awareness of the existential self and after they are clearer about where the self ends and the other begins, they must then develop a sense of the difference between people and inanimate objects. Consideration of this distinction raises two critical theoretical issues. First, there is the issue of the *content* of the infant's knowledge of the other. The term "social cognition" (Shantz, 1975) has been said to encompass: "the child's intuitive or logical representation of others, that is, how he characterizes others and makes inferences about their covert, inner psychological experiences [p. 258]." Apart from the issue of how infants represent the physical aspects of others, inferences that infants may make about others' inner states have hardly been attended to in the small amount of research on infant social cognition. As Lamb and Sherrod (1981) have argued, it is easier for psychologists to study people as physical stimuli for infants than as infants' social partners whose behaviors have meanings and functions apart from infants' behavior. A good example is the important issue of how and when the infant recognizes and attributes meaning to the facial expressions of others (Oster, 1981).

The second issue has to do with the *process* by which knowledge of the other is acquired. Chandler (1977) has argued that researchers who study social cognition share a common responsibility, namely, to address the: "extent to which persons, as opposed to inanimate or nonsocial objects, are seen as possessing special qualities or characteristics that might substantially alter the nature of the process by which they are understood [p. 94]." Glick (1978) has argued that there may indeed be different ways of knowing about social and nonsocial objects because:

> Physical events are in principle specifiable because they are stable and involve determined reactions to identifiable forces. Accordingly, they afford the development of logical systems which allow for knowledge that transcends physical particulars. Social events, on the other hand, display less stability in principle and hence should involve knowledge structures of a more probabilistic sort. Social knowledge therefore should be more uncertain and more sensitive to current informational conditions (contexts) than physical knowledge [pp. 2–3].

Given infants' initially poor ability to perceive contingencies between events above certain time intervals (see Watson, in press), the postulated increased variability in the timing of social as opposed to nonsocial events may well have an impact on the infant's processing of these events.

Turning now to more pragmatic concerns, there are three reasons why it would be important for infants to make a preliminary distinction between social and nonsocial objects. First, with regard to the infant's perception and understanding of events in the world, consider the "reduction of uncertainty" (Gibson, 1969) that will take place when infants realize that the likely sources of many of the events in their world are animate objects, usually people. Second, it will be useful for the infant to know to whom to address appeals for assistance and how to conduct those appeals. Events involving people require no physical contact but distal communicative appeals; events involving nonsocial objects require proximal contact between the infant and the object. Third, to the extent that the infant has the same expectations and categories that the adult does for how the world's events occur, it will be much easier for the child to solve the problem of how language maps onto events.

Gelman and Spelke (1981) have generated what needs to be the first step in studying the distinction between people and objects: a taxonomy of the various ways in which these categories and the broader categories of animate and inanimate objects differ. For example, they point out that only people can act reciprocally, reverse roles, and have the potential to deliver communications. Furthermore, some animate beings and all people have faces which go through various elastic transformations when in motion. Golinkoff, Carlson-Luden, Harding, and Sexton (in press) consider, as do Gelman and Spelke (1981), animate objects' ability to act to be a critical distinction. Golinkoff et al. (in press) write:

> . . . while there are borderline cases such as natural forces like the wind and avalanches, one very important distinction [between animate and inanimate objects] concerns these objects' capabilities. Animate objects (including the self, others, animals, and insects) are capable of moving and initiating actions without the impetus of any external force. Inanimate objects in contrast, such as cars, tables and rocks, cannot ordinarily perform actions and cannot move unless they are affected by gravity or used instrumentally by animate objects.

After perceptual distinctions, these functional differences between people and objects are probably some of the first to be detected by infants. The literature on the development of communication in the last quarter of the first year speaks specifically to infants' recognition that people, not objects, can act autonomously. Furthermore, many psycholinguistic accounts of the semantic underpinnings of early speech presume that the second-year infant can distinguish between the roles people and animate objects, in contrast to inanimate objects, play in events (Bloom, 1970; Brown, 1973; see also Golinkoff, 1981a). However, it is my contention that we know far less about when infants discriminate between social and nonsocial objects than is often claimed. Thus, at an early point in the infant's development what some might refer to as "social" objects may not be social objects at all from the infant's perspective. Paradoxically, I argue that researchers may not have been giving infants who *can* distinguish between social and nonsocial objects enough credit about their knowledge of social objects. That is, infants between about 5 and 8 months of age, and certainly between 9 and 12 months, may have more of a sense of what to expect from social objects— specifically, people—than has been heretofore assumed. Inasmuch as the vehicle for considering these issues is the literature on communication development, it is important to make a distinction between the types of communication that the infant is capable of initiating in the first year of life.

THE NATURE OF COMMUNICATION IN THE FIRST YEAR OF LIFE

In the literature a common distinction is that between the infant's use of preintentional and intentional communication. Bates, Camaioni, and Volterra (1975) suggest that during most of the first year of life communication occurs by virtue of the fact that adults interpret the baby's behaviors as containing and conveying meaning. In other words, communication occurs through the adult's reading of child behaviors (e.g., postural changes, facial expressions, vocalizations, bodily noises, eye gazes, etc.), which are not necessarily used in service to communicative ends at all (see Snow, 1977). Bates et al. (1975) call this the "perlocutionary" period of communicative development. At some point in development, however, the infant begins to try in a purposeful way to contact others. As Schaffer (1977) puts it: "The contrast is between the baby who cries because he has a pain and the baby who cries in order to summon his mother to deal with the pain: the one responding reactively, the other with an eye to the future [p. 10]." "Intentional communication" is operationally defined by the alternation of gaze between a desired object and the adult's eyes or by the use of gesture (e.g., pointing) with alternating eye contact and/or by infant behaviors such as handing an object to the mother, which functions as a request to operate it (Bates et al., 1975; Bruner, 1975; Harding & Golinkoff, 1979; Lock, 1976; Sugarman-Bell, 1978). These intentional communicative behaviors may occur with or without preverbal vocalization.

But it seems to be the case that the intentional communication appearing at approximately 9 months of age is not the infant's first attempt to communicate intentionally, although it may well be the first time the infant has attempted to communicate with the goal of having the adult serve as his or her agent. Communication may first occur as the infant attempts to make social contact—contact during alert periods in which no distress is evident—probably some time around the third month of life. I refer to the first type as "intentional communication for interactional purposes" and to the second type as "intentional communication for instrumental purposes." Trevarthen (1977) makes a similar distinction between "primary" and "secondary" intersubjectivity," as does Sugarman-Bell (1978). The implications of these types of communication for the development of social cognition are addressed elsewhere in this chapter.

The rest of this chapter is concerned with what the child knows of the self and of social and nonsocial objects in the first year of life. The first year is divided into the following three periods, each primarily associated with the achievement of a basic concept in infant social cognition: During the neonatal period (0–2 months) the infant recognizes the existential self; the discrimination between the self versus the other is accomplished in the period from 3 to 8 months; and the distinction between social and nonsocial objects occurs between 9 and 12 months.

The Neonatal Period (0–2 Months)

The Existential Self.   Does the neonate (or perhaps even the fetus) have a sense of the existential self? Over the years some theorists have argued that the neonate has a primitive and unrealistically powerful sense of self because it has not yet differentiated an awareness of a mothering agent. In psychoanalytic theory the omnipotent self begins to dimly recognize its limitations as its every wish is not sated (see Mahler, Pine, & Bergman, 1975).

On the other hand, some theorists have claimed that the neonate does not have a sense of self—let alone an omnipotent one—but more a sense of confusion and undifferentiation. At first as Piaget (1954) argues (in sensorimotor Stages 1 and 2, up to about 4 months), there is no distinction between the self, people, and objects. Further, Piaget does not believe that the infant is capable of acting with intention until about 3 months. When infants succeed in bringing their thumbs to their mouths (primary circular reaction), cause and effect are fused. Bruner (1973), on the other hand (see Harding, 1982, for a comparison of these views), believes that the ability to operate with intention is present from birth. In making this judgement Bruner relies less than Piaget on completed motor acts by the infant. For example, Bruner (1973) has examined adjustments neonates make in their hand movements when presented with objects of various sizes. He argues that the intention to grasp is apparent from these differential hand movements, although it will be months before the skilled act of grasping appears. The appearance of intentions is an important issue for the emergence of self. As Lewis and Brooks-Gunn (1979) have argued it is logically inconsistent to claim that an organism who has intentions and/or plans does not have a self. At a minimum, from the research on early conditioning and observations of primary circular reactions, neonates are probably vaguely aware that they have some ability to manipulate their bodies. For example, Hartka, Lewis, and Brooks-Gunn (1981) have found that by 2 months of age infants will look longer at displays they create with their actions than at equivalent displays not contingent on their actions. In a related finding, Watson (1967) found that 2-month-old infants seemed to greatly enjoy manipulating a mobile contingent upon their behavior. Such results seem to point to the infant's recognition of a relationship between efforts of the self and effects in the world—a primitive existential self.

The Self Versus the Other.   Whether the infant has at this time fully sorted out the difference between self and other is doubtful, however. When events occur infants may still not be sure who else caused and experienced them. The fact that neonates will often show ''crying contagion'' and cry when they hear another infant cry (and not in reaction to equally loud nonhuman sounds) (Sagi & Hoffman, 1976) and the fact that they will seem to respond to the distress of others (see Hoffman, 1977) suggests that the boundary between self and other may not be drawn clearly yet.

For this developmental period, the literature on the development of communication may be overestimating infant knowledge. It seems to presuppose the existence of the self–other distinction since the further assertion that infants can discriminate between social and nonsocial objects is often made. The next section evaluates this stronger claim.

The Distinction Between Social and Nonsocial Objects: A Critique of the Literature in Communication Development.   The literature leads us to believe that the neonate may be genetically predisposed toward interacting with humans by virtue of the following: the neonate's apparent preference for stimulus properties possessed by human beings (Fantz, 1963; Wolff, 1966); the neonate's relatively involuntary production of some of the rudiments of human communicative signals (Trevarthen, 1974), including human emotional displays (Izard, 1977); neurologically based timing mechanisms, which contribute to the impression that the infant takes turns in social interaction (Stern, 1977); and the neonate's growing appreciation of contingencies between its behavior and environmental events (Watson, 1967). At least the Western adult caretaker seems to capitalize on these aspects of the baby's repertoire and treats the infant as a person, attributing communicative significance to many of its behaviors from birth (Bullowa, 1979; Shotter, 1978). However, none of the preadaptations just mentioned mean that the infant knows a social from a nonsocial object. The alerting and arousal neonates are said to show in the presence of social objects (e.g., Brazleton, 1979) may well be a result of the unique combination of multimodal stimulation the infant receives when it interacts with a person. In addition to the dynamic tactile, auditory, visual, and olfactory stimulation people produce, the infant's own vocalizations and facial expressions are reflected back to the infant (at least by the mother) *contingent* on the infant's production of these behaviors (Stern, 1977).

Despite these obvious confounds the literature is replete with claims about how infants are innately predisposed to respond to other humans. Trevarthen (1974) has made this claim and the further claim that infants possess separate behavioral repertoires for interacting with people and inanimate objects: "At the latest by three weeks after birth, infants are adapted to approach persons and objects quite differently [p. 233]." Stern (1977) and Brazleton, Koslowski, and Main (1974) argue similarly. On the other hand, Schaffer (1977) has written about the "need to postulate some degree of social pre-adaptation" in the human infant, although not about social responses being directed exclusively at social objects. This certainly seems a more defensible position. Schaffer (1977) writes:

> A neonate may be an essentially asocial creature in the sense of not being capable as yet of truly reciprocal social relationships and of not having the concept of a person. However, the nature of his early interactive behavior is such that it is increasingly difficult to avoid the conclusion that in some sense the infant is already prepared for social intercourse. Not that this should surprise us: if an infant arrives in the world with a digestive system . . . and a breathing apparatus . . . , why should he not also be prepared to deal with that other essential attribute of his environment, people? [p. 5].

Other researchers who study early social development have resisted declaring that infants can distinguish between social and nonsocial objects from birth. Lewis and Brooks-Gunn (1979), for example, conclude that the earliest this distinction could possibly emerge is at 2 months of age because it is only at that time that infants reliably scan the interior of the human face (Haith, Bergman, & Moore, 1977; see Sherrod, 1981, for a review). However, it is my contention that what may pass for a distinction between social and nonsocial objects at this early age is only the perceptual precursor of such a distinction. The distinction between social and nonsocial objects means having a differential set of expectations about objects in these categories and not being fooled by stimuli (e.g., moving toys), which have properties that mimic properties possessed by people. A case in point is the research by Watson (1967), which illustrates how young infants display social behavior and positive affect to mobiles that move contingent upon the infant's movement.

As an example of research that credits the infant with more knowledge than it probably possesses, Trevarthen (1974, 1977) has claimed that neonates engage in pointing behaviors—primitive gesticulations used for communicative purposes—in the presence of their mothers. However, controlled experiments have not been conducted on the incidence of pointing in the presence of a moving and/or responsive toy, or an object of comparable size to a person, compared with a pointing baseline obtained during an aroused state. Further, the research that makes such claims is often fraught with additional methodological difficulties. For one thing, such conclusions are often drawn from highly selected episodes in which the infant is interacting with a skilled adult partner. The extent to which infants are genuinely contributing to such interactions as opposed to having their behaviors *appear* to be contributions because of their mother's sensitivity to timing and overlap is an issue in that literature (e.g., see Trevarthen, 1979). Another major methodological problem has to do with the failure of many such studies to use observers who are blind to whether an adult is present or not, let alone what precedes or follows the segment of interaction the observer is focusing on. As Contole and Over (1981) stated in their criticisms of such studies: "When such conditions apply, observers may attribute to the infant capabilities that really reflect the competence of the other participant in the interaction [p. 22]." In sum, in the endless rush to endow the young infant with more and more capabilities, some researchers are willing to credit the neonate with the capacity to distinguish between people and objects based on relatively inadequate evidence. On the other hand, adherence to a more conservative position need not deny that infants may engage in what has been called "protoconversations" or "protodialogues" (Stern, 1977) nor that by the end of the second substage of infancy (about 4 months) infants may show much positive affect in the presence of humans (see Contole & Over, 1981). However, to attribute positive affect and social engagement to a distinction infants make between people and inanimate objects may be to overstate the basis for the infant's responses.

Research by Contole and Over (1981) seems to be moving in the direction of falsifying some of the broader, less data-driven claims in this area. With the introduction of additional control conditions their paradigm could also be used to assess infant's discrimination between people and inanimate objects. Contole and Over (1981) have filmed infants at 15 and 30 weeks of age while the infants were either alone or in the presence of the mother or a stranger who either interacted with the infant or remained passive. Judges who did not know which condition the infant was in performed signal-detection analyses of whether an adult was present or absent and, if present, passive or interactive. Microanalyses of various social (e.g., smiling) and nonsocial (e.g., arm movement) behaviors were also performed. By 15 weeks infants' behaviors could be distinguished when an adult was present or absent, although it did not seem to matter whether the adult was the infant's mother or a stranger or whether the adult was interactive or passive. By 30 weeks infants' behaviors reflected whether the adult was passive or interactive. At a minimum, it can be said that by about 13 weeks the infant performs more social behaviors (smiling and looking) when a social object is present than when one is not. Whether the infant's social behaviors would differ in the presence of a person or an inanimate object could be tested by performing the same analyses on the infant's behavior when a person and a comparably sized inanimate object were present. The inanimate object's physical features could be constructed systematically to approximate the characteristics of persons to try and ascertain what features seem most salient for eliciting social behaviors. (The research on face perception could serve as a model, e.g., see Gibson, 1969.) Such research would go far toward establishing when the discrimination in question actually occurs. However, whether this paradigm or another is used is not the point. The point is that statements about the young infant's knowledge of social and nonsocial objects must proceed from a carefully built empirical base.

Analogies with the present line of argument may be made in the areas of face perception and imprinting. Initial overestimates of infants' (both human and infrahuman) abilities have, through research, yielded to more circumscribed and specific statements. In the area of infants' perception of faces, the argument was made that neonates *prefer* human faces above other, similar stimuli. In the area of imprinting, initial descriptions of the phenomenon (Sluckin, 1965) emphasized the particular prosocial species' presumably innate capability to follow a *member of its species*. Both initial generalizations have since been refined in important ways. In face perception, it has been shown that when faces are shown with other complex and symmetrical stimuli the human face is not necessarily preferred before 2 months of age (Brennan, Ames, & Moore, 1966; Hershenson, 1964). In the area of imprinting, others (e.g., Hess 1959) have shown that species who imprint will often follow the first moving object they see—be it animate or inanimate and regardless of whether it is a member of the same species.

It may be that researchers who accept assertions that young infants can distinguish people from objects may be unconsciously acting much as Western parents do when they treat their infants as socially responsive partners and credit them with all types of capabilities (e.g., see Bullowa, 1979). The result is often an anthropomorphizing of the infant to the detriment of science, but to the possible benefit of infant development if one values the perpetuation of the Western mind! However, the specification of the parameters of infants' responsiveness to social and nonsocial objects must be mapped and not taken for granted. The very origins of social cognition—the infants' distinction between social and nonsocial objects—has yet to be pinned down conclusively. To summarize, in the neonatal period the evidence that has been reviewed seems to support the existence of the existential self, but confusion over the self–other distinction and total absence of the distinction between people and inanimate objects.

The Period from 3–8 Months

The Consolidation of the Self–Other Distinction.   The major social-cognitive achievement of this period is the clearer demarcation of where the self ends and the other begins. Researchers who use the recognition of the visual features of the self (e.g., Lewis & Brooks-Gunn, 1979), rather than communicative behaviors as their dependent variables, place the self-other discrimination only at the conclusion of this period. However, examination of the research on receptive communication suggests that the self-other distinction is made earlier. During this period there is evidence that the infant begins to utilize the experiences of others to augment his own.

Two pieces of empirical data, not previously brought to bear on these issues, lead us to attribute the self versus other distinction to the infant. First, there is a phenomenon that Scaife and Bruner (1975) and others (Collis, 1977) have referred to as "joint attention" or "visual co-orientation," which consists of both members of the interacting dyad looking at the same point outside the dyad. For example, the baby may look at a mobile. Then the mother follows the baby's gaze to the mobile, and joint attention is established. Scaife and Bruner (1975) claim that at about 6 months the infant becomes capable of following the *mother's* gaze to an object. The implication of this finding is that infants recognize the perspective of someone outside themselves who is not doing the same thing they are doing. The second phenomenon has been referred to by Campos and Stenberg (1981) as "social referencing." The term is meant to capture the infant's apparent attempt to evaluate some new stimulus through seeking out and interpreting (in some way) the emotional displays provided by another person, in this case, the mother. They have studied this phenomenon in a situation in which the infant and mother are seated side by side, somewhat separated, and facing a new, unusual stimulus that suddenly appears in front of them. Infants at 6 months of age are reported to turn to their mother when the stimulus enters, presumably to ascertain her reaction. The mother can be told to act as if she was fearful of the new stimulus or intensely interested. The infants who look at their mothers are likely to produce an emotional response in line with hers. The important point here is that the infant turns to and looks at the mother's face upon the presentation of a new stimulus. Thus, the phenomenon of social referencing implies that 6-month-old infants can distinguish between the self and others and recognize at some level that the emotional responses of another person may provide useful information about the evaluation of a new event.

What both these phenomena (following another's gaze and social referencing) seem to have in common is that they involve the *reception* or decoding of another person's behavior. That is, the infant looks to someone outside the self to see, on the one hand, what the other is looking at (joint attention) and, on the other hand, how the other is responding to what it is looking at (social referencing). Behaviors such as these imply that the infant has made a distinction between the self and the other and perhaps that the infant is aware that it can modify its own perceptions or emotions by using those of another. On the other side of the coin, when the infant does not wish to engage in communicative interaction with another person it is during this period that the infant develops strategies to avoid doing so. Stern (1981) argues that by 6 months of age infants have the necessary neck muscle control to use gaze and head orientation to initiate, maintain, terminate, or avoid communicative interactions. The presence of infant behaviors designed to shut the other out also suggests that the infant has consolidated the self-other distinction. I say "consolidated" because rudiments of this distinction may be present earlier although infants may lack the motor control to reveal it to observers.

The Categorical Self.   With regard to knowledge of the categorical self, Lewis and Brooks-Gunn (1979) have established that self-recognition can be demonstrated with mirrors or in conditions using video tape. Infants also seem to prefer social objects like themselves, as indicated by greater frequency of smiling to the same-sex parent than to the opposite-sex parent (Brooks-Gunn & Lewis, 1979).

The Distinction Between Social and Nonsocial Objects.   At about 4 or 5 months, the infant's ability to make many sorts of *perceptual* discriminations between people, such as age, gender (Fagan & Singer, 1979), and facial expression (Charlesworth & Kreutzer, 1973), is evidenced. It is also at around 3 months (and not in the neonate as earlier accounts claimed, e.g., Wolff, 1966) that the human voice seems to acquire some special salience for the infant. At that time it becomes the most effective pacifier over other auditory stimuli (Kopp, 1970). Further, at about 6 months of age infants become capable of categorizing a set of male voices versus a set of female voices (Miller, 1981). These findings suggest that infants can discriminate between people and nonsocial objects at this time. However, even if this were so, and the evidence has not been adduced, the *perception of differences is only the first step;* these discriminations need to be endowed with *meaning* and come to have some significance for the infant. For example, differences in the perception of social and nonsocial objects need to signal to infants that they should produce different behaviors in the presence of these objects. Olson (1981) has stated this position well:

> In order to demonstrate that a concept of a person has been formed, it is not sufficient to show merely that persons as stimuli are responded to differently than nonpersons. Discrimination is a necessary but not a sufficient condition. The infant's behavior must at some level be distinctive or appropriate. This can be indexed by the appearance of specific patterns of behavior based on prior learning. For example, the increase in the frequency of smiling and its primary application to persons (or person-like stimuli) would be an example of such evidence [p. 51].

The study alluded to earlier by Contole and Over (1981) is relevant once again. Although their study was not conducted in the most ecologically valid way (a point the authors readily concede) in that the person interacting with the infant had to maintain a certain distance from the infant for technical purposes, their attempt to look for social and nonsocial behaviors in the presence (or absence) of human beings is the type of research this area needs. Their results indicated that although infants at both 15 and 30 weeks acted differently in the presence of a person (mother or stranger) in contrast to when no person was present, only the 30-week-olds acted differently in the presence of an interactive and a passive adult. Microanalyses revealed that the older group looked and smiled significantly more to the interactive than to the passive adult. No significant differences were found for the dependent variable of arm movement—a finding I interpret to mean that these infants were making social responses and not just exhibiting general arousal. These findings suggest that when the infant is about 15 weeks old people act like releasers of social behaviors. Whether the person is interacting or not, the 15-week-old is "off and running" producing social behaviors. By 30 weeks however, infants may have some expectations about what people should be doing in potentially social situations. When the adult's responses to the infant's social bids are not forthcoming, the infant recognizes this and modulates or inhibits his or her social behaviors. As Contole and Over (1981) stated, when the infant is "between 3 and 7 months . . . adults may change from being releasers of infant behavior to true conversational partners [p. 33]."

Summary. The major accomplishment of the period from 3 to 8 months is the infant's discrimination of the self versus the other. This discrimination was revealed through two receptive communicative abilities as well as the infant's ability to avoid communicating with the other.

Also during this period the infant has made many perceptual discriminations between people and nonsocial objects. Further, these perceptual discriminations may have been endowed with some meaning by the infant because, at least at the end of this period, the infant begins to use social behaviors more discriminatively. Distinctions between people and objects on other dimensions, however, may not be evident. For example, when it comes to the infant causing events (intentional communication for instrumental purposes) the 6-month-old infant may still not know that people and objects need to be treated differently and may appeal directly to objects (Harding, 1981). However, infants may recognize that some behaviors work better with (i.e., are reinforced more by) people versus inanimate objects. One study by De Blauw, Dubber, Van Roosmalen, and Snow (1978) suggests that at 6 months (but not at 3 months) infants will direct their distress to people more than to inanimate objects. One means by which infants may initially endow the distinction between people and inanimate objects with significance is through conditioning. People reinforce infant's social overtures and are associated with the reduction of various physiological tensions; clearly, objects by themselves cannot serve these ends.

The Period from 9–12 Months

The Distinction Between Social and Nonsocial Objects. The 9-month-old, approaching the transition from prelinguistic to linguistic communication, is a skilled social partner relative to the 6-month-old of the prior period. In addition to the self versus other distinction, infants in this period may have more knowledge about people than researchers have given them credit for. Once again the literature focusing on infants' communicative behaviors, specifically intentional communication for instrumental purposes, assists researchers in uncovering what infants know about social objects.

It is during the last quarter of the first year that intentional communication for instrumental purposes appears. The presence of this type of intentional communication, in which the infant seeks to influence the behavior of someone outside the self, implies the existence of four prerequisites (Golinkoff, 1981b): (1) the ability to distinguish self from nonself; (2) the ability to maintain some topic in mind to communicate about; (3) the ability to see events as ordered causal sequences with one event (the infant's gestures or vocalizations) occurring prior to and capable of causing later events; (4) the ability to see people as potential agents, capable of serving as a means to an end. Thus, the ability to distinguish self from nonself is not sufficient; infants must distinguish *between* the categories of nonself objects in the world. Initially (and even after the onset of intentional communication for instrumental purposes), the infant directs many communicative behaviors directly to the object it desires, perhaps endowing the object itself with the capacity for self-motivated movement (Harding, 1981; Harding & Golinkoff, 1979).

According to Piaget (1954), in Stage 5 of the sensorimotor period (approximately 12 to 18 months in Piaget's account but appearing at around the end of the first year in many American studies) infants recognize that people can be autonomous centers of action in their own right and that they need to be contacted and activated in distal ways as compared to the way in which one activates inanimate objects. Several lines of evidence support Piaget's assertions. First, Bates et al.'s (1975) preliminary observations of three infants' communicative development found a rough correspondence between Stage 5 causal abilities and the onset of intentional communication for instrumental purposes. Second, Harding and Golinkoff (1979) assessed causal abilities and communicative skill in a controlled laboratory situation and established the necessity of Stage 5 causal development for the infant's use of intentional vocalizations. That is, those infants who used vocalizations simultaneously with eye gaze at their mothers also acted as if they recognized that: (1) people could not be "set into motion"; (2) events have causes apart from their own actions. Both of these insights are Stage 5 causal abilities. Thus, using communicative behaviors with the intent to influence another's behavior is an implicit recognition, on the one hand, of the limitations of the powers of the existential self and, on the other, of the potential power of other social beings.

A longitudinal study of communicative development recently completed by Harding (1981) replicates and extends the finding that infants must recognize people as autonomous beings, capable of self-motivated action (Stage 5), before they can use communication instrumentally. Harding (1981, 1982), drawing on Piaget (1954) and Ryan (1970), developed a model of "intention" as it relates to the development of communication. Her model incorporates distinctions relevant to the discrimination between the powers of social and nonsocial objects. For example, based on her model Harding predicted that communication for instrumental purposes would not be recognized by the infant as a goal until the infant recognized the mother as an autonomous agent (Stage 5 causal level). Before that time, in attempting to achieve a goal such as obtaining a toy, the infant would use communicative behaviors but direct them at objects (including the mother's hand) as if to set the object into motion (Stage 4 causal behaviors). For three assessments on each of Harding's 12 infants (36 observations of causal level and level of communicative development done between 6 and 12 months), all but two supported her predictions about the relationship between cognitive and communicative development. The recognition that others may be agents independent of the self (Stage 5 causality) appeared once again to be prerequisite to the infant's ability to use intentional communication for instrumental purposes.

The Infant's Knowledge of Social Objects.   A study by Carlson-Luden (1980) further supports the argument that infants can discriminate between the capabilities of social and nonsocial objects to serve as agents. By 10 months of age infants seem *not* to expect that the same causal schemes will work with people and objects. In her study 10-month-old infants were taught by their mothers to push a knob on a panel to see a stimulus. On some trials infants knew they could produce an inanimate event (a picture) behind a window. On other trials they could produce an animate event involving a person. In that case a knob push led a person situated on the apparatus to wave and say "hi!" Infants learned to push the knob to cause the inanimate event but failed to learn to cause the animate event sequence. Further, infants pushed the knob significantly more often *toward* the window even in the condition when a push away from the stimulus caused the appearance of the picture. In contrast, there was no difference in the number of knob pushes made in either direction when the reinforcement was the experimenter. It was as if infants appreciated that in the human case contact was not essential. Perhaps 10 months of social interaction was sufficient for infants to realize that pushing a manipulandum should not trigger a positive social response. In fact infants may have considered it disconcerting to be in a situation where human actions were triggered in a mechanistic way. Anecdotal reports (Murray, 1980, personal communication) support this preliminary interpretation. Murray noted that both his children greatly enjoyed playing a game where a press on his nose made his tongue appear. Perhaps they realized that it was anomalous to trigger a person's actions in the same way that one triggers the movements of objects. On the flip side of the coin, infants may not expect inanimate objects to move on their own and act as agents. Golinkoff and Harding (1980) created a scenario in which a real chair in the laboratory appeared to move on its own. Although infants as young as 9 to 12 months were not tested, approximately 39% of the 16-month-olds and 78% of the 24-month-olds responded with either surprise, fear, or smiles and laughter. If we were in fact violating infants' expectations as these results suggest, then at least some infants at these ages may find a self-propelled inanimate object to be as remarkable as a person who is triggered into action like a machine.

During the period between 9 to 12 months infants also act as if they expect people to be able to reverse roles with them. This is a recognition of the fact that people can act reciprocally and exchange the roles of agent and patient of action. Bruner (1975) and Gustafson, Green, and West (1979) have noted that infants start *initiating* established games with their mothers at that time. Notes on my son indicate that at 9 months he put a towel over his head and waited for me to say "peekaboo." He also fed *me* for the first time at 8 months. Additional communicative behaviors that appear during this last quarter of the first year are "showing" and "pointing" for others. Both behaviors (see Lempers, Flavell, & Flavell, 1977) imply that the infant has certainly worked out the self–other distinction. Because the infant does not seem to engage in showing or pointing for the benefit of inanimate objects, infants provide further evidence that they are sensitive to the use of people (and not objects) as targets for communicative contacts.

Some theorists have argued that the social-cognitive abilities noted in the foregoing review may not be sufficient to capture what the child knows about social objects between 9 and 12 months of age. Bretherton, McNew, and Beeghly-Smith (1981), building on the work of Shields (1978) and Premack and Woodruff (1978), have speculated that in order to engage in intentional communication for instrumental purposes infants must have a "theory of mind." Bretherton et al. (1981) argue that "in order to communicate intentionally a baby must have recognized that his mind can be *interfaced* with that of a partner," an interfacing which is possible because: "both partners a) share a *framework of meaning* and b) share *an interfacible medium* (language or conventional gestures) into which underlying intentions can be encoded by the speaker and from which they can be decoded into something corresponding to the speaker's underlying intentions by the addressee [p. 340; their emphasis]." It is called a "theory of mind" because children impute unobservable mental states to themselves and others and use these states to make predictions about the behavior of others (Premack & Woodruff, 1978). Some of the other concepts suggested by Shields (1978) which infants require to engage in intentional communication are as follows:

> . . . Persons are self moving or animate, and influence over the course of their behavior has to be negotiated by invoking interest or a shared frame of constraint. persons identify each other and can react to each other. persons can see, feel, hear, touch, smell, i.e., they have a perceptual field. persons intend their actions. . . . persons have an action potential, i.e., things they can and can't do. Persons can retain previous experience and structure their present behavior by it [pp. 553–554].

Shields has essentially outlined many of the empirical questions the area of infant social cognition will probably be addressing in years to come. There is woefully little data on these abilities now.

To summarize what has been said about the period from 9 to 12 months, at least some obvious perceptual aspects of the categorical self seem to be present. The existential self emerged earlier, and evidence for the further awareness of its limitations and capabilities appears in this period. On both perceptual and salient functional dimensions, infants do seem to appreciate differences between people and inanimate objects.

SUMMARY AND CONCLUSIONS

This chapter has explored three social-cognitive achievements, all evident in some ways during the first year of life, from the perspective of the research on the development of communication. The first achievement—the recognition that there is an existential self, which has feelings and inchoate intentions and serves as an agent—was seen as being present even in the neonatal period. However, evidence was also reviewed suggesting that the infant had not yet ascertained where the self ended and the other began. The second distinction, that between the self and the other, was seen as emerging sometime after the second month and evolving further during the period from 3 to 8 months. The third achievement—the infant's division of nonself objects into people (social objects) and inanimate objects—was seen as emerging in two parts: (1) in perceptual discriminations between 3 and 8 months; (2) in functional discriminations that carry meaning for the infant between 9 and 12 months. My claims in this chapter about when two of these major social-cognitive achievements (self versus other; social versus nonsocial objects) occur are more conservative than claims found in the literature. A critical examination of the research on the development of communication outlines a clearer picture of early social-cognitive development available elsewhere. However, many complex, unanswered questions remain.

Infant's work on these dimensions is not complete as they finish their first year of life. As with all knowledge, there will be continual reconstructions and refinements of what is known. Certainly, there are varying degrees of consciousness about the key concepts discussed. What starts out as implicit, inaccessible knowledge in the first year is transformed into an explicit, verbally expressable understanding in the second year (Bretherton et al., 1981; Lewis & Brooks-Gunn, 1979). At this time the typical infant becomes able to discuss, in a limited way, aspects of the existential self. Some infants can label their emotions, perceptions, and physiological states, as well as the corresponding states in others. Clear empathic responses will be seen then, as in the example of an 18-month-old child offering its security blanket to its crying mother (Zahn-Waxler, Radke-Yarrow, & King, 1979). Infants also begin to label aspects of the categorical self, such as their sex.

Throughout life, as personality and social psychologists can attest, our under-standing of ourselves and others will continue to be transformed as each of us constructs our naive theories of ''human nature,'' the fundamental question in psychology. Furthermore, through formal and informal schooling, humans learn to make finer and finer classificatory cuts among the class of other objects in the world. Social and biological scientists represent the best examples of how knowl-edge is continually reworked and formalized in these two conceptual domains. But even the experts started out as infants, constructing their knowledge first through perception and action. It is my hope that subsequent research will chal-lenge and refine the assertions set forth in this paper on when and how the infant comes to know the self versus the other and people from objects.

ACKNOWLEDGMENTS

I wish to thank Carroll Izard, Karen Gouze, Leslie Rescorla, Susan Scanlon, and Carol Harding for feedback on earlier drafts of this chapter. I also wish to acknowledge the support of the Department of Psychology at the University of Pennsylvania where parts of this paper were written on my sabbatical leave in the fall of 1980.

REFERENCES

Bannister, D., & Agnew, J. The child's construing of self. In A. W. Landfield (Ed.), *Nebraska Symposium on Motivation* (Vol. 24). Lincoln: University of Nebraska Press, 1976.

Bates, E., Camaioni, L., & Volterra, V. The acquisition of performatives prior to speech. *Merrill-Palmer Quarterly, 1975, 21,* 205–226.

Bloom, L. *Language development: Form and function in emerging grammars.* Cambridge, Mass.: MIT Press, 1970.

Bornstein, M. H., Gross, C. G., & Ferdinandsen, K. *Perception of symmetry in infancy.* Paper presented at the International Conference on Infant Studies, New Haven, Conn., April 1980.

Brazleton, T. B. The epigenesis of conversational interaction: A personal account of research development. In M. Bullowa (Ed.), *Before speech: The beginning of interpersonal communica-tion.* Cambridge, Mass.: Cambridge University Press, 1979.

Brazleton, T. B., Koslowski, B., & Main, M. The origins of reciprocity: The early mother–infant interaction. In M. Lewis & L. Rosenblum (Eds.), *The effect of the infant on its caregiver.* New York: Wiley, 1974.

Brennan, W. M., Ames, N. W., & Moore, R. W. Age differences in infants' attention to patterns of different complexities. *Science, 1966, 151,* 354–356.

Bretherton, I., McNew, S., & Beeghly-Smith, M. Early person knowledge as expressed in gestural and verbal communication: When do infants acquire a ''theory of mind''? In M. Lamb & L. Sherrod (Eds.), *Infant social cognition.* Hillsdale, N.J.: Lawrence Erlbaum Associates, 1981.

Brooks, J., & Lewis, M. Infants' responses to strangers: Midget, adult, and child. *Child Develop-ment, 1976, 47,* 323–332.

Brooks-Gunn, J., & Lewis, M. Why ''mama and papa''?: The development of social labels. *Child Development, 1979, 50,* 1203–1206.

Brown, R. *A first language.* Cambridge, Mass.: Harvard University Press, 1973.

Bruner, J. S. Competence in infants. In J. S. Bruner (Ed.), *Beyond the information given: Studies in the psychology of knowing*. New York: Norton, 1973.

Bruner, J. S. The ontogenesis of speech acts. *Journal of Child Language*, 1975, *2*, 1–19.

Bullowa, M. (Ed.). *Before speech: The beginning of interpersonal communication*. Cambridge, Mass.. Cambridge University Press, 1979.

Campos, J. J., & Stenberg, C. R. Perception, appraisal and emotion: The onset of social referencing. In M. Lamb & L. Sherrod (Eds.), *Infant social cognition*. Hillsdale, N.J.: Lawrence Erlbaum Associates, 1981.

Carlson-Luden, V. Infant causality: Is it the same for social and nonsocial events? Paper presented at the International Conference on Infant Studies, New Haven, Conn. April 1980.

Chandler, M. Social cognition: A selective review of current research. In W. R. Overton & J. M. Gallagher (Eds.), *Knowledge and development, Vol. I. Advances in research and theory*. New York: Plenum Press, 1977.

Charlesworth, W., & Kreutzer, M. Facial expressions of infants and children. In P. Ekman (Ed.), *Darwin and facial expression*. New York: Academic Press, 1973.

Collis, G. M. Visual co-orientation and maternal speech. In H. R. Schaffer (Ed.), *Studies in mother–infant interactions*. London: Academic Press, 1977.

Contole, J., & Over, R. Change in selectivity of infant social behavior between 15 and 30 weeks. *Journal of Experimental Child Psychology*, 1981, *32*, 21–35.

Cooley, C. H. *Human nature and the social order*. New York: Scribner's, 1912.

De Blauw, A., Dubber, C., Van Roosmalen, G., & Snow, C. E. Sex and social class differences in early mother–infant interaction. In O. Garnica & M. King (Eds.), *Language, children, and society*. New York: Pergamon, 1978.

Epstein, S. The self-concept revisited. *American Psychologist*, 1973, *28*, 404–416.

Fagan, J. F. III, & Singer, L. T. The role of simple feature differences in infant's recognition of faces. *Infant Behavior and Development*, 1979, *2*, 39–45.

Fantz, R. L. Pattern vision in newborn infants. *Science*, 1963, *140*, 296–297.

Gelman, R., & Spelke, E. The development of thoughts about animates and inanimates: Implications for research on social cognition. In J. H. Flavell & L. Ross (Eds.), *Social cognitive development: Frontiers and possible futures*. Cambridge, England: Cambridge University Press, 1981.

Gibson, E. *Principles of perceptual learning and development*. New York: Appleton-Century-Crofts, 1969.

Glick, J. Cognition and social cognition: An introduction. In J. Glick & K. A. Clarke-Stewart (Eds.), *The development of social understanding*. New York: Gardner Press, 1978.

Golinkoff, R. M. The case for semantic relations: Evidence from the verbal and nonverbal domains. *Journal of Child Language*, 1981, *8*, 413–438. (a)

Golinkoff, R. M. The influence of Piagetian theory on the study of the development of communication. In I. Sigel, D. Brodzinsky, & R. M. Golinkoff (Eds.), *New directions in Piagetian theory and practice*. Hillsdale, N.J.: Lawrence Erlbaum Associates, 1981. (b)

Golinkoff, R. M., Carlson-Luden, V., Harding, C. G., & Sexton, M. The infant's perception of causal events: The distinction between animate and inanimate objects. *Infant Behavior and Development*, in press.

Golinkoff, R. M., & Harding, C. G. *The development of causality: The distinction between animates and inanimates*. Paper presented at the International Conference on Infant Studies, New Haven, Conn., April 1980.

Gustafson, G. E., Green, J. A., & West, M. J. The infant's changing role in mother–infant games: The growth of social skills. *Infant Behavior and Development*, 1979, *2*(4), 301–318.

Haith, M. M., Bergman, T., & Moore, M. J. Eye contact and face scanning in early infancy. *Science*, 1977, *198*, 853–855.

Harding, C. G. *A longitudinal study of the development of the intention to communicate*. Unpublished doctoral dissertation, University of Delaware, 1981.

Harding, C. G. The development of the intention to communicate. *Human Development*, 1982, *25*, 140–151.

Harding, C. G., & Golinkoff, R. M. The origins of intentional vocalizations in prelinguistic infants. *Child Development*, 1979, *50*, 33–40.

Hartka, L., Lewis, M. & Brooks-Gunn, J. *Age changes in contingency learning*. Paper presented at the meetings of the Eastern Psychological Association, New York City, April, 1981.

Hershenson, M. Visual discrimination in the human newborn. *Journal of Comparative and Physiological Psychology*, 1964, *58*, 270–276.

Hess, E. H. Imprinting. *Science*, 1959, *130*, 133–141.

Hoffman, M. L. Empathy, its development and prosocial implications. In C. B. Keasey (Ed.), *Nebraska Symposium on Motivation* (Vol. 25). Lincoln: University of Nebraska Press, 1977.

Izard, C. *Human emotions*. New York: Plenum Press, 1977.

Kopp, C. B. *A comparison of stimuli effective in soothing distressed infants*. Unpublished doctoral dissertation, Claremont University, 1970.

Lamb, M. E. Developing trust and perceived effectance in infancy. In L. P. Lipsitt (Ed.), *Advances in infancy research* (Vol. 2). Norwood, N.J.: Ablex, 1981.

Lamb, M. E., & Sherrod, L. R. Infant social cognition: An introduction. In M. E. Lamb & L. Sherrod (Eds.), *Infant social cognition*. Hillsdale, N.J.: Lawrence Erlbaum Associates, 1981.

Lempers, T., Flavell, E., & Flavell, T. H. The development in very young children of tacit knowledge concerning visual perception. *Genetic Psychology Monographs*, 1977, *95*, 3–53.

Lewis, M., & Brooks-Gunn, J. *Social cognition and the acquisition of self*. New York: Plenum Press, 1979.

Lock, A. Acts not sentences. In W. von Raffler-Engle & Y. Lebrun (Eds.), *Baby talk and infant speech*. Holland: Sivets and Aeitlinger V. B. V., 1976.

Lock, A. *The guided reinvention of language*. London: Academic Press, 1980.

Mahler, M. S., Pine, F., & Bergman, A. *The psychological birth of the human infant*. New York: Basic Books, 1975.

Mead, G. H. *Mind, self and society*. Chicago: University of Chicago Press, 1934.

Miller, C. L. *Development in the discrimination of male and female voices by infants*. Paper presented at the meeting of the Canadian Psychological Association, Toronto, 1981.

Olson, G. M. The recognition of specific persons. In M. Lamb & L. Sherrod (Eds.), *Infant social cognition*. Hillsdale, N.J.: Lawrence Erlbaum Associates, 1981.

Oster, H. Recognition of emotional expression in infancy? In M. Lamb and L. Sherrod (Eds.), *Infant social cognition*. Hillsdale, N.J.: Lawrence Erlbaum Associates, 1981.

Piaget, J. *The origins of intelligence in children*. New York: International Universities Press, 1952. (Originally published, 1936.)

Piaget, J. *The construction of reality in the child*. New York: Ballantine, 1954.

Piaget, J., & Inhelder, B *The psychology of the child*. New York: Basic Books, 1969.

Premack, D., & Woodruff, G. Does the chimpanzee have a theory of mind? *The Behavioral and Brain Sciences*, 1978, *1*, 515–526.

Ryan, T. A. *Intentional behavior*. New York: Ronald Press, 1970.

Sagi, A., & Hoffman, M. L. Empathic distress in newborns. *Developmental Psychology*, 1976, *12*, 175–176.

Scaife, M., & Bruner, J. The capacity for joint visual attention in the infant. *Nature*, 1975, *253*, 365–366.

Schaffer, H. R. Early interactive development. In H. R. Schaffer (Ed.), *Studies in mother–infant interaction*. London: Academic Press, 1977.

Schieffelin, B., & Ochs, E. A cultural perspective on the transition from prelinguistic to linguistic communication. In R. Golinkoff (Ed.), *The transition from prelinguistic to linguistic communication*. Hillsdale, N.J.: Lawrence Erlbaum Associates, in press.

Shantz, C. V. The development of social cognition. In E. M. Hetherington (Ed.), *Review of child development research* (Vol. 5). Chicago: University of Chicago Press, 1975.

Sherrod, L. R. Issues in cognitive-perceptual development: The special case of social stimuli. In M. Lamb & L. Sherrod (Eds.), *Infant social cognition*. Hillsdale, N.J.: Lawrence Erlbaum Associates, 1981.

Shields, M. M. The child as psychologist: Construing the social world. In A. Lock (Ed.), *Action, gesture and symbol. The emergence of language*. London: Academic Press, 1978.

Shotter, J. The cultural context of communication studies: Theoretical and methodological issues. In A. Lock (Ed.), *Action, gesture, and symbol: The emergence of language*. New York: Academic Press, 1978.

Sluckin, W. *Imprinting and early learning*. Chicago: Aldine, 1965.

Snow, C. The development of conversation between mothers and babies. *Journal of Child Language*, 1977, *4*, 1–22.

Stern, D. *The first relationship: Infant and mother*. Cambridge, Mass.: Harvard University Press, 1977.

Stern, D. The development of biologically determined signals of readiness to communicate, which are language resistant. In R. Stark (Ed.), *Language behavior in infancy and early childhood*. New York: Elsevier North Holland, 1981.

Sugarman-Bell, S. Some organizational aspects of preverbal communication. In I. Markova (Ed.), *The social context of language*. New York: Wiley, 1978.

Suomi, S. J. The perception of contingency and social development. In M. Lamb & L. Sherrod (Eds.), *Infant social cognition*. Hillsdale, N.J.: Lawrence Erlbaum Associates, 1981.

Trevarthen, C. Conversations with a two-month old. *New Scientist*, 1974, *62*, 230–235.

Trevarthen, C. Descriptive analyses of infant communicative behavior. In H. R. Schaffer (Ed.), *Studies in mother-infant interaction*. London: Academic Press, 1977.

Trevarthen, C. Communication and cooperation in early infancy: A description of primary intersubjectivity. In M. Bullowa (Ed.), *Before speech: The beginning of interpersonal communication*. Cambridge, Mass.: Cambridge University Press, 1979.

Watson, J. S. Memory and "contingency analysis" in infant learning. *Merrill-Palmer Quarterly*, 1967, *12*, 55–76.

Watson, J. S. Bases of causal inference in infancy: Time, space, and sensory relations. *Infant Behavior and Development*, in press.

Wolff, P. H. The natural history of crying and other vocalizations in early infancy. In B. M. Foss (Ed.), *Determinants of infant behavior* (Vol. IV). London: Metheun, 1966.

Zahn-Waxler, C., Radke-Yarrow, M., & King, R. Child rearing and children's prosocial invitations toward victims of distress. *Child Development*, 1979, *50*, 319–330.

10
The Role of Knowledge and Ideation in the Development of Delay Capacity

Walter Mischel
Stanford University

I suspect that the results of the program of research described in this chapter must surely be anticipated somewhere in Piaget's formidable *oevre*. I offer this summary of some of my work here not for its potential surprise value to Piagetians— they have anticipated much of experimental child psychology. Rather, these studies may fit comfortably in this volume to illustrate how a very different route of theorizing and methodology yields conclusions that seem highly compatible with those Piaget might have predicted. For me, the essence of the compatibility is that the present work makes one thing plain: What is in the child's head, not just what is in the stimulus, must be considered seriously if we seek to understand behavior. In addition, the work illustrates the potential power of the child as intuitive psychologist and as an increasingly competent expert on the rules of behavior. Finally, the work is intended to show that it is fruitful to analyze both the cognitive processes that underlie the child's developing competencies and the characteristic qualities in the child associated with those competencies.

CHILDREN'S KNOWLEDGE OF PSYCHOLOGY

The core of this chapter is the role of ideation in the development of the child's delay capacity. But I want to digress even before I begin. I want first to report some findings that speak to the larger issue of the child as intuitive psychologist who knows about our science more broadly. This digression, I believe, may have relevance for how one views the child's developing competencies and his or her role as ''scientist.''

In the context of a larger program of research on cognitive social-learning person variables (Mischel, 1973, 1979), Harriet Nerlove Mischel and I have been trying to assess aspects of the child's developing cognitive competencies and knowledge. In a fashion surely compatible with a Piagetian perspective, although not directly influenced by it, we construe children as potentially sophisticated intuitive psychologists who develop increasing awareness of psychological principles for understanding social behavior, and learn to use them to guide, master, and control their environments with increasing efficacy. To study the development of children's cognitive competencies, we have begun examining selected features of their growing understanding of psychological principles that underlie a wide range of social behavior. Studies of specific areas of children's developing cognitive competence, pioneered by Piaget, continue to be the focus of voluminous research (e.g., Brown, 1977; Flavell & Wellman, 1977). Indeed, our own research into the principles of self-regulation has recently begun to assess children's growing understanding of effective strategies for specific aspects of self-regulation, such as delay of gratification (Mischel & Mischel, 1983, in press).

In one study, we attempted to measure everyday knowledge of some of the basic rules and principles of psychology, particularly those underlying social behavior. The status of the layperson's awareness of such principles and rules remains highly controversial, in spite of the recent "cognitive revolution" in psychology and the acknowledgment of the extensive role cognition plays in human conduct. Therefore, it seemed potentially interesting to assess the degree to which some of the most basic empirical discoveries of psychological research might be available to the ordinary "untutored" person and especially to young children before their exposure to formal tuition concerning the contents of scientific psychology. We wanted to see which insights, if any, from the basic principles and concepts of psychology would become known to youngsters in the course of early development. With that general purpose, we devised objective tests containing highly specific multiple choice questions that asked fourth and sixth grade children to predict the probable outcome of classical experiments in psychology (Mischel & Mischel, 1979).[1] The experiments were described in detail, with the jargon deleted, and using age-appropriate language.

For example, we described research on the effect of intermittent reinforcement on extinction by showing pictures of a white pigeon and a gray pigeon in their Skinnerian worlds. We then described and illustrated each pigeon pecking at a bar. For one pigeon, pieces of food were dropped into a cup continuously for each of many bar-presses; for the other pigeon reward delivery was on an intermittent schedule. After the end of food for bar-pressing was described, the child had to choose the sentence that best says what each pigeon will then do:

---

[1]A form for use with preschoolers and primary grade school children has been developed and piloted with a small number of subjects. The attempt to question young children about psychological principles seems feasible and promising, but our efforts in this direction are still only preliminary.

1. The gray pigeon (who had gotten food some of the time it pressed the bar) will completely stop pressing the bar sooner than the white pigeon.
2. The gray pigeon (who had gotten food some of the time it pressed the bar) and the white pigeon (who had gotten food every time it pressed the bar) will both completely stop pressing the bar at the same time.
3. The white pigeon (who had gotten food every time it pressed the bar) will completely stop pressing the bar sooner than the gray pigeon.

Our subjects were 38 fourth graders and 49 sixth graders attending the Nixon Elementary School in Stanford, California. The children were volunteers who came in groups after school hours to a small room at their school. All procedures were conducted by two female adults. Specifically, each child was given a booklet containing descriptions of over a dozen psychology experiments in language the children could easily understand. Among the experiments summarized were Pavlov's demonstration of classical conditioning (1927/1960), Asch's study of conformity (1956), Bandura's demonstration of the effect of modeling on aggressive behavior (Bandura, Ross, & Ross, 1961), and the bystander intervention experiments of Latané and his colleagues (Latané & Darley, 1968; Latané & Rodin, 1969). Also included were several examples of basic psychological principles associated with more than one series of experimental studies (e.g., the contrast effect in perceived water temperature, better memory performance when measured by recognition than by recall). A summary of results, a complete list of the principles and experiments, and the sources on which they were based is in Table 10.1.

Note that even the 10-year-olds knew a great deal about the basic principles of social behavior. They knew, for example, that children who have seen an adult playing aggressively will subsequently play more aggressively, that live modeling with guided participation is more effective in reducing snake phobic behavior than covert desensitization or modeling alone, that frightened baby monkeys prefer to cling to a soft surrogate mother rather than a wire one that provides milk, and that not attending to either immediate or delayed rewards facilitates delay. Fourth graders did not know that a bystander will be more likely to help when alone than when in a group but by the time they were in grade six they did know this widely cited nonobvious insight of social psychology. Do not conclude, however, that the children's psychological knowledge was limitless. For example, they did not know Pavlov's discovery about classical conditioning (although they did know that intermittent reinforcement makes Skinner's pigeons peck longer after the food stops). They also were wrong about conformity in the Asch situation, the importance of physical attractiveness in future dating behavior, and the effects of cognitive dissonance.

Some of our subjects had Stanford Binet or WISC scores on record at the school. These scores were made available to us through parental permission for nine fourth graders and ten sixth graders. The correlations between these scores

TABLE 10.1
Summary of Children's Predictions of Psychological Principles

Experiment or Principle	grade	χ^2	df	right	wrong	NS
1. Group pressure can distort visual judgment (Asch, 1956)	4	25.28	1		<.001	
	6	.082	1			x
2. Not attending to the rewards facilitates delay (Mischel, Ebbesen, & Zeiss, 1972)	4	38.42	3	<.001		
	6	30.59	3	<.001		
3. The same water temperature feels cooler on a hot day than on a cool day (based on principle of effect of context, Helson, 1964)	4	12.80	2	<.002		
	6	54.03	2	<.001		
4. Classical conditioning: after repeated pairing of light and food, dog will salivate to food alone (Pavlov, 1927)	4	2.14	1			x
	6	4.0	1		<.05	
5. Children who have seen an adult behave aggressively will subsequently behave more aggressively than a control group (Bandura, Ross, and Ross, 1961)	4	21.16	3	<.001		
	6	78.26	3	<.001		
6. Modeling with guided participation is more powerful than covert desensitization or modeling alone in the treatment of phobic behavior (Bandura, Blanchard, & Ritter, 1969)	4	59.26	3	<.001		
	6	103.08	3	<.001		
7. The absence of object permanence at age 3 months (Piaget, 1954)	4	16.96	2		<.001	
	6	4.2	2			x
8. The attainment of object permanence by age 1½ years (Piaget, 1954)	4	2.53	2			x
	6	12.87	2	<.002		
9. Narrative stories are an aid to memory for lists of words (Bower & Clark, 1969)	4	10.04	2	<.007		
	6	48.38	2	<.001		
10. Frightened, infant monkeys prefer soft surrogate mothers to wire ones that produce milk (Harlow & Zimmerman, 1959)	4	21.54	2	<.001		
	6	23.35	2	<.001		
11. Memory performance is better when measured by recognition vs. recall (Achilles, 1920)	4	44.15	2	<.001		
	6	70.71	2	<.001		
12. Inhibition of bystander intervention						
a) Two person groups are less likely than an individual alone to offer help to an injured woman (Latané and Rodin, 1969)	4	4.23	2			x
b) Three person groups are less likely than an individual alone to report a fire (Latané and Darley, 1968)	6	15.87	2	<.001		
13. Extinction of a response is more rapid following continuous vs. intermittent reinforcement (Ferster & Skinner, 1957)	4	12.72	2	<.002		
14. The absence of conservation of quantity of liquid at age 4 years (Piaget, 1965)	4	44.89	4	<.001		
15. The attainment of conservation of quantity of liquid by age 10 years (Piaget, 1965)	4	114.89	4	<.001		

(continued)

TABLE 10.1 (*Continued*)

Experiment or Principle	Prediction					
	grade	χ^2	df	right	wrong	NS
16. Physical appearance is more important in determining future dating behavior than opinions, intelligence, or school grades (Walster, Aronson, Abrahams, & Rothman, 1966)	6	51.17	3		<.001	
17. Attitude change is greater after a $1 reward for forced compliance than after a $20 reward (Festinger & Carlsmith, 1959)	6	34.02	2		<.001	

and knowledge scores were: fourth graders, $r = .11$ (ns), sixth graders, $r = .93$, $p < .001$, with a combined r of .54, $p < .005$. Although these results are based on small samples and should be viewed only as suggestive, they do encourage us to believe that the antecedents and correlates of children's growing understanding of psychological principles merits serious attention, and we hope to pursue that route more deeply.

CHILDREN'S KNOWLEDGE OF SELF-CONTROL

We also have been investigating in a more detailed fashion children's understanding of psychological principles for self-regulation. Here we employed a two-pronged strategy. First, we try to discover the objective conditions that make self-regulation (and particularly delay of gratification and resistance to temptation) either difficult or easy (e.g., Mischel, 1974; Mischel & Moore, 1980; Mischel & Patterson, 1976; Moore, Mischel, & Zeiss, 1976). Second, we are assessing the child's own developing understanding of effective strategies for self-regulation (e.g., Mischel & Mischel, 1983, in press; Yates & Mischel, 1979), an effort that is made possible by the availability of empirical data that clarify the conditions and processes that govern effective self-regulation.

The role of reward-relevant ideation is the aspect of delay of gratification that seems to have especially interesting theoretical implications. Little has been learned until recently about the way in which mental representations of rewards and outcomes affect the individual's pursuit of them. This ignorance is especially surprising given the crucial importance of the concept of reinforcement in psychology. For the last few years our research has focused on the problem of reward representation when people are attempting to delay immediate smaller gratification for the sake of more desirable but deferred goals. Our intent has been to understand more deeply how the mental representation of the relevant rewards in a contingency might influence voluntary delay for those outcomes. In the remainder of this chapter I want to summarize first our work on the "objective" rules of effective reward representation and then our research on children's knowledge of those rules.

THEORIES OF MECHANISMS UNDERLYING DELAY CAPACITY

One of the few theoretical discussions of how delay of gratification may be bridged is Freud's (1911/1959) pioneering analysis of the transition from primary to secondary process. He proposed that ideation arises initially when there is a block or delay in the process of direct gratification discharge (Rapaport, 1967). Briefly, Freud suggested that the child constructs a hallucinatory wish-fulfilling image of the need-satisfying object during the externally imposed delay period. With increased exposure to the imposed delay of satisfying objects, and as a result of the development of greater ego organization, the child substitutes hallucinatory satisfactions and other thought processes that convert "free cathexes" into "bound cathexes" (e.g., Freud, 1911/1959; Singer, 1955) and allow "time binding." The exact process that supposedly occurs here does not seem entirely clear, although there has been much psychoanalytic theorizing and speculation about how the mental representation of blocked gratifications may function in the growth of the capacity to delay gratification.

Theorists other than psychoanalysts, guided by a learning orientation, suggest that the capacity to bridge delay of gratification or "time-binding" also may be helped by self-instructional processes through which the person makes the delayed consequences of the waiting behavior more salient (Mischel, 1974). If so, any factors (situational or within the individual) that make delayed consequences more vivid should serve to increase waiting time. Such a view, consistent with learning theories, also implies the operating of covert self-reinforcement processes through which individuals may reinforce their own delay behavior by anticipating some of the rewarding outcomes that will be produced by waiting. Likewise, one could also expect that young children would easily forget the deferred outcomes for which they are waiting and therefore stop waiting unless they are reminded of the relevant contingencies and rewards during the course of the delay period itself.

Given these arguments, any circumstances that help the child to attend mentally to the delayed reward for which he or she is waiting should lead to greater or easier delay. Any cues in the situation that increase the salience of the delayed gratifications (for example, by letting the person focus on them, by picturing them in imagination, or by thinking of the awaited object) should enhance waiting behavior. Therefore we initially predicted that voluntary delay behavior would be greater when people convert the delayed object into more concrete form by making it psychologically more immediate, as by providing themselves with physical cues about it. It seemed to us that the most direct way to increase the salience of the deferred outcomes and to focus attention on them would be to have them physically present in front of subjects so that they can attend to them vividly and easily. To investigate how attention to delayed and immediate outcomes influences waiting behavior for them, we varied the availability of those outcomes for attention during the delay period (Mischel, 1974).

STUDYING ATTENTION TO THE REWARDS:
SOME UNEXPECTED EFFECTS

A method was developed in which very young children would be willing to wait by themselves in an experimental room for at least a short time without becoming excessively upset (Mischel & Ebbesen, 1970). After the usual brief play periods to establish rapport, each child was taught a "game" in which he or she could immediately summon the experimenter through a simple signal. The children practiced this procedure until they clearly understood that they could immediately end the waiting period alone in the room by signaling for the experimenter's return. The child was then introduced to the relevant contingency. Specifically, each child was shown two objects (e.g., snack-food treats). One of these the child clearly preferred (as determined by pretesting), but to get the preferred object required waiting for it until the experimenter returned "by himself." Throughout this delay period the child was entirely free to signal anytime for the experimenter to return; children who signaled could have the less preferred object at once but would forego the more desirable one later.

To systematically vary the extent to which children could attend to the rewards while they were waiting for them, the reward objects were available to the child's view in all attentional combinations. In one condition the children waited with both the immediate (less preferred) and the delayed (more preferred) rewards facing them in the experimental room so that they could attend to both outcomes. In a second group, neither reward was available for the child's attention, both rewards having been removed from sight. For children in the remaining two groups either the delayed reward only or the immediate reward only was left facing them and available for attention while they waited. The dependent measure was the length of time before each child voluntarily terminated the waiting period, recorded in seconds.

We found the very opposite of what we had predicted. We had expected that attention to the delayed rewards in the choice situation would facilitate delay behavior while waiting. We discovered, instead, that attention to the rewards significantly and dramatically decreased delay of gratification. The children waited longest when *no* rewards faced them during the delay period; they waited significantly less long when they faced the delayed reward, or the immediate

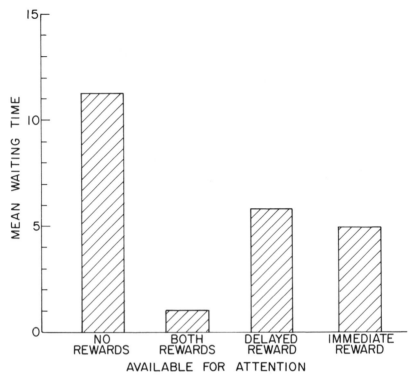

FIG. 10.1   Mean minutes of voluntary waiting time for the delayed reward in each attention condition (from Mischel & Ebbesen, 1970).

reward, or both rewards, as Figure 10.1 indicates, with no significant differences between the reward conditions but a trend for shortest delay when the children were facing both rewards.

To begin to understand these unexpected results, we attempted to see just what the children were doing while they were waiting. Therefore, we observed them closely by means of a one-way mirror throughout the delay period as they sat waiting for their preferred outcomes in what had turned out to be the most difficult situation, (i.e., when both the immediate and delayed outcomes faced them). Our ally here was "Mr. Talk Box," a device that consisted of a tape recorder and a microphone that announced its name to the youngster and cheerfully said, "Hi, I have big ears and I love it when children fill them with all the things they think and feel, no matter what." Thereafter, Mr. Talk Box adopted a Rogerian nondirective attitude and acceptingly "uhemed" and "ahad" to whatever the child said to him. Many of the children seemed quick to treat Mr. Talk Box as an extension of their psyche and participated enthusiastically in dialogues with themselves.

From these observations we obtained some leads about the possible mechanisms through which the children seemed to mediate and facilitate their own goal-directed waiting. Some children had remarkably simple but powerful delay strategies. They seemed able to wait for the preferred reward for long periods apparently by converting the aversive waiting situation into a more pleasant nonwaiting one. They did this by elaborate self-distraction techniques through which they spent their time psychologically doing almost anything other than waiting and suffering. Instead of focusing their attention for long on the rewards, they avoided them altogether. Some of these children covered their eyes with their hands, rested their heads on their arms, and discovered other similar techniques for averting their eyes from the rewards. Many children also seemed to try to reduce the frustration of delay of reward by creating their own diversions: They talked quietly to themselves, sang ("This is such a pretty day, hurray"), played games with their hands and feet, and when all other distractions seemed exhausted even tried to go to sleep during the waiting situation—as one child did successfully, falling into a deep slumber in front of the signal bell. Anyone who has ever been the victim of a boring lecture is surely familiar with such techniques.

How can we make sense theoretically of these intuitively sensible (albeit, post-hoc) impressions? When the children are experiencing conflict and frustration about wanting to end the delay but not wanting to lose the preferred, delayed outcome, then cues that enhance attention to the elements in the conflict (i.e., the two sets of rewards) seem to make waiting more aversive. So, when the children attend to the immediate reward their motivation for it increases and they want to take it but become frustrated because they know that if they do they cannot get the more preferred reward later. When the children attend to the preferred but delayed outcome they become increasingly frustrated because they then want it more now but cannot have it yet. When they focus attention on both objects, both of these sources of frustration occur and further delay becomes most aversive; therefore the child soon terminates. This line of reasoning, consistent with frustrative nonreward theory (Amsel, 1962), suggests that conditions that decrease attention to the rewards in the choice contingency and that distract the child from the conflict and the frustrative delay would make it less aversive to continue goal-directed waiting and therefore lead to a longer delay of gratification period.

COGNITIVE DISTRACTION FROM THE REAL REWARDS FACILITATES DELAY

The theorizing so far suggests that delay of gratification and frustration tolerance should be facilitated by conditions that help the person to transform the aversive waiting period into a more pleasant nonwaiting situation. Children could achieve such a transformation by converting their attention and thoughts away from the frustrative components of delay of gratification. They should be able to enhance voluntary delay of reward by any overt or covert activities that serve as distractors from the rewards and thus from the aversiveness of the situation. Through such distraction they could presumably convert the frustrative delay-of-reward situation into a less aversive one. Any cognitions or activities that serve to distract the children from the reward objects therefore should increase the length of time that they would be able to wait for their preferred but delayed outcomes.

The challenge was how to devise a way to affect what the child is going to think about so that we could test these propositions experimentally. We stumbled quite a bit before discovering that even at age 3 and 4 our subjects could give us vivid examples of the many things that led them to feel happy (such as finding frogs, singing, or swinging on a swing with mommy pushing). We, in turn, instructed them to think about those fun things while they sat waiting alone for their preferred outcomes. The immediate and delayed rewards were physically not available for direct attention during the waiting period in some of these studies. Here we manipulated the children's attention cognitively to the absent rewards by different types of instructions given before the start of the delay period. The findings showed that cognitions directed toward the rewards substantially reduced, rather than enhanced, the duration of time that the children were able to wait. Thus, attentional and cognitive mechanisms that enhance the salience of the rewards greatly decreased the length of voluntary delay time. In contrast, overt or covert distractions from the rewards (e.g., by prior instructions to think about fun things) facilitated delay of gratification (Mischel, Ebbesen, & Zeiss, 1972), as Figure 10.2 summarizes graphically.

Taken as a whole, the findings disconfirm theories that predict mental attention to the reward objects will enhance voluntary delay by facilitating "time binding" and tension discharge (through cathexes of the image of the object). The results also undermine any "salience" theories which would suggest that making the outcomes salient by imagery, cognitions, and self-instructions about the consequences of delay behavior should increase voluntary delay. In contrast to theoretical expectations that images and cognitions relevant to the gratifications should sustain delay behavior, looking at the rewards or thinking about them in their absence was found to decrease voluntary delay of gratification. We therefore concluded that, at least in the present delay paradigm, effective delay does not appear to be mediated by consummatory fantasies about the rewards; instead, it seems to require suppressive and avoidance mechanisms to reduce frustration during the delay period. Situational arrangements or self-induced conditions that allow one to shift attention more readily from the reward objects seem to facilitate voluntary waiting times.

Of course, the transformations and distractions that occur during delay do not erase the role of the reward contingencies in the waiting situation. We see that from data which showed that there was little persistence in "thinking fun" or playing with a toy when there was no reward contingency for waiting. Although the distracting activity itself was pleasant enough to maintain the waiting for a contingent reward, it did not in itself keep the children in the room for more than a minute when the contingency was removed. Moreover, the children easily

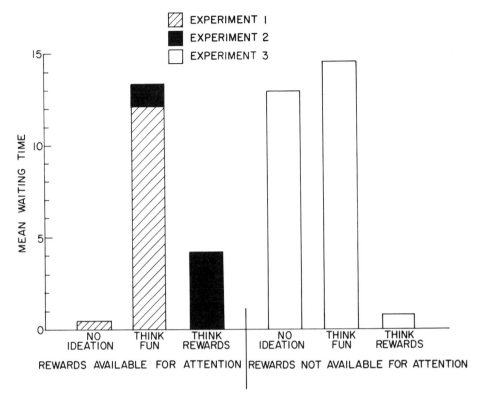

FIG. 10.2   Mean minutes of voluntary waiting time for treatment conditions in Experiments 1, 2, and 3, comparing different ideation instructions with controls (from Mischel, Ebbesen, & Zeiss, 1972).

reproduced (verbally or by appropriate action) the contingencies at the end of the waiting period, thus further showing that the contingency was available mentally to them throughout the waiting period. Children who had been busily distracting themselves for the full 15 minutes, playing with a toy or singing songs, immediately and spontaneously ate the appropriate food reward when the experimenter returned. It is evident that the transformation of the aversive waiting experience into a pleasant play period did not efface the task-oriented purpose of the behavior and presumably the two processes somehow coexist. The children remained guided by their goals, even when they were absorbed in distractions intended to obscure them or reduce their intensity. Of course the way the contingency was operating remains an interesting issue for speculation. Perhaps the contingency was available but was never reproduced mentally until the end of waiting. Perhaps the children have reminded themselves of the contingency occasionally throughout the waiting period. As mentioned before, children often verbalized the contingency when they left their distracting play for a moment and seemed about to end their waiting. It is as if the children periodically remind themselves of the goal for which they are waiting, remember it but distract themselves from it to make delay less frustrative, and then repeat the process throughout the period thus bridging the delay time. In this way they can transform the noxious situation into an easy one and make waiting and "will power" manageable and less formidable than psychological theories originally suggested.

SYMBOLICALLY-PRESENTED REWARDS FACILITATE DELAY

Given the complex cognitive activity that seems to mediate delay behavior it becomes important to consider and control more precisely the covert activities in the subject during the waiting period. The most relevant condition for further study at this point seemed to be the one in which the subject is attending cognitively to the reward objects although the rewards are physically absent. Freud's (1911/1959) formulation of delay of gratification suggested that delay capacity begins when the child develops images (mental representations) of the delayed reward in the absence of the object itself. That view suggests that the hungry infant may gain some satisfaction by forming a "hallucinatory" image of the mother's breast when she is physically unavailable. While originally we tried to manipulate attention to the actual rewards by varying their presence or absence in the child's visual field, we had not manipulated the availability of an *image* of the relevant objects in their physical absence. Mischel and Moore (1973) tried to approximate this condition at least crudely by *symbolic* presentations of the absent objects during the delay period. We therefore exposed children to slide-presented images of the absent reward objects while they were waiting for them. The design of this study compared the effect on delay behavior of exposure to such images of the "relevant" objects (i.e., the rewarding outcomes for which the subject was waiting) with exposure to images of similar objects that were irrelevant to the delay contingency.

Preschool children in this study first had to choose between two rewards. Then they were allowed to wait for their preferred choice or to signal at any time to obtain the less preferred outcome immediately, just as in the Mischel et al. (1972) study. Two different pairs of reward choices were employed: half the children chose between two marshmallows and a pretzel and half between two pennies and a token. During the delay period, we exposed the children to realistic color slide-presented images on a screen that faced them. In one condition the images were slides of the rewards between which the children had chosen ("relevant imagery"); in another condition, the slides showed the objects that the child had not seen before ("irrelevant imagery"). For example, if a child had been given a choice between two marshmallows and a pretzel, each relevant imagery slide would show those reward objects, whereas each irrelevant imagery slide would depict the other objects (two pennies and a token) to which he or she had not been exposed previously (i.e., the irrelevant rewards with respect to the contingency). Children in a third condition were exposed to a blank slide (no picture but illuminated screen). The fourth condition was a no-slide control group.

The slides with *relevant* imagery produced the longest delay times in all conditions, and the contents of slide-presented images yielded a highly significant main effect ($p < .001$). The effects of relevant slide-presented rewards thus turned out to be the opposite of those we had found for exposure to the real rewards. Although attention to the real objects makes it much harder for preschool children to delay, for them slide-presented symbolic presentations of those rewards substantially increases waiting time. Further, these opposite effects were found reliably within the same basic subject population and experimental paradigm at the same preschool. The provocative question here was why this difference occurred.

Mischel and Moore (1980) tried to resolve this discrepancy and to clarify why symbolic reward presentations enhance self-imposed delay although attention to the actual outcomes makes it more difficult. We reasoned that the highly significant effects obtained for the mode of presentation of the reward stimuli (real vs. slide-presented) occurred because they led children to ideate about the rewards in different ways. We thought, extrapolating from Berlyne's (1960) and Estes' (1972) distinctions, that a stimulus may have a motivational (consummatory, arousal) function and an informational (cue) function. The actual reward stimuli (i.e., the real objects) probably have a more powerful motivational effect than do their symbolic representations (i.e., slide images). But symbolic representations of the objects (e.g., through slide pictures) would have a more abstract cue function. When children view the actual goal objects their motivation is increased, but a picture of the rewards reminds them of the desired objects without producing as much affective arousal. The motivational arousal generated by attention to the real rewards themselves is frustrative because it increases the child's desire to make the blocked consummatory responses appropriate to the outcome (e.g., eat it, play with it). This arousal function of the real stimulus makes the frustration effect even greater (because the person cannot let himself make the consummatory response), thereby rendering delay more difficult (Mischel et al., 1972). In contrast, the cue (informative) function of the symbolic reward stimulus may guide and sustain the individual's goal-directed delay behavior, by reminding one of the contingency in the delay situation (''if I wait, I'll get . . .'') but without being so real that it is frustratively arousing.

In sum, we reasoned at this point that when preschool children are exposed to the real reward stimuli and must wait for them they become excessively aroused; such arousal is frustrative for them because it makes them ready to perform the terminal response in a situation in which they cannot do so. In contrast, when they are exposed to the symbolic representations of the objects (in the form of pictures or slides) the stimuli retain their cue function but do not generate excessive arousal. (After all, pictures and slides cannot be consumed.) Mischel and Moore (1980) attempted to test this general conceptualization more systematically. We varied the children's consummatory ideation by manipulating their attention to the arousing qualities of the reward objects through instructions. We simultaneously varied the slide-presented stimulus content that faced the child during the delay period. This design allowed us to isolate the role of consummatory ideation and of symbolic presentations of the rewards in the delay of gratification paradigm.

Specifically, we hypothesized that the key variable would be the child's ideation about the rewards and not their physical representation during the delay period. For this purpose, we tried to replicate the major Mischel and Moore (1973) finding that exposure to slides of the rewards in the delay contingency leads to significantly longer delay than does exposure to slides of comparable rewards that are irrelevant to the delay contingency. And we also predicted that this enhancing effect of the slide-presented rewards can be completely eliminated and even reversed when children are instructed (before the delay period) to ideate about the consummatory qualities of the relevant rewards while they are waiting for them. Using the self-imposed delay of gratification paradigm (e.g., Mischel et al., 1972), we systematically varied the contents of slide-presented images of the rewards and the instructions to the children about ideation during the delay (Mischel & Moore, 1980).

The results clearly supported our expectations. We replicated the original finding that exposure to slides of the relevant rewards leads to significantly longer self-imposed delay than does exposure to slides of the comparable rewards that are irrelevant to the delay contingency (Mischel & Moore, 1973). But interestingly, we also found that the delay-enhancing effects of the relevant slides can be entirely eliminated when subjects are instructed before the delay interval to ideate about the consummatory qualities of the relevant rewards (e.g., the taste and texture of food objects) while waiting for them. Thus the delay-enhancing effects of exposure to the symbolic presentation of the rewards in the waiting contingency depend on their allowing the child to ideate about them but in a nonconsummatory fashion. In contrast, consummatory ideation about the relevant rewards, whether induced by instructions (as in this study), or by exposure to the actual rewards (Mischel & Ebbesen, 1970; Mischel et al., 1972), makes effective delay of gratification difficult. It is the child's consummatory ideation about the rewards, and not the content of the slide the child faced during the waiting period, that seemed to be the crucial determinant.

For example, instructions to dwell on the consummatory qualities of the rewards in the delay contingency consistently led to the shortest delay times. When instructed to ideate about the consummatory qualities of the objects in the waiting contingency ("relevant rewards") the children delayed gratification significantly less long than when they were given the same instructions directed at comparable rewards irrelevant to the delay contingency. The debilitating effect of consummatory ideation about the rewards in the contingency were found regardless of the physical stimulus that faced the children while they were waiting (see Figure 10.3).

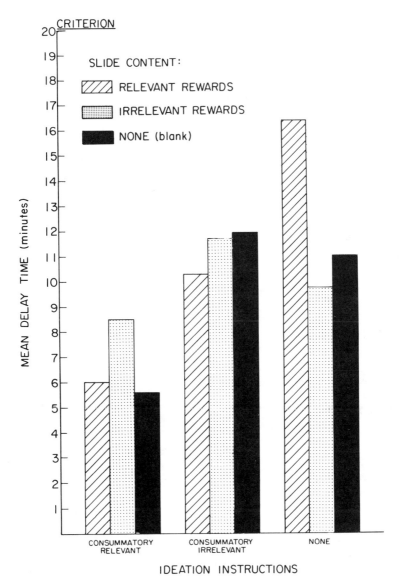

FIG. 10.3 Effects of ideation and slide content on delay time (from Mischel & Moore, 1980).

TRANSFORMING THE STIMULUS BY COGNITIVE OPERATIONS

The results thus far suggest that the effects of attention to the rewards upon delay behavior probably depend on *how* the children attend to them rather than simply on whether or not they do. If so, then attention focused at the nonconsummatory (more abstract, "cool," informative) cue properties of the reward stimuli, should facilitate delay. In contrast, attention to the motivational or arousing ("hot") qualities of the rewards should increase the frustrativeness of delay and make effective self-control more difficult. If Freud's (1911/1959) conceptualization of the positive role of the "hallucinatory image" of the blocked gratification in the development of delay of gratification refers to the motivational properties of the image, he was probably incorrect. But if his formulation referred to the nonconsummatory, more abstract cue properties of the image, it may still prove to be of value in understanding the total process.

We have been testing these theoretical possibilities in various ways. Some of our studies have explored how the impact of attention to the rewards in the delay paradigm can be modified by the child's specific *cognitive transformations* of them. In these studies, just before the delay period begins, we give children brief instructions intended to encourage them to ideate in different ways during the actual delay time. To illustrate, in one study we compared the effects of instructions to ideate about the motivational (consummatory) qualities of the "relevant" rewards with comparable instructions to ideate about their nonmotivational (nonconsummatory) qualities and associations (Mischel & Baker, 1975). We also used the same two types of instructions for the "irrelevant" rewards. (Relevant and irrelevant were operationalized as in the Mischel and Moore studies.) All children had to wait while facing the relevant rewards in the contingency.

Guided by these instructions children seem able to cognitively transform the reward objects that face them during the delay period in ways that either permit or prevent effective delay of gratification. For example, when the children have been instructed to focus cognitively on the consummatory qualities of the relevant reward objects (such as the pretzel's crunchy, salty taste or the chewy, sweet, soft taste of the marshmallows) it becomes difficult for them to wait. Conversely, if they cognitively transform the stimulus to focus on the nonconsummatory qualities (by thinking about the pretzel sticks, for example, as long, thick brown logs, or by thinking about the marshmallows as white, puffy clouds or as round, white moons), they can wait for long periods of time (Mischel & Baker, 1975). Table 10.2 summarizes the main results.

Most interesting, transformations of the reward objects that focus on their nonconsummatory qualities provide more than mere cognitive distraction. Thus, the Mischel and Baker study compared the effects of instructions that focus on nonconsummatory qualities of the relevant reward objects (i.e., those for which

TABLE 10.2
Mean Delay Time in Each Ideation Instruction Condition
(from Mischel and Baker, 1975)[a]

	Content of Ideation	
Rewards in Ideation	Consummatory	Nonconsummatory
Relevant[b]	5.60	13.51
Irrelevant[b]	16.82	4.46

[a]Maximum possible delay time is 20 minutes. All subjects facing the rewards. Data are in minutes.
[b]To contingency in the waiting situation.

the subject is actually waiting) with the same instructions for irrelevant rewards. When the children had been instructed to ideate about nonconsummatory qualities of the relevant rewards their mean delay time was more than 13 minutes (20 minutes was the maximum amount of time possible). In contrast, when the children had been given the same instructions with regard to the irrelevant rewards (i.e., comparable but not in the delay contingency) their average delay time was less than 5 minutes. Thus, attention to the nonconsummatory qualities and associations of the actual reward objects in the delay contingency substantially enhances the ability to wait for them, and does so more effectively than when the same ideation instructions focus on comparable objects irrelevant to the delay contingency.

Might the relatively low delay time obtained when instructions dealt with ideation for the irrelevant rewards reflect that young children simply have trouble thinking about reward objects that are not present? That interpretation seems unlikely given that the longest mean delay time (almost 17 minutes) occurred when subjects were instructed to ideate about those same objects but with regard to their consummatory qualities (see Table 10.2). This finding also is provocative theoretically. It suggests that while consummatory ideation about a potentially available object makes it difficult to delay gratification, similar consummatory ideation about an outcome that is simply unattainable in the situation (i.e., the irrelevant rewards), rather than being aversive, is highly pleasurable and may serve to sustain prolonged delay behavior. Thus, consummatory ideation about reward objects that are not expected and not available in the delay contingency (the irrelevant rewards) may serve as an interesting effective distractor, hence facilitating waiting. But in contrast, similar ideation about the relevant but blocked rewards heightens the frustration of wanting what one expects but cannot yet have and, by making the delay more aversive, decreases one's waiting time.

Additional support for the important role of cognitive transformations in delay behavior also comes from studies that show how instructions allow children to easily transform the real objects (present in front of them) into an abstract version (a "color picture in your head"), or to transform the picture of the objects (i.e., a slide projected on a screen in front of them) into the "real" objects by pretending in imagination that they are actually there on a plate in front of them. These instructions yield the predictable opposite effects on delay time shown by the children. Thus Moore et al. (1976) exposed preschoolers either to a slide-presented image of the rewards or to the actual rewards. Half the children in each of these conditions were instructed before the start of the delay period to imagine a "picture" of the reward objects during the delay period. To illustrate:

> . . . Close your eyes. In your head try to see the picture of the _____ (immediate and delayed rewards). Make a color picture of (them); put a frame around them. You can see the picture of them. Now open your eyes and do the same thing. (more practice) . . . From now on you can see a picture that shows _____ (immediate and delayed rewards) here in front of you. The _____ aren't real; they're just a picture. . . . When I'm gone remember to see the picture in front of you.

Conversely, half the children in each of the conditions were instructed before the delay period (with similar techniques) to imagine the *real* rewards actually present in front of them while waiting. Details of the instructions were adapted to make them plausible in each condition, and a maximum delay time of 20 minutes was possible. The findings suggested that the crucial determinant of delay behavior was the subject's cognitive representation, regardless of what was actually in front of the child. When imagining the rewards as a picture, the mean delay time was almost 18 minutes, regardless of whether the real rewards or a picture of them actually faced the child. But when representing the rewards cognitively as if they were real, subjects' delay time was significantly and very substantially lower, regardless of whether the slide or the actual set of rewards was objectively in front of them (see Table 10.3).

The findings on cognitive stimulus transformation taken as a whole thus seem to clearly show that how children represent the rewards cognitively (not what is physically in front of them) determines how long they delay gratification in this paradigm. Regardless of the stimulus in the children's visual field, if they imagine the real objects as present they cannot wait very long for them; if they imagine pictures (abstract representations) of the objects they can wait for long time periods (and even longer than when they are distracting themselves with abstract representations of objects that are comparable but not relevant to the rewards for which they are waiting). One can completely alter (in fact, reverse) the effects of the physically present reward stimuli in the situation, and cognitively control delay behavior with substantial precision by means of ideation-inducing instructions. Arousal-generating cognitions about the real objects in the contingency significantly impede delay, whereas cognitions about their nonconsummatory (nonmotivational) qualities or about their abstract representations have the opposite effect. In sum, cognitive representations of the rewards (goals,

TABLE 10.3
Mean Delay Time as a Function of Cognitive Transformations
(from Moore, Mischel and Zeiss, 1976)[a]

Objectively Facing Subject	Cognitive Representation of Rewards as:	
	Pictures	Real
Picture of Rewards	17.75	5.95
Real Rewards	17.70	7.91

[a]Maximum possible delay time is 20 minutes. Data are in minutes.

outcomes) that emphasize their motivational (consummatory, arousal) qualities, seem to prevent effective delay by generating excessive frustration, at least in young children. The more the person focuses on the arousing qualities of the blocked goals, the more intense and aversive the choice conflict and the delay become. Conversely, cognitive representation of the same objects that focuses on their nonconsummatory (more abstract, less arousing) qualities appears to facilitate the maintenance of goal-directed behavior and make delay of gratification achievable even by the young child.

STUDYING CHILDREN'S DEVELOPING KNOWLEDGE OF DELAY RULES

So far we have summarized some evidence about conditions that may facilitate waiting for deferred outcomes. The results make it possible to infer more clearly the mechanisms underlying delay behavior. But until recently little was known about the child's own understanding and strategies for coping with various types of delay. Do preschool children know that consummatory ideation about the rewards will make self-imposed delay more difficult? When and how does such awareness develop? Although we now know a good deal about conditions that affect delay, children's own awareness of effective attentional strategies during delay of gratification has only recently become a focus of research. Thus, in one recent set of studies we began to explore young children's verbal preferences and actual use of different attentional strategies for sustaining delay of gratification (H. N. Mischel, 1982; H. N. Mischel & W. Mischel, 1983, in press; W. Mischel & H. N. Mischel, 1979; Yates & Mischel, 1979). We hope that these results ultimately will help clarify the degree to which young children know and utilize delay-facilitating attentional strategies when they face situations in which they must wait for deferred outcomes.

As one step to investigate children's preferred attentional strategies for delaying gratification, Yates and Mischel (1979) modified the delay paradigm. We developed equipment that allowed the child to self-regulate the presentation of stimuli throughout the delay period instead of placing fixed stimuli in front of the child throughout the delay. Thus each child had available for self-presentation one of the types of stimuli that facilitates self-imposed delay (SID) and one of the types of stimuli that hinders it. For example, the child could see the relevant real reward or a picture of the reward. The amount of time that the children actually viewed the different types of stimuli during self-imposed delay of gratification was assessed.

The younger children, rather than preferring objectively effective stimulus conditioning, seemed to spontaneously prefer to view the real stimuli while waiting for them. Interestingly, this result seems to be congruent with Freud's (1911/1959) classical theory of wish-fulfilling ideation during delay: when the desired object is blocked, the frustrated child tries to self-present it, to "have it." But our previous research suggests that in so doing, the young children are making self-imposed delay not less but more difficult for themselves, creating poor conditions for effective waiting. This occurs because reward-relevant ideation increases the child's desire and hence enhances the frustrativeness of the delay (e.g., Mischel, 1974)—especially if this ideation is consummatory rather than more abstract (Mischel & Baker, 1975; Moore, Mischel, & Zeiss, 1976). The youngsters are then trapped in a delay-defeating cycle, attending to the consummatory qualities of what they really want and becoming increasingly frustratively aroused, thereby making it even harder to wait successfully. Thus, young children's preference for attending to the real rewards rather than to more symbolic representations of them helps to explain why it is so difficult for them to tolerate voluntary delay of gratification. By attending to the real rewards young children may make such delay especially frustrative and arousing, thereby defeating their own ability to wait for what they want. These interpretations receive some support from the repeated finding that attention to the real stimuli makes self-imposed delay more frustrative and shortens delay time (Mischel, 1974; Schack & Massari, 1973; Toner & Smith, 1977).

THE DEVELOPMENT
OF SELF-CONTROL COMPETENCIES

More recently, Harriet Nerlove Mischel and I have been discovering that children show a clear developmental progression in their knowledge of effective delay rules. In these studies, we presented the delay situation to children varying in age from preschool to sixth grade, adapting the standard procedure described earlier in this chapter. Briefly, the children were asked to suppose that they really wanted to get the delayed outcomes and to choose whether it would help them wait if the rewards were exposed or covered during the delay period. Afterwards, the children were further instructed to suppose that the rewards would be ex-

TABLE 10.4
Ideation Alternatives*

Hot:	"The marshmallows taste yummy and chewy."
Cool:	"The marshmallows are puffy like clouds."
Task-Contingency:	"I am waiting for the two marshmallows."

*Subjects chose between hot versus cool and hot versus task-oriented ideation. (The table shows the alternatives when the delayed rewards were two marshmallows.)

posed. They were then asked what they could say to themselves to help waiting with the rewards in front of them, and we explored with them how that would help them wait.

Finally, a "hot" (consummatory) ideation (focusing on the consummatory properties of the rewards) was paired with either a "cool" (abstract) ideation (focusing on the nonconsummatory, abstract properties) or a task-oriented one (focusing on the contingency, see Table 10.4). Thus, each child chose hot versus cool and hot versus task-contingency ideation. All children also were asked to indicate why they had chosen as they did after making each selection.

The overall data, summarized in Table 10.5, clearly reveal an orderly developmental sequence in children's knowledge of rules for effective delay of gratification. Let us consider this sequence for each choice measure separately.

Obscuring the Rewards Helps Delay.   Table 10.5 shows in the developmental progression in children's awareness that it helps to obscure (cover) the rewards rather than expose them during the delay period. Preschoolers chose to have the rewards exposed somewhat more often than covered, but this difference was not significant ($\chi^2 < 1$). By third grade, children systematically indicated that it would help to have the rewards obscured during the delay period ($\chi^2 = 4.36$, $df = 1$, $p < .05$), and sixth graders showed the same preference most

TABLE 10.5
Number at Each Age Level Choosing Each Strategy to Help Delay*

	Expose vs. Cover Rewards		Hot vs. Task-Contingency Ideation		Hot vs. Cool Ideation	
Preschool	14	10	13	10	11	10
Grade 3	10	23	7	26	16	17
Grade 6	8	27	6	28	6	26

*Based on data in Mischel & Mischel, 1983, in press.

markedly ($\chi^2 = 9.26$, $df = 1$, $p < .002$). Thus, there was a significant linear age effect ($\chi^2 = 8.35$, $df = 2$, $p < .01$). By grade three, children have shifted from no systematic preference (or a tendency to expose the rewards) to a clearly significant preference for obscuring the rewards to help wait for them (see Table 10.5).

Task-Contingency Ideation Helps More Than Hot Ideation.   Preschoolers showed no systematic preference for the hot versus the task-contingency ideation. Third graders strongly preferred the task-contingency ideation over hot ideation ($\chi^2 = 9.82$, $df = 1$, $p < .002$), and sixth graders showed an overwhelming preference for the task-contingency ideation ($\chi^2 = 12.97$, $df = 1$, $p < .001$). There was a strong linear age effect on this choice ($\chi^2 = 11.60$, $df = 2$, $p < .003$). Table 10.5 suggests that by grade three most children understood that task-contingency ideation helps delay more than does hot ideation about the rewards.

Cool Ideation Helps More Than Hot Ideation.   Neither preschoolers nor third graders showed a significant preference for cool versus hot ideation. Sixth graders, however, strongly indicated that cool ideation would help delay more than hot ideation ($\chi^2 = 11.28$, $df = 1$, $p < .001$). The linear age effect again was significant ($\chi^2 = 8.38$, $df = 2$, $p < .01$).

Correlations Between Age and Knowledge.   Correlational analyses confirmed the picture provided by the chi-square analyses. Each child was assigned a ''knowledge score'' from 0 to 3 for the number of correct answers given about delay rules (cover/expose, hot/task-contingency, hot/cool). The correlation between total knowledge and age was .452 ($N = 94$, $p < .001$) for the total sample.

Correlations between knowledge subscores and age for the total sample were also highly significant but understandably somewhat more modest. Specifically, age correlated .288 ($p < .01$) with knowledge that covering the rewards helps more than exposing them, .316 ($p < .01$) with knowledge that task-contingency ideation helps more than hot ideation, and .283 ($p < .01$) with knowledge that cool ideation helps more than hot ideation. Interestingly, correlations between knowledge scores (collectively and separately) and age *within* each grade level were generally erratic and did not reach statistical significance, suggesting that age is an excellent predictor of knowledge of effective delay strategies but only over a relatively broad age range.

The clear linear relationship between age and knowledge of delay scores is also revealed by examining the mean scores for knowledge at each of the three age levels sampled. These means were 1.29, 1.89, and 2.31 for preschool, third grade, and sixth grade children, respectively.

HOT VERSUS COOL IDEATION PREFERENCES
IN NONDELAY CONTEXT

We also included a control to assess whether any age-related changes in preferences for hot versus cool ideation about the rewards might merely reflect age
changes in children's preferences for either type of ideation apart from its specific role for facilitating waiting in the delay situation. To assess this possibility,
about half the children at each age level served as their own control, first making
the choice between hot and cool ideation about the reward objects imbedded in a
nondelay context before the delay contingency was introduced. In this preliminary nondelay situation, hot ideation (focusing on the consummatory properties
of the rewards) was strongly preferred to cool ideation by all age groups. This
preference for consummatory hot ideation in a nondelay situation occurred both
for marshmallows and pretzels at each age level, with no significant differences
in preferences due either to the specific item or to the child's age. These data
show that in a nondelay context children of all ages greatly preferred hot rather
than cool ideation about the same objects that later served as the contingent
rewards ($\chi^2 = 6.72$, $df = 1$, $p < .01$). But as we saw, in the delay context
preschoolers shifted from a clear preference for hot ideation to random choice,
both third and sixth graders avoided hot ideation and preferred task-contingency
ideation, and sixth graders greatly preferred cool ideation over hot ideation.
Hence, it is clear that the development with age of a strong avoidance for hot
ideation as a delay strategy does not merely reflect a general tendency for older
children to avoid hot ideation about objects. It reflects instead a development of
the realization that hot ideation about the rewards specifically makes delay difficult in spite of the fact that such ideation about the same objects in a nondelay
context is preferred to cool ideation at all the sampled age levels. Finally, note
that in the delay situation the preferred delay strategies of children tested for
nondelay ideation preferences at every grade level were similar to those of the
children who did not have this preliminary measure, ruling out the possibility of
an effect from the control condition assessment itself.

THE METACOGNITION OF DELAY: CONCLUSIONS

The sample of preschoolers tested in the study just described was small, hence it
would be erroneous to reach firm conclusions about the lack of delay knowledge
exhibited by these young children. A larger scale follow-up by the same investigators was conducted more recently (Mischel & Mischel, 1983, in press). The
total results indicated that children begin to understand two basic rules for effective delay of gratification by about the end of their fifth year: cover rather than
expose the rewards and engage in task-oriented rather than in consummatory

ideation while waiting. In the delay paradigm, young 4-year-olds seem to create self-defeating dilemmas for themselves, by choosing (or even creating) a tempting environment without adequately anticipating that they will be unable to execute strategies to overcome the temptation. This preference for the delay-defeating strategy (exposing the rewards) waned toward the end of the fourth year and was replaced by a growing preference for the delay facilitating strategy (covering the rewards). In sum, although most children below the age of 5 do not seem to generate clear or viable strategies for effective delay, by the age of 5 to 6 years the majority do know that covering the rewards will help them in waiting, whereas looking at them or thinking about them will make it difficult in our paradigm.

We also find that by third grade most children spontaneously generate and reasonably justify a number of potentially viable strategies and unequivocally understand the basic principles of resistance to temptation. For example, they avoid looking at the rewards because: "If I'm looking at them all the time, it will make me hungry . . . and I'd want to ring the bell." Often they focus on the task and contingency, reminding themselves of the task requirement and outcomes associated with each choice ("If you wait you get _____; if you don't you only get _____"). They also often indicate the value of distraction from the rewards or of negative ideation designed to make them less tempting ("Think about gum stuck all over them"). A small minority still suggest that positive ideation about the rewards ("The marshmallow looks good and fluffy") will help, and one wonders if these are the very youngsters for whom delay is likely to be most difficult. Most third graders clearly know that task-contingency ideation helps delay more than hot reward ideation, but they still do not know that cool reward ideation is better than hot reward ideation. By the time they reach sixth grade, the children's spontaneous strategies (just like their formal preferences) show considerable sophistication. Now most of these youngsters seem to clearly recognize the advantage for delay of cool rather than hot ideation about the rewards. The basic delay rules have been firmly mastered. The details of the developmental progression are described in Mischel and Mischel (1983, in press).

In conclusion, a comprehensive, coherent account of the genesis of knowledge about delay of gratification seems to be emerging. In the course of development, children show increasing awareness of effective delay rules and come to generate the strategies necessary for effectively reducing frustration and temptation. They progress from a systematic preference for seeing and thinking about the real blocked rewards and hence the worst delay strategy (Mischel & Mischel, 1983, in press; Yates & Mischel, 1979) to randomness and to a clear avoidance of attention to the rewards, particularly, consummatory hot reward ideation. Systematically, they come to prefer distraction from the temptation, self-instructions about the task-contingency, and cool ideation about the rewards themselves. These developmental shifts seem to reflect a growing recognition by the child of the principle that the more cognitively available and hot a temptation, the more one will want it and the more difficult it will be to resist. Armed with this insight, the child can generate a diverse array of strategies for effectively managing otherwise formidable tasks and for overcoming so-called "stimulus control" with self-control.

EFFECTIVE DELAY AS A PERSON VARIABLE

Our focus in this chapter has been on ideational processes that facilitate delay and the child's growing knowledge of those processes. But there is another side of the research program that also requires mention to allow a more complete view of the meaning of the child's delay behavior.

Concurrent with our investigations of the situational and cognitive processes underlying delay behavior, we also have been exploring the meaning of delay behavior as a quality of the person. For this purpose we have been assessing the cognitive and social correlates of effective goal-directed delay behavior in the course of development. Delay of gratification has been recognized as a key personality indicator ever since Freud (1911/1959) first called attention to it. In earlier studies, a network of meaningful correlations associated with children's choice preferences for delayed, more valuable versus immediate, less valuable outcomes (e.g., Mischel, 1966, 1974) was uncovered. For example, individuals who predominantly choose larger, delayed rewards or goals for which they must either wait or work are more likely to be oriented toward the future, to plan carefully for distant goals, to have high scores on "ego-control" measures, to have high achievement motivation, to be more trusting and socially responsible, to be brighter and more mature, to have a higher level of aspiration, and to show less uncontrolled impulsivity (for details see Mischel, 1966; Mischel & Metzner, 1962). While these results are of interest, little has been known until very recently about the possible correlates of actual waiting time in the delay paradigm described in this chapter.

In one direction, to help clarify the meaning of delay as a quality of the child, Mischel and Peake (1982 a, b) exposed preschool children (with a mean age of 53 months) at Stanford's Bing School to the delay situation. For most children, responses to the 100-item California Child Q Set or CCQ (Block, 1961) also were obtained concurrently from both parents. These ratings provide brief personality characterizations of the rated child. The composited mother–father Q-item correlates that reached or tended to approach statistical significance for waiting time in the standard delay situation were highly meaningful. For example, there were low-level but statistically significant associations between the seconds of waiting time on the standard delay measures and such ratings as "is competent, skillful"; "is planful, thinks ahead"; "has high standards of performance for self"; "can acknowledge unpleasant experiences and admit to own negative feelings"; "uses and responds to reason"; "is verbally fluent, can express ideas well in language''; ''is curious and exploring, eager to learn, open to new experiences''; ''is reflective, thinks and deliberates before he or she speaks or acts.'' In sum, these ratings illustrate the occurrence of modest, generally theory-consistent associations between concurrent parental ratings and the preschool child's delay time on the same behaviors whose predictable responsiveness to situational and cognitive variables have been demonstrated experimentally, and provide reassuring evidence for the ecological validity and meaningfulness of the delay measure itself.

In a related vein, we also have started to explore the possible association between the preschool child's delay behavior and indices of coping and competence obtained not concurrently but years later. Namely, at the same time that we pursued the experimental strategy for studying delay mechanisms summarized in this chapter, we also have been engaged in a longitudinal study of children who participated in these delay of gratification experiments when they were preschoolers in the years from 1967 to 1974 at Stanford's Bing Nursery School. During that time, over 650 preschool children (with a mean age of about 53 months) were subjects in one or more studies of waiting behavior. All delay situations were versions of the standard (experimenter-absent during delay) waiting paradigm (Mischel, 1974), on which numerous experimental variations were conducted (e.g., by manipulating the ideation instructions to the child or the presence of the rewards). Some children also were administered various individual differences measures. In addition, the parents of a subsample of these children provided ratings of their child's ability to delay rewards and made predictions (in minutes) of the child's probable waiting times in specific delay situations like those in which the child was actually tested. These ratings were obtained while the child was still in preschool. In follow-ups starting in 1979, after time intervals of about 10 years had elapsed, we also have begun to collect data to assess the child's cognitive and social competence and coping patterns in the adolescent years.

In these data we are obtaining highly significant continuities that link the preschooler's delay time while waiting in our experiments to his or her cognitive and social competence, coping skills, and school performance years later. For example, the number of seconds preschoolers delayed the first time they had an opportunity to do so in our 1967–1974 preschool studies, regardless of the specific delay situation they encountered, significantly predicts their social competence as high school juniors and seniors as rated by their parents ($r = .30, N = 99, p < .01$).

CONCLUSIONS

In sum, the preschooler's waiting behavior in the delay paradigm is highly predictable from knowledge of the particular situational and cognitive variables operating in the specific context. It is clearly a measure of considerable ecological validity. A set of principles or rules that characterize the relevant psychological processes have emerged and allow fine-grained predictions of delay time in the specific situation. These rules allow one to account for a substantial portion of the variance in children's delay behavior. Nevertheless, the same behavior can significantly predict the child's competence and coping assessed a decade later in development, and yields a stable network of coherent correlates that depict a generally cognitively and socially competent child. The strength of these relations is modest in absolute terms, generally averaging not more than about .30. Yet these correlations seem impressive given that they are based on a specific preschool behavior, that they span at least a 10-year period of development, and that they occur even for a single early act (i.e., seconds of first delay time).

Perhaps most interesting in the present context, the attributes suggested by the adolescent correlational data are nicely congruent with the analyses of the delay process provided by the experimental research. The former yields a general picture of the adolescent who delayed in preschool as bright, resourceful, able to concentrate, planful, competent, and able to cope and deal with stress (e.g., Mischel, 1983). The latter gives a more fine-grain, specific analysis of the essential ingredient for effective delay in the waiting paradigm; the ability to divert and control attention, focusing it away from the frustrativeness of the situation and the "stimulus pull" of the rewards while maintaining the goal directed perseverance required for their attainment. Taken together, the experimental and correlational efforts provide a more complete view both of the psychological demands of the delay situation and of the children who are likely to meet them effectively.

It will be important to trace further not only the development of this cognitive competence but also to clarify more fully its nature and timetable. In future work we will be especially alert to the interface of the development of the child's self-control knowledge and its effective application to relevant self-control tasks. We also will continue to explore the conditions that might impede or enhance the developmental progression. While knowledge of self-control rules is only one component of the growth of effective self-control, it appears to follow a predictable developmental sequence of potential theoretical and practical importance. We will want to know not only when do children know what rules, but also what determines the cognitive availability, the accessibility of those rules when they are needed and their activation to guide behavior, so that we can understand more fully the links between cognitive competence and effective self-regulatory behavior. And we look forward to seeing how our present and future research will articulate with Piaget's work, confident that it will do so, but leaving that task to other scholars.

ACKNOWLEDGMENTS

The research reported in this chapter is also presented in Mischel, 1981. This research was supported in part by Grant MH 36953 from the National Institute of Mental Health and by Grant HD MH 9814 from the National Institute of Child Health and Human Development.

REFERENCES

Achilles, E. M. Experimental studies in recall and recognition. *Archives of Psychology*, 1920, *44*.

Amsel, A. Frustrative nonreward in partial reinforcement and discrimination learning. *Psychological Review*, 1962, *69*, 306–328.

Asch, S. E. Studies of independence and conformity: A minority of one against a unanimous majority. *Psychological Monographs*, 1956, *70*(9, Whole No. 416).

Bandura, A., Blanchard, E. B., & Ritter, B. Relative efficacy of desensitization and modeling approaches for inducing behavioral, affective, and attitudinal changes. *Journal of Personality and Social Psychology*, 1969, *13*, 173–199.

Bandura, A., Ross, D., & Ross, S. A. Transmission of aggression through imitation of aggressive models. *Journal of Personality and Social Psychology*, 1961, *63*, 575–582.

Berlyne, D. E. *Conflict, arousal, and curiosity*. New York: McGraw-Hill, 1960.

Block, J. *The Q-sort method in personality assessment and psychiatric research*. Springfield, IL: Thomas, 1961.

Bower, G. H., & Clark, M. C. Narrative stories as mediators for serial learning. *Psychonomic Science*, 1969, *14*, 181–182.

Brown, A. Development, schooling and the acquisition of knowledge about knowledge. In R. Anderson, R. Spiro, & W. Montague (Eds.), *Schooling and the acquisition of knowledge*. Hillsdale, N.J.: Lawrence Erlbaum Associates, 1977.

Estes, W. K. Reinforcement in human behavior. *American Scientist*, 1972, *60*, 723–729.

Ferster, C. B., & Skinner, B. F. *Schedules of reinforcement*. New York: Appleton, 1957.

Festinger, L., & Carlsmith, J. M. Cognitive consequences of forced compliance. *Journal of Abnormal and Social Psychology*, 1959, *58*, 203–210.

Flavell, J. H., & Wellman, H. M. Metamemory. In R. V. Kail & J. W. Hagen (Eds.), *Perspectives on the development of memory and cognition*. Hillsdale, N.J.: Lawrence Erlbaum Associates, 1977.

Freud, S. Formulations regarding the two principles in mental functioning. In *Collected papers* (Vol. 4). New York: Basic Books, 1959. (Originally published, 1911.)

Harlow, H. F., & Zimmerman, R. R. Affectional responses in the infant monkey. *Science*, 1959, *130*, 421–432.

Helson, H. *Adaptation-level theory*. New York: Harper & Row, 1964.

Latané, B., & Darley, J. M. Group inhibition of bystander intervention in emergencies. *Journal of Personality and Social Psychology*, 1968, *10*, 215–221.

Latané, B., & Rodin, J. A lady in distress: Inhibiting effects of friends and strangers on bystander intervention. *Journal of Experimental Social Psychology*, 1969, *5*, 189–202.

Mischel, H. N. The growth of children's knowledge of delay of gratification strategies. Paper presented at the *Meetings of the American Psychological Association*, Division 7, Washington, D.C., August, 1982.

Mischel, H. N., & Mischel, W. The development of children's knowledge of self-control strategies. *Child Development*, 1983, in press.

Mischel, W. Theory and research on the antecedents of self-imposed delay of reward. In B. A. Maher (Ed.), *Progress in experimental personality research* (Vol. 3). New York: Academic Press, 1966.

Mischel, W. Toward a cognitive social learning reconceptualization of personality. *Psychological Review*, 1973, *80*, 252–283.

Mischel, W. Processes in delay of gratification. In L. Berkowitz (Ed.), *Advances in experimental social psychology* (Vol. 7). New York: Academic Press, 1974.

Mischel, W. On the interface of cognition and personality: Beyond the person-situation debate. *American Psychologist*, 1979, *34*, 740–754.

Mischel, W. Metacognition and the rules of delay. In J. Flavell & L. Ross (Eds.), *Social cognitive development: Frontiers and possible futures.* New York: Cambridge University Press, 1981.

Mischel, W. Delay of gratification as process and as person variable in development. In D. Magnusson & V. P. Allen (Eds.), *Human development: An interactional perspective.* New York: Academic Press, 1983, in press.

Mischel, W., & Baker, N. Cognitive appraisals and transformations in delay behavior. *Journal of Personality and Social Psychology,* 1975, *31,* 254–261.

Mischel, W., Ebbesen, E. B., & Zeiss, A. R. Cognitive and attentional mechanisms in delay of gratification. *Journal of Personality and Social Psychology,* 1972, *21,* 204–218.

Mischel, W., & Metzner, R. Preference for delayed reward as a function of age, intelligence, and length of delay interval. *Journal of Abnormal and Social Psychology,* 1962, *64,* 425–431.

Mischel, W., & Mischel, H. N. *Children's knowledge of psychological principles.* Unpublished manuscript, Stanford University, 1979.

Mischel, W., & Moore, B. Effects of attention to symbolically-presented rewards on self-control. *Journal of Personality and Social Psychology,* 1973, *28,* 172–179.

Mischel, W., & Moore, B. The role of ideation in voluntary delay for symbolically-presented rewards. *Cognitive Therapy and Research,* 1980, *4,* 211–221.

Mischel, W., & Patterson, C. J. Substantive and structural elements of effective plans for self-control. *Journal of Personality and Social Psychology,* 1976, *34,* 942–950.

Mischel, W., & Peake, P. In search of consistency: Measure for measure. In M. P. Zanna, E. T. Higgins, & C. P. Herman (Eds.), *Consistency in social behavior: The Ontario symposium* (Vol. 2). Hillsdale, N.J.: Lawrence Erlbaum Associates, 1982. (a)

Mischel, W., & Peake, P. K. Beyond déjà vu in the search for cross-situational consistency. *Psychological Review,* 1982, *89,* 730–755. (b)

Moore, B., Mischel, W., & Zeiss, A. Comparative effects of the reward stimulus and its cognitive representation in voluntary delay. *Journal of Personality and Social Psychology,* 1976, *34,* 419–424.

Pavlov, I. P. *Conditioned reflexes* (G. V. Anrep, trans.). London: Oxford University Press, 1927. (New York: Dover, 1960).

Piaget, J. *The construction of reality in the child.* New York: Basic Books, 1954.

Piaget, J. *The child's conception of number.* New York: Norton, 1965.

Rapaport, D. On the psychoanalytic theory of thinking. In M. M. Gill (Ed.), *The collected papers of David Rapaport.* New York: Basic Books, 1967.

Schack, M. L., & Massari, D. J. Effects of temporal aids on delay of gratification. *Developmental Psychology,* 1973, *8,* 168–171.

Singer, J. L. Delayed gratification and ego development: Implications for clinical and experimental research. *Journal of Consulting Psychology,* 1955, *23,* 428–431.

Toner, I. J., & Smith, R. A. Age and overt verbalization in delay-maintenance behavior in children. *Journal of Experimental Child Psychology,* 1977, *24,* 123–128.

Walster, E., Aronson, V., Abrahams, D., & Rottman, L. Importance of physical attractiveness in dating behavior. *Journal of Personality and Social Psychology,* 1966, *4,* 508–516.

Yates, B. T., & Mischel, W. Young children's preferred attentional strategies for delaying gratification. *Journal of Personality and Social Psychology,* 1979, *37,* 286–300.

Learning and Development Through Social Interaction and Conflict: A Challenge to Social Learning Theory

Frank B. Murray
University of Delaware

The Genevans and their colleagues have not studied delay of gratification phenomena because the epistemic subject—besides having no social class, sex, nationality, culture, or personality—also has no fun, and thus no fun can be delayed. The gratification of delay in Mischel's sense could only be interesting for the Genevans in any case when the object of gratification had a logically necessary connection to the events at the beginning of the delay period. Ironically, in this case, no delay could be imposed by an experimenter or the subjects themselves because logic transcends time and space.

Were the topic to be investigated by the Genevans, it would not be for itself, as it has been with Mischel, but rather as the manifestation of the presence or absence of some regulation or operation. Like delayed imitation or play, we might see in delay of gratification research evidence for representation, although not as the source of representation, which Piaget claims for imitation and play.

Mischel's finding (Chapter 10, this volume), incidentally, that the child's management of the delay interval was ultimately found to be controlled by the child's representation of the gratification stimulus, not by the experimenter's representation of it as an object, picture, or idea, is a striking finding. Although the distinction between the nominal and the functional stimulus is not new in psychology, Mishcel's results provide still another example of the distinction as a caution to the researcher that what he or she takes as the stimulus may not at all be what the subject takes as the stimulus. At the very least, the Genevan literature has dramatized this fact repeatedly, as has the literature on stimulus salience.

It would not be difficult to imagine the delay of gratification phenomenon investigated, along with the rich data Mischel has provided, as one of the behaviors considered in the Genevan projects on the grasp of consciousness or success and understanding. It would or could provide further elaboration of the ontogenetic relationship between "doing" and "knowing."

The finding that the child's knowledge of delay strategies or rules is constrained by the child's cognitive level is no surprise to Piagetian researchers. It would be perfectly clear to them why the preschooler focuses on the consummatory salience of the reward (thereby incidentally making the wait most burdensome), why the 5- and 6-year-olds exhibit primitive delay rules (e.g., covering the reward), why third graders are able to shift their attention to other dimensions (e.g., either to cool abstractions of the hot dimension or to irrelevant or unrelated dimensions altogether), and finally why or how the sixth grader can play the hot and cool aspects of the reward against each other to build an effective, coherent delay strategy. The competence base for the findings ia apparent in the structures of preoperational and operational reasoning. However, explication of this competence base would not provide us with much guidance about what children will do in the delay of gratification tasks set by Mischel and his co-workers. There is no clue in the Genevan research program about how disciplined and self-controlled children would be, or how much guilt or pride they would feel as a result of what they do, because the epistemic subject has no shame either.

Moreover, as is made clearer later, the epistemic subject is preoccupied with things that are necessarily true, that have to be true, that must be true. That which is merely true is not treated well in Piaget's account of intellectual development. We have a theory of knowledge, but not a theory of information; we have a theory of necessary truth, but not a theory of truth.

In many ways, the most interesting and compelling features of Piaget's work are unexplained in the theory, for example, *all* the horizontal decalage events. Because we have more information than knowledge, it is self-evident that within the Piagetian framework we are far from a complete account of intellectual development. Although the form, structure, and purpose of the child's developing mathematics, logic, and physics are set out in genetic epistemology, the content is unspecified. The research of Mishcel (this volume) and others (e.g., Flavell on memory) on the child's psychology fits well with Piaget's corpus on the child's cognition of various subject matter domains (viz., the child's mathematics, physics, biology, etc.). But the point is that the theory does not predict the content of the young child's psychology, or metapsychology as it has been called lately. The early work by the Genevans on the child's understanding of dreams, by the way, may have been the first metacognitive studies.

There are no clues in the theory, for example, about which categories of transformations lead to nonconservation, a matter of paramount interest in educational psychology. Why does a change in an object's shape, texture, or temperature lead children to believe, as they do, that the object's weight has changed as well? Or consider an example from Inhelder and Piaget (1958). A formal account of the stages of the billiard ball problem (angle of incidence equals the angle of reflection) is given in propositional logic in which the concrete operational achievement is the conjunction or correlation ($p.q$, where 'p' and 'q' refer to aspects of the paths of incidence and reflection). The formal operational advance of this achievement is described as the rejection of the hypothetical $\bar{p}.q$ and $p.\bar{q}$ and formation of the disjunction '$p.q$ v $\bar{p}.\bar{q}$', which turns out to be truth functionally equivalent to the biconditional "p if and only if q" or "p is equivalent to q." Inhelder and Piaget take this to be a good description of the fact that the angle of incidence (p) equals the angle of the reflection (q). But in reading the children's protocols, one is struck by all the information the formal account or descriptions omits. For example, how can the formal model account for these facts?

1. Some children see the angles as between the trajectory and the rebound wall; others see them as between the trajectory and an imaginary perpendicular to the rebound point—not a trivial difference in the subject matter of Newtonian mechanics.
2. Some children adopt and reject various hypotheses such as force or the angle is always a right angle.

How does Piagetian theory capture the richness of the child's science?
Or consider how the theory would account for these two responses from children:

1. The child in a conservation of length study who says that the transformed stick is longer than the other because "my mother put it in the oven."
2. The child on an airplane trip who asks his mother when they get smaller.

It is not that Piagetian theory does not acknowledge children's responses of this sort, but the explanation in some way precludes an explanation. Piaget (1959) wrote:

> Childish ideas arise through schemas . . . that do not correspond to analogies or casual relations that can be verified by everybody . . . in the mind of the child, everything is connected with everything else, everything can be justified by means of unforeseen allusions and implications . . . we have no suspicion of this wealth of relations precisely because this very syncretism which causes it is without the means of expression that would render it communicable [p. 227].

Even though the Genevan account of intellectual development and accomplishment must of necessity be incomplete, it still provides powerful challenges to the alternative explanations of the child's intellectual development.

A CHALLENGE TO SOCIAL LEARNING THEORY

One of the most informative discussions of one researcher's work by a researcher who shared the assumptions of a different model of development was Kamii and

Derman's critique (1971) of a paper by Engelmann. Engelmann (1971) claimed that operativity, or at least its manifestations, can be easily taught and acquired by children because the teaching of conservation, for example, required only the teaching of the component skills of conservation, some of which were very simple and others that were already in the child's repertoire of skills and information. Kamii and Derman were given the rare opportunity by Engelmann to test his subjects and probe the genuineness of their alleged accomplishments. They concluded that the children had acquired an algorithm for each task, which was considerably less general and less powerful than the acquisition of operativity would predict. Indeed, the algorithms seemed on occasion to interfere with the children's thinking as, for example, when a child explained the floating of a piece of aluminum foil by saying, "It is lighter than a piece of water the same size" and then when a tiny piece was torn off and sank by saying, "It's heavier than a piece of water the same size." The child was reported as apparently unshakable in thinking the smaller piece was heavier because it sank.

Kamii and Dermon's conclusion has become commonplace in discussions between Piagetians and others and pointless because each debater sees the child's deficiency or error as due to a factor the other sees as tautological and nonfalsifiable. In the most extreme case, where one group claims the factor is an infinite regress of incomplete discriminations or algorithms, the other sees it as hypothetical operation whose meaning is redundant with the behavior it seeks to explain.

Since 1971, however, the results of a number of operativity training procedures have been reported that, despite the pointlessness of paradigm debates, provide some critical additional information for the evaluation of the issue. These reports have their origins in social learning theoretical approaches to thinking, and they are reviewed in the remainder of this chapter.

The Explanation of Necessity

How the child comes to discriminate the large set of statements that are true or false from the smaller set that are necessarily true or false is a significant issue for any theory of the development of the intellect because having a concept of necessity is a criterial attribute of a rational mind. The most parsimonious developmental theories limit the explanation of the causes of the child's idea of necessity and other matters to material and efficient causes, with particular attention to efficient causes in the form of eliciting and maintaining stimuli. Only reductionist theories have seriously treated material causes. Social learning theories are examples of a class of theories that emphasize the efficient cause as the explanation of behavior. Other theorists have felt that an adequate explanation of the causes of the intellect required a specification of formal and final causes in addition to the others. Piaget's explanation is an example of this latter category of theory. These theories require that an account be given of the structure, form, and pattern of the behavior and also its purpose and function.

The Genevans have attempted to diagnose the presence of the child's concept of necessity with many tasks, but most notably with the conservation task. This task has the structure of a transitive inference or deduction once the child makes the assumption that the transformed object is equivalent to the untransformed object. How the child comes to make this assumption has been an important research question with the "parsimonious" theorists searching only for the efficient causes of the assumption. The other theorists continue to point out that the specification of the efficient cause provides an incomplete account of conservation. The added specification of the structure of the conservation response and the "necessity" it diagnostically represents must be given along with the specification of the place and purpose of the concept of necessity in the formation of the mature mind. The initial debates, like the Kamii–Dermon debate with Engelmann, naturally focused upon criteria that would implicate the restricted versus the full range of Aristotelian causes.

The research question (Bandura, 1977) was largely whether conservation "can be induced, eliminated, and reinstated by varying external influences [p. 5]" because it was felt that such a demonstration of the power of these efficient causes would provide such a complete account of the conservation behavior that formal and final accounts would not be required because they could add very little scientifically to a satisfying account based upon efficient causes. The results of a particular category of conservation-inducement technique are instructive to review because they help delineate the assumptions made by the various models of development and because they have practical utility in education. According to Bandura (1977), this category is the group of conservation teaching strategies based on social learning theory in which the "symbolic, vicarious, and self-regulatory processes assume a prominent role [p. 6]."

However, before considering these techniques and their relationship to the assumptions of social learning theory and genetic epistemology, a brief examination of the conservation paradigm and the range of conservation criteria should be undertaken to make the account of the research program clearer.

The Conservation Paradigm and Criteria

A detailed account of the paradigm and criteria is given in Murray (1981), but it is important to realize that the tests of genuine conservation used by the Genevans only make sense insofar as they are attempts to certify that the child's conservation response was a deduction (i.e., a necessary conclusion). A determination of the child's feeling of the necessity of his or her response could be made, but it almost never is (e.g., Murray & Armstrong, 1976). For example, the child could be asked whether the outcome could ever have been different or whether it would always or just sometimes be what the child said it was. Typically, the feeling of necessity is assessed indirectly by one or more of the following five criteria:

1. Durability. Conservation assessment is repeated at later time intervals up to 1 or 2 months on the assumption that the notion of necessity is never given up once it is acquired.
2. Resistance to countersuggestion. In this case, counterevidence, pressure, or argument is offered by the experimenter in an attempt to change the child's conservation response on the assumption that necessary conclusions are not modifiable. Easily changed responses are said to indicate pseudo-conservation, that is, a judgment based upon something other than necessity.
3. Specific transfer. Conservation is assessed with different materials and perhaps with different transformations on the assumption that the logical form of the task should transcend particular task features.
4. Nonspecific transfer. Conservation is assessed in different domains or with different operativity tasks (e.g., seriation, transitivity, class inclusion) to see if the notion of necessity was firmly established.
5. Trainability. This criterion is in some sense the converse of the counter-suggestion criterion because it is applied to the nonconservation response on the assumption that a quick and abrupt change in response after feedback, hints, cues, and so forth indicates that the original nonconservation was not valid (or was pseudo-nonconservation).

Finally, it should be noted that the classical Genevan explanations for conservation (viz., identity, negation, and reciprocity) are valid justifications only in cases where conservation and necessity are presupposed (Murray, 1981).

Less demanding criteria for conservation exist in experimental paradigms that favor alternate explanations of the behavior (e.g., Bever, Mehler, & Epstein, 1968; Braine & Shanks, 1965; Bryant, 1974; Gelman, 1969; Gruen, 1966; Mehler & Bever, 1967). No empirical evidence can clarify or resolve the differences between these competing explanations as they are arguments over different criteria and paradigms and not arguments about the data each has generated (see Reese & Overton, 1970, for an elaboration of this point).

Unfortunately, the conservation problem is not solely a logical reasoning task even though success on it is taken by Piaget (1960) as the best indicator of the presence of the logical groupings of operational thought. The conservation problem tells us as much about children's understanding of certain natural regularities as it does of their understanding of logical necessity. The problem, as Piaget (1971) and others (e.g., Osherson, 1974) have noted, is contaminated by a mixture of logical and physical principles. The information that the clay ball and a clay pancake are equal in weight and the information that weight is transitive both have nonlogical sources. How children come to know these things and how they use what they know is one question that separates the various theories of conservation.

Conservation Training

It is important to be clear about what can be expected from studies that attempt to train conservation. Because a training procedure is effective, for example, is not evidence that conservation is acquired that way "naturally" by any substantial number of children but only that conservation could be acquired that way. In any case, it is not evidence for *the* natural mechanism. Also, it cannot simply be assumed that the theoretical mechanism the researcher addressed in the experimental design was the one the children employed. A social interaction or conflict training design, for example, may allow children to employ cognitive dissonance, modeling, "equilibration," verbal rule learning, recollection, and/or attention mechanisms or strategies in their solutions to the tasks presented to them.

It is useful to bear in mind the competence-performance distinction in considering the results of conservation training studies, particularly with respect to the interpretation of studies in which conservation is acquired with relative ease. As just pointed out, rapid and effortless training indicates that the pupils already possessed the competence to solve the task and that the training procedure addressed peripheral performance features whose acquisition, although required to solve the problem, has no particular theoretical interest (e.g., Gelman, 1978; Hornblum & Overton, 1976). This is an attractive interpretation of studies in which conservation is easily trained, but it must be borne in mind that the question of *relative* ease is complicated enormously by the fact that no one has a reliable idea about how much time is ordinarily needed to acquire the competence to solve operativity tasks, except to say lamely that after 7 or 8 years of experience the child can solve the tasks in a wide range of domains. Doise, Mugny, and Perret-Clermont (1975) and Inhelder, Sinclair, and Bovet (1974) claim only that the acquisition of cognitive operations is an active and relatively slow process. Whether competence or performance was acquired as a result of various training manipulations, however long each may take, is a significant but, regrettably, not an empirical question.

The training literature does illuminate one critical difference between the "efficient cause" theories and "final cause" theories. This is the question of the direction of change because the final cause theories assume and specify a final end point of development toward which all the behavioral changes of interest are directed. Efficient cause theories make no assumptions about the direction of change except perhaps to say that change brings about behavior that is more efficient and economical in the sense that it optimizes the reinforcement contingencies (i.e., change is always in the direction of greater reinforcement). Final cause theories are quite specific about the form of the end point and the points along the way that mark the chid's progress toward it. Thus, it is clear that changes are always from nonconservation to conservation and never the other way around in a final cause theory, although it could be the other way around in an efficient cause theory. In fact, a good case can be made that nonconservation would lead to greater reinforcement because the nonconservation judgment more closely matches environmental events than the conservation judgment does (e.g., larger objects are usually heavier, longer rows usually contain more, taller glasses usually hold more because width is standardized by grip size, etc.).

The specification of the developmental sequence (e.g., Kuhn, 1972) allows some empirical evaluation of the directionality of behavioral change, which separates social learning theories and organismic theories.

Social Interaction Techniques

Since the middle of the 1970s, there has not been any legitimate doubt that conflict and interaction among peers in small classroomlike settings are effective ways to promote cognitive development and the acquisition of conceptual information in the curriculum. Murray (1972) and Silverman and Stone (1972) reported success with conservation training procedures based on the rather simple experimental manipulation of having the nonconserving pupils argue with their conserving peers until they all came to an agreement or stalemate about the various conservation problems. When tested alone after the interaction, 80% to 94% of the nonconservers made significant gains in conservation in these studies compared to very much lower rates of success reported in previous studies of conservation training attempts (Beilin, 1977; Murray, 1978). These gains fulfilled the aforementioned criteria for necessity. Not only do most nonconserving children make significant gains as a result of social interactions with conservers, but the gains are of substantial magnitude. For example, in Murray (1972) 8 out of 15 children who scored 0 out of 12 on the pretest had scores of 11 or 12 out of 12 on the various posttests, a finding which, by the way, clouds the prevailing Genevan notion of stage constraints on training and learning. What has not been clear in this line of research is what in the social interaction experience produced these gains. A number of factors come to mind, and research since 1973 or so has treated many of them.

We know that the social interaction effect can be had in different size interaction groups of one on one (Silverman & Geiringer 1973; Silverman & Stone, 1972), two on one (Murray, 1972), and three on two (Botvin & Murray, 1975) in kindergarten, first, second, third, and fifth grades with normal and learning disabled, although not with those disabled with communication disorders (Knight-Arest & Reid, 1978), with blacks and whites, and with middle and low socioeconomic status (SES) groups. Borys and Spitz (1979), however, did not find social interaction to be especially effective with mentally retarded institutionalized adolescents (IQ = 66, mental age (MA) = 10 yrs., chronological age (CA) = 20 yrs.).

We know also that no unusual information or instruction is presented in the interaction; that is, no researcher has reported children saying anything or manipulating the stimuli in any way that has not been said or demonstrated in the less effective "nonsocial" training procedures, namely, cognitive conflict, cue reduction, phenomenal–real discrimination, verbal rule instruction, reversibility, and the various learning paradigm procedures (Murray, 1978).

Analyses of the course of the interaction yield no surprises either, except perhaps that agreement is often reached quickly. Miller and Brownell (1975) found that nearly half the agreements were reached in less than 50 seconds and rarely took longer than 4 or 5 minutes. It is also surprising that the conservers do not prevail because of any greater social influence or higher IQ or because they are particularly better arguers. In arguments about best TV shows and so forth, conservers won only 41 of 90 arguments, lost 38, and stalemated 11, which leads Miller and Brownell (1975) to conclude: "There was no evidence. . . that conservers and nonconservers differed in relative social influence [p. 994]."

Growth occurs only for nonconservers who yield, which they do 60–80% of the time (Silverman & Geiringer, 1973). The conservers seem to initiate discussion slightly more often, state their answer slightly more often, give the good reasons, counter the nonconservers slightly more often, move stimuli to show reversibility, and appear slightly more flexible in their arguments than the nonconservers who repetitiously center on their original opinion and its perceptual justifications (Miller & Brownell, 1975; Silverman & Stone, 1972). No differences between conservers and nonconservers are found in their modes of communication, considered apart from their content, nor between yielders and nonyielders in this regard (Silverman & Geiringer, 1973); thus, the clues to the success of the procedure are not apparent in the analysis of the form or content of interactions between the children.

Despite the magnitude of the success of the social interaction procedures, the authenticity of the children's newly acquired conservation responses may still be questioned even though, taking the studies as a whole, the principal criteria for conservation were met. It may have been possible for the nonconservers in these studies to have merely parroted or imitated the correct response because a thoughtless repetition of the response, *same,* could have inflated the posttest performance. Although some researchers controlled for such a response set with inclusion of items for which the response, *same,* would be inappropriate, a most demanding test of whether the children did more than imitate their tutors would be the degree to which they explained their new conservation judgments by justifications that differ from those given by the conservers during the social interaction sessions. Silverman and Stone (1972) report only 1 instance out of 14 in which a newly trained conserver gave an explanation not originally offered by his conserving partner in the interaction. However, Botvin and Murray (1975) report significant differences in the types of reasons given by conservers during the interaction and by nonconservers on the posttest. Forty-nine percent of the original conservers tended to give reversibility reasons during the interaction, and 61% of the original nonconservers tended to give identity reasons when they conserved on the posttest. Similarly, Perret-Clermont (reported in Doise et al., 1975) found that over half her children introduced one or more arguments or explanations that had not occurred during the social interaction session. There is evidence that newly acquired conservation has a different basis of justification than seasoned conservation (Gelman, 1978; Murray, 1981), the former being based on identity and the latter on the two reversibilities. Although these latter studies bolster considerably the contention that the nonconservers were not merely imitating the conservers, they do not indicate whether the training procedures merely addressed or activated a pre-existing operational competence.

The group of social interaction conservation training procedures does address the directionality of development issue, which stands between the social learning theories and organismic theories (or between efficient and final cause theories). From a social learning theory perspective, particularly in the dyad interactions, there is no a priori reason to think that the conservers should not be as affected as the nonconservers by the interaction, especially when the "social influence" of the nonconservers is no less than the conservers' (Miller & Brownell, 1975; Silverman & Geiringer, 1973). Yet, shifts from conservation to nonconservation simply are not reported in any significant degree in the literature. Why conservation should be a more firmly held position than nonconservation from a social learning perspective is not clear because environmental and linguisitc support for nonconservation is very great (Murray, 1981). As was noted earlier, because there are so many more large-heavy and small-light objects in the world than large-light and small-heavy, it is not unreasonable to expect nonconservation of weight to result, as it commonly does, from transformations of size and shape. In fact, it is a puzzle in social learning theory why nonconservation eventually breaks down because it seems to serve the child so well for so long.

Silverman and Geiringer (1973) found 5 cases (of 23) and Miller and Brownell (1975) found only 8 instances (of 69) where the conserver yielded his or her position during the social interaction session, but in virtually no case did even these conservers regress to nonconservation on the posttests. Thus, the directionality requirement of the organismic account is sustained in these studies, although it remains to be seen whether more direct or systematic attempts to shift children from conservation to nonconservation would succeed. Still, a heavy burden is placed upon social learning theory to explain the single direction of the behavioral change that results from the social interaction procedures.

The Genevan account for the efficacy of the social interaction treatments in facilitating operational development centers on the claim that logic and operativity have their origins in children's need to prove their point of view to others coupled with the shock of their thought coming up against that of others. Logic and necessity, the critical ingredients in persuasive argument, have their origins in the breakdown of the equilibrium of egocentrism as a result of the child's cooperation with others. The efficacy of the social interaction studies makes sense from the Genevan perspective, although the changes occur over intervals that are too short to be consistent with the general Genevan position that development is a slow process. The question of how much time a qualitative change takes, on the other hand, is meaningless because it involves the contradiction of quantification of a quality.

The Genevan explanation lacks parsimony, and it should come as no surprise that it might be possible to explain the workings of social interaction procedures with more parsimonious mechanisms, such as imitation or modeling.

Modeling and Imitation

Several researchers (Charbonneau & Robert, 1977; Charbonneau, Robert, Bourassa, & Gladu-Bisonnette, 1976; Rosenthal & Zimmerman, 1972; Sullivan, 1969; Waghorn & Sullivan, 1970; Zimmerman & Lanaro, 1974) have demonstrated that nonconservers can acquire conservation merely by observing adults model or perform the conservation tasks, and other researchers (Botvin & Murray, 1975; Cook & Murray, 1973; J. Murray, 1974) have confirmed the result with child models, often showing greater conservation gains here than with adult models.

In a direct comparison of the power of modeling and social interaction procedures, Botvin and Murray (1975) showed they yield equivalent success. In both cases, the conservation gains met the traditional justification, transfer, and durability criteria. As Murray (1972) in his study of social interaction and Rosenthal and Zimmerman (1972) in their study of modeling both used the Goldschmid and Bentler (1968) Concept Assessment Kit, Forms A and B, as the dependent measure, another comparison of the two procedures is possible, at least indirectly. Both studies yielded equivalent posttest scores (Forms A and B) with children of the same age and background. The posttest scores for children who gave *no* evidence of operativity on the pretests were essentially the same in the two studies and met all the major criteria for conservation. There is some evidence (Charbonneau & Robert, 1977; Charbonneau et al., 1976) that some children exposed to a modeling experience fail in the end to meet the full range of conservation criteria (viz., duration and generalization) and also that the cognitive growth that results from modeling is constrained by the intellectual and cognitive level of the observer (Murray, 1974) to a greater degree than it appears to be for children in the social interaction experience. It appears that some children rotely memorize the model's response algorithms, but this fact itself does not rule out the possibility that in other circumstances they would respond operationally. Persons with operativity may still use rotely memorized algorithms as a problem-solving approach in a situation for which they perceive them to be an appropriate, or at least an economical, strategy.

The modeling effects, like the interaction ones, have been shown to hold across various age groups (4 to 8 years), SES levels, language and ethnic groups, and IQ levels. Moreover, they cannot be explained away as merely the nonconserver's assimilation of the information presented by the model because often the information presented outside a modeling condition fails to produce stable conservation gains (Rosenthal & Zimmerman, 1972) and because the conservation gains are sometimes based upon reasons different from those given by the model (Botvin & Murray, 1975; Murray, 1974). Rules and explanations given by the model often, but not always, enhanced conservation gain to be sure (Rosenthal & Zimmerman, 1972; Sullivan, 1969; Waghorn & Sullivan, 1970), but the effect cannot be attributed solely to their presence. Something more is contributed by the modeling aspect of the information transmission. The social attribute of the message appears to be critical for cognitive growth.

Unlike the conservers in the social interaction condition who may yield to the nonconservers and still maintain conservation on the posttests, some researchers (Rosenthal & Zimmerman, 1972) report that conservers who observe nonconservation models regress and imitate the model somewhat. These reports of regression require close examination because potentially they are a serious threat to the strong directionality claims of organismic theories.

It is important to be aware that the mere fact the child now thinks that flattening a clay ball changes its mass, weight, or volume whereas before he or she did not may indicate nothing at all about the child's notion of necessity. Adults, for example, can be routinely fooled about the consequences of a conservation transformation (Murray & Armstrong, 1978; Siegler, 1979; Siegler & Liebert, 1972), and no one supposes they have given up the notion of necessity as a result. Even nonconservation may in certain cases indicate necessity. Murray and Armstrong (1976) reported a sizable number of "nonconservers" felt their judgments necessarily followed from the events of the task. Their error, like the adult's error, was not an error in logic or reasoning but rather stemmed from misinformation about the effects of the particular transformation. Errors of this sort tell us nothing about operativity.

A closer look at Rosenthal and Zimmerman's (1972) 17 "conservers," whose mean scores significantly declined after exposure to a nonconserving adult model, reveals that the conservers had a mean score of only 8.59 out of 12 on the Goldschmid–Bentler assessment kit and could, on that basis alone, be thought to be only partial conservers. Cook and Murray (1973), on the other hand, had 12 conservers with perfect scores on the Goldschmid–Bentler kit observe a nonconserving child model (scores of 0) and found no regression in conservation. The conservers maintained perfect scores on the modeled tasks and on the transfer tasks. Murray (1974) also found no evidence of regression to nonconservation after his conservers observed a nonconserving child model.

These regression effects are not found, it seems, when children serve as the nonconserving model. Robert and Charbonneau (1977, 1978) argue convincingly that regression reports in modeling procedures are artifactual and a function of social control and submissiveness to social influence features of the procedure.

They found that extinction or regression in conservation occurred only in the presence of adults, and even then it appeared that the children only temporarily adopted a nonconservation attitude simply to conform to perceived social demands (Robert & Charbonneau, 1978). Moreover, Kuhn (1972) found little evidence of regression in the modeling of classification in a study that provided a fine-grained portrayal of regression and progression in terms of the Piagetian substages. In balance, the directionality assumption of the organismic developmental model is not seriously threatened by the results of modeling and imitation attempts to extinguish conservation in either "natural" or newly trained conservers.

Although it is plausible that the social interaction effects are explainable as essentially modeling effects, competing explanations are equally plausible. For example, it is possible that given the very short durations of the interactions, the nonconservers merely acquiesced to terminate the argument and simply pretended to conserve. Even though their pretense would not fully explain all the results of the interaction studies, we still might expect that the dissonance between the nonconserver's pretense and his or her true belief, discounting the likelihood of the sufficient justification of the experimental procedure, could motivate cognitive change, as it typically does, in the direction of the subject's public position (viz., the conservation pretense). In this account, the nonconservers would come to believe their public position and genuinely conserve.

Murray, Ames, and Botvin (1977) investigated the dissonance or role-playing hypothesis in two experiments that dramatically confirmed it. Nonconservers with initial scores of 0 scored 14.5 out of 16 in one experiment and 6 out of 8 in the other experiment after they pretended to conserve publicly. All the traditional conservation criteria, including resistance to extinction, were met. In the extinction condition, the newly trained conservers pretended to nonconserve publicly with no ensuing evidence of regression. Thus, they gave all the signs of genuine conservation—justification, transfer, durability, and countersuggestion resistance. "Natural" conservers who pretended to nonconserve also gave no signs of regression, even after a second dissonance manipulation. They maintained nearly perfect scores on the pretest and throughout the posttests. However, there were signs of conservation regression among transitional conservers where their nonconservation pretenses conflicted with their original judgments. An interesting case was that of the transitional conservers who pretended to conserve. On problems where their pretense conflicted with their initial position, they made the maximum gain, but on problems where there was no conflict (i.e., where there was originally a correct judgment without a correct reason), they made only half the gains that could have been made, despite the fact that all the information needed to solve the problem was presented in the pretense.

The picture that is emerging from these "social" training procedures supports a unidirectional and nonreversible change in children's performance on the conservation tasks, which is supported by something more than the presentation of additional useful information. That is, there is in these studies support for the *development* construct and perhaps for the Genevan *equilibration* construct. There is not support for social learning theories because they are unable to explain the general failure of experimenters to undo conservation or operativity through social interaction, conflict, modeling, or dissonance. In social learning theory, it should be as easy to shift children from conservation to nonconservation as it is to shift them from nonconservation to conservation; that is, change should be symmetrical, but the evidence points more certainly to an asymmetrical change.

If the effects of social conflict, interaction, modeling, and dissonance are greater or more potent than the effects from the presentation of the same informational content in nonsocial formats, the question of the "contentfree' motivational aspects of these procedures naturally arises. Inasmuch as unique effects of these procedures are confounded with the information contained in them, it may be possible to unconfound these and generate the unique motivational feature of each by confronting nonconserving children with modeled, dissonant, etc. information that conflicts with their nonconservation judgment but is still equally incorrect. Thus, any gain in conservation could not be attributed to the presentation of the correct answer, so to speak. For example, a child who thought that the taller, narrower glass held more liquid could be confronted by a peer who argues it contains less, by a model who states it contains less, or by his or her own public pretense that it contains less.

Both Murray (1974) and Cook and Murray (1973) found that nonconservers who observed other nonconservers made slight but significant gains in conservation. Similarly, Murray, Ames, and Botvin (1977) found that transitional conservers whose nonconservation pretense did *not* conflict with their original nonconservation position on certain problems made slight gains in conservation on those problems on the posttests. Doise, Mugny, and Perret-Clermont (1976) found that when nonconservers of length were told by an adult that the displaced stick, which the child thought was longer, was shorter when viewed from its other end, a significant number of them (9/20) conserved length on immediate and delayed posttests. Even though they were presented with erroneous information, apparently the fact that it conflicted with their initial position promoted some cognitive growth, although not as much growth as when the nonconservers received correct information. In that case, nearly all the nonconservers conserved on the posttests.

Ames and Murray (1982) also subjected nonconservers to conflicting nonconservation judgments in social interaction dyads, in a model, in a pretense, and in a "nonsocial" information presentation. All social procedures—social interaction, dissonance, modeling—had significant effects on the nonconservers. Virtually all the children changed their responses to at least one of nine tasks presented, but just a few children (12%) changed only to conservation. Most (57%) changed to another nonconservation judgment (i.e., the conflicting version), and about 31% changed to conservation on some tasks and to another nonconservation judgment on some others. The changes to conservation on the posttests were virtually all from children in the social interaction group. Significant differences in conservation were found between the social interaction and all other groups in mean posttest scores. Insignificant differences were found among all the other groups and the retesting control. Still, the gains in conservation were modest with final mean posttest scores slightly better than 4 ($sd = 5$) out of 18. These modest gains nevertheless did fulfill the justification, transfer, and durability criteria. Three nonconservers scored between 16 and 18 out of 18, and eleven scored between 5 and 15.

Thus, this approach provides some support for cognitive motivation but little support for a unique equilibration function in any procedure but the social interaction condition. Here it is shown that conflict *qua* conflict is not only cognitively motivating but that the resolution of the conflict is likely to be in the progressive directions described by the equilibration model. In this limited way, two wrongs come to make a right. Lower change rates from these social procedures occur when nonconservation information content is presented than when conservation information content is presented; this indicates that conservation and nonconservation information are not equivalent. The child more easily changes from nonconservation to conservation than from nonconservation to another form of nonconservation. Except in the organismic or final cause theories, there is no a priori reason for this difference in the potency of the two kinds of information.

Finally, there is the question of the source of cognitive growth in the social interaction condition in which no one is in possession of the information needed to solve the problem. From where did the conservation come? There does not appear to be an external source.

REFERENCES

Ames, G., & Murray, F. *When two wrongs make a right: Promoting cognitive change by social conflict.* Va., *Developmental Psychology*, 1982, *18*(6), 892–895.

Bandura, J. *Social learning theory*. Englewood Cliffs, N.J.: Prentice-Hall, 1977.

Beilin, H. Inducing conservation through training. In G. Steiner (Ed.), *Psychology of the 20th century, Piaget and beyond* (Vol. 7). Zurich: Kindler, 1977.

Bever, T., Mehler, J., & Epstein, J. What children do in spite of what they know. *Science*, 1968, *162*, 921–924.

Borys, S., & Spitz, H. Effect of peer interaction on the problem-solving behavior of mentally retarded youths. *American Journal of Mental Deficiency*, 1979, *84*, 273–279.

Botvin, G., & Murray, F. The efficacy of peer modeling and social conflict in the acquisition of conservation. *Child Development*, 1975, *46*, 796–799.

Braine, M., & Shanks, B. The development of the conservation of size. *Journal of Verbal Learning and Verbal Behavior*, 1965, *4*, 227–242.

Bryant, P. *Perception and understanding in young children*. New York: Basic Books, 1974.

Charbonneau, C., & Robert, M. Observational learning of quantity conservation in relation to the degree of cognitive and conflict. *Psychological Reports*, 1977, *44*, 975–986.

Charbonneau, C., Robert, M., Bourassa, G., & Gladu-Bissonnette, S. Observational learning of quantity conservation and Piagetian generalization tasks. *Developmental Psychology*, 1976, *12*(3), 211–217.

Cook, H., & Murray, F. *Acquisition of conservative through the observation of conserving models.* Paper presented at the meetings of the American Educational Research Association, New Orleans, March, 1973.

Doise, W., Mugny, G., & Perret-Clermont, A-N. Social interaction and the development of cognitive operations. *European Journal of Social Psychology*, 1975, *5*(3), 367–383.

Doise, W., Mugny, G., & Perret-Clermont, A-N. Social interaction and cognitive development: Further evidence. *European Journal of Social Psychology*, 1976, *6*(2), 245–247.

Engelmann, S. Does the Piagetian approach imply instruction. In D. Green, M. Ford, & G. Flammer (Eds.), *Measurement and Piaget*. N.Y.: McGraw-Hill, 1971.

Flavell, J. *Cognitive Development*. Engelwood Cliffs, N.J.: Prentice Hall, 1977.

Gelman, R. Conservation acquisition: A problem of learning to attend to relevant attributes. *Journal of Experimental Child Psychology*, 1969, *7*, 167–187.

Gelman, R. Cognition development. *Annual Review of Psychology*, 1978, *29*, 297–332.

Goldschmid, M., & Bentler, P. *Concept assessment kit-conservation manual*. San Diego, Cal.: Educational and Industrial Testing Service, 1968.

Gruen, G. Note on conservation: Methodological and definitional considerations. *Child Development*, 1966, *37*, 977–984.

Hornblum, J., & Overton, W. Area and volume conservation among the elderly: Assessment and training. *Developmental Psychology*, 1976, *12*, 68–74.

Inhelder, B., & Piaget, J. *The growth of logical thinking from childhood to adolescence*. New York: Basic Boosk, 1958.

Inhelder, B., Sinclair, H., & Bovet, M. *Learning and the development of cognition*. Cambridge, Mass.: Harvard University Press, 1974.

Kamii, C., & Derman, L. Does the Piagetian approach imply instruction? In D. Green, M. Ford, & G. Flammer (Eds.), *Measurement and Piaget*. New York: McGraw-Hill, 1971.

Knight-Arest, I., & Reid, D. *Peer interaction as a catalyst for conservation acquisition in normal and learning disabled children*. Paper presented at the eighth annual symposium of the Jean Piaget Society, Philadelphia, May 1978.

Kuhn, D. Mechanisms of change in the development of cognitive structures. *Child Development*, 1972, *43*, 833–844.

Mehler, J., & Bever, T. Cognitive capacity of very young children. *Science*, 1967, *158*, 141–142.

Miller, S., & Brownell, C. Peers, persuasion, and Piaget: Dyadic interaction between conservers and nonconservers. *Child Development*, 1975, *46*, 992–997.

Murray, F. The acquisition of conservation through social interaction. *Developmental Psychology*, 1972, *6*, 1–6.

Murray, F. Teaching strategies and conservation training. In A. M. Lesgold, J. W. Pellegrino, S. Fokkema, & R. Glaser (Eds.), *Cognitive psychology and instruction*. New York: Plenum Press, 1978.

Murray, F. The conservation paradigm: Conservation of conservation research. In D. Brodzinsky, I. Sigel, & R. Golinkoff (Eds.), *New directions in Piagetian theory and research*. Hillsdale, N.J.: Lawrence Erlbaum Associates, 1981.

Murray, F., Ames, G., & Botvin, G. The acquisition of conservation through cognitive dissonance. *Journal of Educational Psychology*, 1977, *69*(5), 519–527.

Murray, F., & Armstrong, S. Necessity in conservation and nonconservation. *Developmental Psychology*, 1976, *12*, 483–484.

Murray, F., & Armstrong, S. Adult nonconservation of numerical equivalence. *Merrill-Palmer Quarterly,* 1978, *12*(4), 255–263.

Murray, J. Social learning and cognitive development: Modeling effects on children's understanding of conservation. *British Journal of Psychology,* 1974, *65*, 151–160.

Osherson, D. *Logical abilities in children* (Vols. 1 & 2). Hillsdale, N.J.: Lawrence Erlbaum Associates, 1974.

Piaget, J. *Judgment and Reasoning in the Child.* Princeton, N.J.: Littlefield Adams and Co., 1959.

Piaget, J. *Logic and psychology.* New York: Basic Books, 1960.

Piaget, J. The theory of stages in cognitive development. In D. Green, M. Ford, & G. Flammer (Eds.), *Measurement and Piaget.* New York: McGraw-Hill, 1971.

Reese, H., & Overton, W. Models and theories of development. In L. R. Goulet, & P. Baltes (Eds.), *Life-span development psychology.* New York: Academic Press, 1970.

Robert, M., & Charbonneau, C. Extinction of liquid conservation by observation: Effects of model's age and presence. *Child Development,* 1977, *48*, 648–652.

Robert, M., & Charbonneau, C. Extinction of liquid conservation by modeling: Three indicators of its artificiality. *Child Development,* 1978, *49*, 194–200.

Rosenthal, T., & Zimmerman, B. Modeling by exemplification and instruction in training conservation. *Developmental Psychology,* 1972, *6*, 392–401.

Siegler, R. Children's thinking: The search for limits. In G. Whitehurst & B. Zimmerman (Eds.), *Functions of language and cognition.* New York: Academic Press, 1979.

Siegler, R., & Liebert, R. Effects of presenting relevant rules and complete feedback on the conservation of liquid quantity task. *Developmental Psychology,* 1972, *7*, 133–138.

Silverman, I., & Geiringer, E. Dyadic interaction and conservation induction: A test of Piaget's equilibration model. *Child Development,* 1973, *44*, 815–820.

Silverman, I., & Stone, J. Modifying cognitive functioning through participation in a problem-solving group. *Journal of Educational Psychology,* 1972, *63*, 603–608.

Sullivan, E. Transition problems in conservation research. *Journal of Genetic Psychology,* 1969, *115*, 41–45.

Waghorn, L., & Sullivan, E. The exploration of transition rules in conservation of quantity (substance) using film mediated modeling. *Acta Psychologica,* 1970, *32*, 65–80.

Zimmerman, B., & Lanaro, P. Acquiring and retaining conservation of length through modeling and reversibility cues. *Merrill-Palmer Quarterly of Behavior and Development,* 1974, *20*, 145–161.

Author Index

Numbers in *italics* indicate pages with bibliographic information.

Subject Index